Invitation to

Talcott Parsons' Theory

Invitation to
TALCOTT PARSONS' THEORY

Pat N. Lackey

Associate Professor of Sociology
California State University, Fullerton

**CAP and GOWN
PRESS**

HOUSTON

Copyright © 1987 by Cap and Gown Press, Inc.

Cap and Gown Press, Inc.
Box 58825
Houston, Texas 77258
U.S.A.

Library of Congress Catalog Card Number 84-71504

Photograph of Talcott Parsons courtesy of Lois Lord, New York

Library of Congress Cataloging in Publication Data

Lackey, Pat N.
    Invitation to Talcott Parsons' Theory.

    Bibliography: p. 167.
    Includes index.
    1. Parsons, Talcott, 1902-1979.   2. Sociology—
United States—History. I. Title.
HM22.U6P3749 1987   301'.092'4   84-71504
ISBN 0-88105-052-0

Printed in the United States of America

Contents

List of Figures

Preface

For almost half a century Talcott Parsons elaborated a sociological theory which he thought was so general that it could be used to explain a wide range of phenomena. The philosophical perspective of the theory was set forth in 1937 in *The Structure of Social Action*. However, it was not until 1951 (*The Social System* and *Toward a General Theory of Action*) that the structure of the theory began to take shape. Then, in 1953 (*Working Papers in the Theory of Action*) and 1956 (*Economy and Society*) the theory's structure was more clearly defined. After 1956 the theory was refined as a result of writings on political power (1963), influence (1963), value-commitments (1968), and the university system in the United States (1973). Parsons' elaboration of a theory of social action systems provoked sociologists to examine the epistemological foundations of their discipline with a thoroughness which probably would not have been possible without the Parsonian perspective.

Since his death in 1979, an assessment of Parsons' impact on sociology has commenced. Certainly we will not engage that issue here except to propose that most sociologists would probably agree that Parsons' most widespread effects have stemmed from the philosophical debates which his philosophy stimulated. Although Parsons did respond to his critics, his prolificacy and persistency in propounding his theory leaves one with the impression that, for the most part, he remained aloof from the debates.

The most enduring controversies have been about the usefulness of deductive or inductive theory and the conceptual validity of structural -functional theory compared to conflict theory. Parsons subscribed to the deductive method of arriving at theory. Even if a student avoids learning Parsons' theory it is impossible to avoid the deductive/inductive issue. It is quintessential in philosophy.

Although since 1970 Parsons repeatedly disclaimed the labeling of his theory as structural-functional, theory textbooks continued to use the label, usually in contrast with the conflict theory of Karl Marx. The structural-functional/conflict controversies are neither settled nor compromised. However, from time to time, one or the other position has been favored. During the turbulence of the 1960's structural-functional theory was out of fashion and conflict theory was in. Then, in the early '80's, a renewed interest in Parsons' theory seemed to have left the old structural-functional/conflict polemics by the wayside. Studies of Parsons' works were invigorated by turning attention to his systems perspective. Now, a working knowledge of his theories and an awareness of the philosophical debates which he stimulated have become prerequisites for being well-read in sociology.

This book was written as a beginning to understanding Parsons. Although the intellectual environment requires that students of sociology have some familiarity with Parsons' work, there is so much information about it that in attempting to come to grips with the Parsonian perspective, a student hardly knows where to begin. Besides, the abstrusity in his writings can easily give a student an impression that the theory is so complex it is impossible to comprehend. It is not. There is even a tale which circulates among those who have struggled with Parsons' turgidity. The story goes that Sorokin and Parsons were in a Harvard departmental meeting during which Parsons announced that one of his books had just been translated into the *nth* foreign language. Sorokin was reported to have retorted, "but has it been translated into English yet?"

Parsons' theory depicts social activities as forming vertical and horizontal organizations. In discussing such organizations, it provides a multiplicity of frames of reference which can be mindboggling. Another source of confusion results from Parsons' willingness to communicate his reasons for defining concepts in a particular way. Often he mingled commentary with definitions of concepts, requiring a reader to ferret out the definitions from the commentary. Also, he referred to analogies in other disciplines and in his later writings, he related a topic of discussion to his previous writings. If a reader is not familiar with the knowledge underlying the analogies or has not read the earlier writings the references can be confusing; to the novice, they provide more information than desired.

The multiple frames of reference within which theoretical concepts are used and Parsons' imprecise definitions have made it difficult to put together an accurate and concise glossary of terms. Instead of a glossary a detailed index has been included so that the context within which Parsons used concepts can be identified. Also, by distinguishing the theoretical core from the derived theory the book facilitates a student's understanding that the same theoretical perspective is applied to different systems and that Parsons used different words to denote one theoretical concept.

Many of us, professors and students, lament the fact that, due to the time constraints of a single academic term and the voluminousness of the works of theorists such as Freud, Marx, Weber, and Parsons, students can only sample the original writings of theorists. A sampling here and there of what has been, for a theorist, an all-consuming lifetime's work too frequently results in an uninformed disparagement of ideas or a vulgar interpretation implied by an evaluator's facetious comments.

This book was written as a concise and accurate statement of the basic structure of Parsons' theory. One objective has been to provide a guide to understanding Parsons' theory so that reading his original writings and others' evaluations of his perspective will be easier and more enjoyable for persons who do not have a background in philosophy. This book was written for advanced undergraduate students and first-year graduate students of theory in the social sciences. Perhaps the work will also be informative and useful to social scientists who are not familiar with Parsons' theory.

When students read secondary sources on theory they need to be able to distinguish between what the theorist says in the theory and what a writer describing the theory has said about it. In order to eliminate a reader's dilemma of having to distinguish this writer's opinions from Parsons' own theoretical statements there has been an attempt to minimize evaluative statements about the theory; such statements are relegated to the last chapter herein. Although the phrase ''Parsons says'' has not been used frequently, all of this book has come from his publications. However, some of the commonsense examples demonstrating concepts have been mine. Attempting to understand a theory through some logic which is external to the theory can result in incorrect information and superficial understanding. Desiring to assist the reader in understanding the internal logic of Parsons' theory, statements about the theory have been couched in terms of the theory itself. Hence, after definitions and examples of the concepts of Parsons' core theory are stated in Chapters 2 and 3, these concepts are not redefined nor reexemplified; they are used to define other concepts (Chapters 4 through 7). The intention has been to let Parsons explain Parsons. Insofar as a nonevaluative stance toward the theory is a by-product of such an approach, it should not be interpreted as an apology for the Parsonian perspective.

Everything Parsons wrote about has not been covered here. The book contains information about the basics of the theory. His theory was put forth as a general theory which could explain myriad phenomena. Parsons used it to explain such things as the human condition, the American university system, the economy, and the political system. All of these and other applications of this theory are not discussed here. Parsons also commented on social issues, such as youth, maturity, illness, death, McCarthyism, and Fascism. Since these essays do not definitively relate his theory to the topic of an essay they are not included here.

Throughout his long and productive career Parsons' critics were numerous and clamorous. Any studied evaluation of Parsonian theory must not only be addressed to Parsons' thought, but also to the critics, as well as to the critics of the critics. That sort of an endeavor is beyond the scope of this work. Nevertheless, a list of publications in which the theory is evaluated has been included. It contains ample resources for surveying the opinions of the critics, the critics of the critics, and Parsons' responses to both. Since some evaluations have been premised on incorrect information about Parsons' writings, persons who are not familiar with the history of Parsons' works should read several evaluations and some of the more recent ones.

Some writers have stated that Parsons wrote about more than one theory. Of those taking that position, and especially those who are interested in the theory's development, he is most usually said to have had two theories: action theory and systems theory, or three theories: structural-functional theory, action theory, and systems theory. Since this book presents Parsons' developed theory and ignores the historical sequence in which it was developed, *the position here is that his writings culminated in one theory, a theory of social action systems.*

Information about the theory has been organized so that concepts are introduced in a logical order of complexity. This is not always the sequence in which Parsons developed his ideas; however, it is an order which is logical and conducive to understanding. From time to time Parsons' theories were revised and concepts were changed. Changes have been noted in that if one concept was referred to by two different words, the most recent, appropriate word is used to denote the concept.

Since the book has been written for students who do not have a background in philosophy, the philosophical foundations of Parsons' work have been of minor interest. Obviously, Parsons disagreed with Lipset, who said "It is a foolish man who believes that he knows the sources of his ideas" (*The First New Nation*, p. viii), because Parsons gave greater attention to documenting the sources of his ideas than most writers of his stature. The definitive work tracing the roots and strands of philosophical influences on his ideas has yet to be written. At the present time the best source for such information is Parsons' own writings.

Considering the amount of information contained in the theory, empirical tests of it are disproportionately scanty. Reports of analytical applications and research on the theory have been included in this work for the sole purpose of illustration. There has been no attempt to make a complete survey of such studies.

Using analogies from theories in biology, economics, psychoanalysis, and sociology, Parsons integrated some of the dominant themes in 20th -century philosophy into his core theory. Figure i is a schematic outline of the structure of the core theory and theories derived from it. It is a cognitive map to assist the reader in understanding the organization of this book.

In Figure i the uniqueness of Parsons' work appears in the combination of the general theory of action (Chapter 2) and systems theory (Chapter 3) from which he arrived at a theory of social action systems (Chapter 3). The theory of social action systems was then used to describe conditions for action (Chapter 3), society (Chapter 4), and some characteristics of stratification (Chapter 6) and personality (Chapter 7).

A second theoretical core combined the theory of social action systems and evolutionary theory (Chapter 5). It describes the development of stems. Parsons used it to account for social change (Chapter 5) and personality development (Chapter 7), as well as stratification processes associated with evolutionary development (Chapter 6).

Chapter 1 contains a cursory statement of some of the influences on Parsons' thought. The influences of Durkheim, Weber, and Freud are emphasized. In discussing their ideas it is assumed that the reader has some familiarity with their writings. The core of the theory - action theory, systems theory, and a theory of social action systems - is described in Chapters 2 and 3. More illustrations and examples of concepts are provided in these chapters than in Chapters 4 through 7 which deal with applications of the basic theory to empirical systems. These latter chapters assume that the reader understands the core theory. Chapters 4 through 7 contain Parsons' use of the theory to describe structures of society and personality and the processes of socialization, stratification, and social change. Some of the main criticisms of the theory are briefly discussed in Chapter 8.

The information in Chapter 8 is by no means a thorough or penetrating evaluation of Parsons' works. It provides a general orientation to some of the major criticisms of the Parsonian approach to theory. It is addressed to undergraduate students who do not have a background in philosophical analysis and scientific methodology. Graduate students are advised to use the list of references in the bibliography. Since the literature on Parsons' thought follows the historical development of his theory, evaluations of his theory changed. In surveying others' ideas about the theory, students should study many critics, reading both early and recent evaluations.

Figure i

The Structure of Parsons' Theory

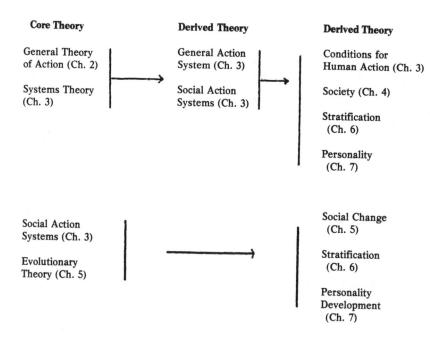

Core Theory	Derived Theory	Derived Theory
General Theory of Action (Ch. 2)	General Action System (Ch. 3)	Conditions for Human Action (Ch. 3)
Systems Theory (Ch. 3)	Social Action Systems (Ch. 3)	Society (Ch. 4)
		Stratification (Ch. 6)
		Personality (Ch. 7)

Social Action Systems (Ch. 3)		Social Change (Ch. 5)
Evolutionary Theory (Ch. 5)		Stratification (Ch. 6)
		Personality Development (Ch. 7)

Acknowledgments:

Early drafts of the manuscript were improved as a result of constructive evaluations by Professors Daniel Glaser and Mike Mend. Students, too many to name, interested in sociological theory, provided what, at times, seemed necessary prodding by asking, "have you finished?" The constructive comments of Professor Eugene B. Gallagher provided stimuli for final revisions. Don Schweitzer, Dean of the School of Humanities and Social Sciences at California State University, Fullerton, provided funds for scanning of the typed manuscript onto computer disks which facilitated final revisions on a personal computer. The camaraderie and collegiality of Helaine Feingold, Perry Jacobson, and Mike Mend, faculty in the sociology department, have enhanced the intellectual environment within which the project was completed. Special thanks to Jacobson for the habitualness of his receptivity to discussions of others' intellectual dilemmas. Most importantly, the editor of Cap and Gown Press, E. Gartly Jaco's knowledge and expertise, encouragement and patience have been indispensable contributions to the project.

Talcott Parsons

Photo by Lois Lord, New York

1

Chapter 1

A Survey of Parsons' Career and Work

While an account of Parsons' life history is of only tangential interest to this work, it does serve as an introduction to his perspective. This chapter provides a summary statement about his career, his approach to theory, and similarities between his thought and that of Durkheim, Freud, and Weber.

Biographical Sketch

Parsons was born in 1902 in Colorado Springs, Colorado. His father was a Congregational minister and president of Marietta College in Ohio. Martel (1979) reports that the family moved to New York City where Parsons attended the Horace Mann experimental boys' high school of Columbia University. As an undergraduate at Amherst, anticipating a medical career, Parsons studied biology. Medicine remained one of his major interests. His interest in medicine was later expressed as the study of the social environment of medical practice, a study which seemed to have been reinforced by his having associations with several persons in the medical profession.

He studied at the London School of Economics as a nondegree student in 1924-25 where the social anthropologist Bronislaw Malinowski had a major influence on Parsons' view of rationality. Later he studied at Heidelberg where one of his examination topics was economics. At Heidelberg his main teacher was Max Weber's brother, Alfred Weber; he was also instructed by Karl Mannheim and Karl Jaspers. Max Weber had taught at Heidelberg, and although he died five years before Parsons arrived there, his works had an enduring impact on Parsons. Writing a dissertation on "The Concept of Capitalism in Recent German Literature,"

3

Parsons received the Philosophiae Doctor in 1929. Later he translated Weber's *The Protestant Ethic and the Spirit of Capitalism* and (with A. M. Henderson) *The Theory of Social and Economic Organization.*

After returning to the United States he was an instructor of economics at Amherst. In 1927 he became an instructor of economics at Harvard and of sociology in 1931. Throughout his academic career he remained at Harvard, except for visiting appointments both prior to and following his retirement in 1973. At Harvard, he assisted in the reorganization of instruction in sociology, social anthropology, and social and clinical psychology into the Department of Social Relations. He chaired that department for ten years. An active participant in professional associations, he was elected president of the Eastern Sociological Society, the American Sociological Association, and the American Academy of Arts and Sciences. In 1979 he returned to Heidelberg where he was honored on the 50th anniversary of his dissertation. After delivering lectures in Heidelberg and Munich, he died in Munich in 1979.

Parsons' work is based on a firm foundation of scholarship. His formal studies continued throughout his career, in interdisciplinary seminars, discussion groups with students and colleagues, as preparations for writing papers and delivering lectures. He inferred that his degree at Heidelberg was somewhat inferior to an American doctorate, involving only three semesters of credits, oral examinations, and a dissertation, and that in his early years of teaching at Harvard he continued to study economics. Martel (1979) reported that he audited F. W. Taussig's graduate course on economic theory which emphasized the work of Alfred Marshall. He also took formal training in psychoanalysis in 1946. While a visiting professor at the University of Cambridge in 1953 and 1954, his interest in economics was renewed.

Parsons had an enduring interest in systems theory, probably initially stimulated by studies in biology and macro-economics. From about 1952 to 1957 he participated in conferences on systems theory and reaffirmed his conclusion that systems theory, including the principles of cybernetic control and homeostasis, is an appropriate frame of reference for the analysis of social action.

Early in his career the difficulties inherent in the study of social change were discussed, and in the 1960s, that problem was tackled. He was familiar with classical anthropological theories of social change and he had studied Weber and Durkheim's works which used a comparative analysis of social change. In 1963, this area of study was updated in a seminar on the problems of social evolution.

In the early 1950s, Parsons' writings focused on social roles; i.e., the normative and motivational aspects of roles in a family, in the professions, in social interactions, small groups, and deviancy, as well as relationships between role performances on the one hand and stratification and institutional processes on the other. It was during that period that Bales identified four phases of action in the role performances of members of small groups. Parsons generalized the phases as system problems and although he continually refined his theory, from about 1956 to the end of his career his major interest seemed to be the application of these four problems to all sorts of systems.

Intellectual Influences

Much of Parsons' insight was a result of his liberal use of concepts and analogies from theories in anthropology, biology, economics, medicine, cybernetics, and psychoanalytic psychology. He used this strategy throughout his career. In all of his writings there is a consistent affinity for the ideas of Emile Durkheim, Sigmund Freud, and Max Weber. The sources of Weber and Durkheim's effects are specified in *The Structure of Social Action* (1937). Freud's influence is most evident in writings about the family and the socialization of children.

There are four motifs threaded through Parsons' theory. In this chapter they are discussed in a general manner and related to historical influences on his thought. In later chapters they are referenced to the specifics of his theory. The four motifs are: (1) normatively rational action, (2) symbolic communication, (3) organic systems, and (4) analytic abstraction.

Parsons' view that action is normatively rational explains behavior as being influenced by social values and norms. His use of the word "action" instead of behavior indicates a concern for the conditions, situations, and motivations associated with a behavior. There is also an interest in an end state of affairs to which behavior is directed.

Action is rational if it is organized so that means are used to attain ends. Action is normatively rational when actors use beliefs, values or norms to justify or guide their choices of means and ends. Parsons was committed to the idea that actors use values and norms in making decisions. He would tell us that, no doubt, everyone has a desire for "a good life" and many activities are used as means for attaining it. Nevertheless, unless one assumes that individuals have some ideas or beliefs which define "a good life" and which also suggest ways of attaining it, they will be unable to bring it about. From this perspective, he criticized utilitarian and positivistic theories of rationality because he thought that they did not explain how actors choose means and ends. His criticism of these theories was a precursor of his own theory of normative rationality and he based his theory on the writings of others, especially those of Emile Durkheim and Max Weber.

In *The Structure of Social Action* the theories of Emile Durkheim, Alfred Marshall, Vilfredo Pareto, and Max Weber were analyzed in order to demonstrate that each theorist converged on a perspective that rational action is influenced by social values and beliefs. Parsons evaluated the thoughts of the four theorists, contrasting their ideas with earlier utilitarian philosophy and proposed his version of action theory.

Early utilitarian philosophy had defined rationality as the selection of the means most appropriate for the attainment of ends. Parsons said that utilitarian philosophers defined ends as variable and random, and failed to suggest criteria for an "actor's" choice of ends. Consequently, failing to identify ends and not defining the criteria used by actors to select means made it impossible to specify rationality as a relationship between means and ends.

Radical positivists modified the utilitarian view of rationality by assuming that hereditary and environmental conditions influence actors' choices; they also assumed that actors know about the conditions which affect their decisions. Based on these assumptions, positivists were inclined to define rationality as the selection of the empirically or scientifically appropriate means for the attainment of ends. Parsons thought such a view required an actor to have more knowledge than was available to him.

Parsons thought these theories ignored significant cultural influences which affect actors' selections of means and ends. He argued that individuals' choices of means and ends are guided by cultural beliefs and values and that Marshall, Pareto, Durkheim, and Weber had thought so, too.

A review of Alfred Marshall's work in economics led Parsons to conclude that Marshall had been aware that values influence economic activity, but he did not pursue the consequences of such influence. After discussing Marshall's idea of wealth-getting actions being affected by values or attitudes, Parsons surmised that Marshall rejected utilitarian views. He was judged to have assumed that economic actions are not motivated solely by desires for acquisition of wealth but, on the contrary, are carried out as expressions of values or attitudes.

Pareto was considered to have extended the analysis of the effects of values a bit further than Marshall. He permitted subjective elements to enter the means-end schema and suggested that individuals' acts could stem from the values of a group, a premise central to Durkheim's theories.

In *The Division of Labor* and *Suicide*, Durkheim demonstrated the thesis that a social order controls the conduct of individuals. In studies of religion, he emphasized the importance of sacred values as guidelines for human choices, proposing that an individual's choice could stem from a commitment to values which are shared with others. Durkheim also analyzed religious rituals from two perspectives, noting that rituals are expressions of individuals' beliefs and also are symbols of a group's beliefs about morality. Parsons adopted Durkheim's views and proposed that social values and beliefs be studied as to their effects on culture, society, and personality.

In Weber's theory an actor's beliefs in values, laws, rules, charisma, and traditions are used to justify choices of means and ends. Parsons concluded that although Weber and Durkheim differed in the manner in which they approached the problem of explaining actor's choices, both assumed that cultural values can be used to explain behavior. He then suggested that sociological theory should be concerned with understanding relationships between values and actions.

In concluding *The Structure of Social Action*, Parsons proposed an alternative theory about relationships between means and ends. He called it a voluntaristic theory of action systems. It was proposed as a general schema in the social sciences, with four subschemata:

(a) economics, utilizing a supply-demand schema;
(b) political power relationships;
(c) sociology, dealing with groups, and
(d) psychology, dealing with attitudes and personality.

The suggestion was made in 1937, and in 1956 in *Economy and Society*, four subsystems of a society were defined as similar to the above. The four subsystems were:

(1) an economy produces facilities for a society (similar to (a) above); (2) a polity uses power for attaining society's goals (similar to (b)); (3) an integrative subsystem (later called a societal community) creates solidarity for a society by controlling individuals so that their behavior conforms to the groups to which they belong (similar to (c)); and (4) a pattern-maintenance subsystem (later called a fiduciary subsystem) regulates individuals' values and belief so that the values of the various units of a society are maintained (similar to (d) above).

Charles Horton Cooley, George Herbert Mead, and Sigmund Freud explained the manner in which social values and norms come to be incorporated into individual personalities. One of Parsons' more important contributions has been his specification of the internalization process and its relationship to social institutions. In that part of his theory he extended Freud's model, emphasizing that not only the superego but also the id and ego are affected by social environments. While Durkheim and Weber's works had given him the idea of the internalization of beliefs and values, Freud's theory of socialization was used as a model for his own theory of socialization. In his theory of socialization, individuals' instincts, drives, and cognitive categories are socialized and through a superego they are integrated with the values and beliefs of a society.

In Parsons' theory, symbolic communications maintain relationships between persons and between institutions. The importance of symbolic processes can be related to Freud's use of symbols in psychoanalysis, as well as to Cooley and Mead's theories of socialization. The latter assume that children learn social roles as a result of having first understood symbolically the meanings associated with behavior patterns observed in their environments. Parsons embraced these ideas. He also agreed with Mead's view of the requirements for social interaction. Both Mead and Parsons thought that meaningful interaction between two persons requires each person to internalize relevant dimensions of the other's role.

Parsons' categories for analyzing the normative control of action, the pattern variables, were also used to describe social institutions. Initially they were proposed as useful in describing values and motivations underlying an actor's definition of a situation. Of course, the term "definition of the situation" was generalized first by W. I. Thomas to account for shared meanings and values of persons in interaction.

The pattern variables evolved from Ferdinand Toennies' *gemeinschaft* and *gesellschaft* distinctions. In dichotomizing types of social relationships, Toennies defined a communal (or *gemeinschaft*) type of relationship as one based on affectual or traditional feelings that persons belong together. He defined an associative (or *gesellschaft*) type of relationship as based on rationally motivated self interests, interests based on values of expediency. In an essay on the "Professions and Social Structure," in 1939 (*Essays,* 1949; 1954) Parsons attempted to use the dichotomy from Toennies. He compared the role of the medical practitioner to other occupational roles. As a result of the analysis, he found that Toennies' categories did not apply to the classification of the role of a physician; some aspects of that role were associational and some were communal. For instance, the physician was expected to comply with the ethic of science, a *gesellschaft*-type interest; on the other hand, he was also expected to be interested in his patients' welfare; in this respect, his role was of the *gemeinschaft* type. Parsons concluded that to reduce the role relationship of physician and patient to those features which could be described by *gesellschaft* and *gemeinschaft* oversimplified the relationship. He developed the following categories to describe the physician's role: ego-altruistic interests, universalistic scientific orientations, particularistic aspects of the physician-client relationship, disinterestedness, and specificity of function in the physician's role.

In *The Social System* (1951), Parsons noted the need to add Ralph Linton's distinctions of ascription and achievement (later also referred to as quality and performance) for describing role relationships. In that publication, and in *Toward a General Theory of Action* (1951), the pattern variables were stated in a form which remained relatively constant. The pattern variables classify guidelines for action as cathectic, cognitive, or moral. Freud's influence is apparent in Parsons' use of cathexis to describe the condition by which an object acquires motivational significance as a result of its having been a source of gratification for an individual. Cathectic, cognitive, and moral evaluations are analytically distinguished by Parsons and each is treated as a dimension of evaluation. The importance of the moral basis of action stems from the Durkheim influence. The cathectic-cognitive distinction was clearly made by Weber in defining two ideal types of rational action as affectively rational and value rational. In discussing three mental functions, cathexis, cnition, and morality were also analytically distinguished by Freud.

In explaining interpersonal interaction Parsons postulated four expectations which actors have: approval, response, esteem, and acceptance. These are similar to W. I. Thomas' four wishes: wish for new experience, security, response, and recognition.

Parsons' study of economics culminated in a formal analysis, with Smelser in 1956, of economic activity as a system. The cultural dimensions of action had already been worked out in *The Social System* (1951), and in the Parsons-Smelser book, *Economy and Society*, relationships between cultural, economic, social, and political activities were further specified. That latter work, more clearly than any other, specified relationships between major social institutions. The theories of economists, such as Alfred Marshall, J. M. Keynes, and J. A. Schumpeter, were cast in the perspective of the theory of social action systems. The book's major objective was a demonstration that economic processes are conditioned by noneconomic social factors. It is an example of Parsons' penchant for taking ideas from others' theories and incorporating them into his own frame of reference.

After the analysis of the economy, much of Parsons' work was stimulated by analogies from economic theory. In the work with Smelser four subsystems of a society were defined and characterized as being specialized in types of inputs-outputs. Then, inputs-outputs were used to explain relationships between the subsystems. It was assumed that relationships among subsystems maintain a system. These ideas were analogically arrived at from economic theory in which land, labor, capital, and organization are treated as factors in production.

Another important analogy from economics evolved from Parsons' treating power, influence, and value-commitments as similar to money in economic activity. The idea that money is a symbol of economic value was used as a heuristic device for identifying other symbols by which communication within a society can be maintained. After 1956, as each type of system was defined, the appropriate symbolic media were specified.

After the subsystems of a society had been defined, no doubt, it was for Parsons a foundation firm enough for him to propose a satisfactory theory of social change. This objective dominates his writings on the evolution of societies. He had discussed difficulties in analyzing social change. Judging that sociology was not sophisticated in the description of what society was, he queried: How could social change be explained if we did not first describe society, the entity which changed. He had been impressed with Weber's comparative analysis of religions and Weber's enduring interest in the historical conditions for the development and change of economic institutions in modern societies. Parsons' early writings on social change were mere tentative suggestions of the nature of the problem. Being familiar with the evolutionary theories of Darwin and Herbert Spencer, and after participating in a seminar on social evolution, he studied the history of Christianity, and the civilizations of Rome, Israel, and Greece. Then he applied his four-problem paradigm to the analysis of the evolution of societies.

Prior to Parsons' work, the evolutionary perspective had had a significant impact on social theorists. Parsons' use of evolutionary theory rests on the historically antecedent theories using organic analogies in the study of society. The analogies of Herbert Spencer, A. R. Radcliffe -Brown, and Emile Durkheim characterized social life as similar to organic life. Parsons adopted the analogies. The more immediate influences on him seem to have been Darwin's evolutionary theory, the positivistic organicism of Comte, and functional theory in anthropology. He borrowed from biology and stated that societies have processes analogous to physiological processes by which an organism maintains itself separate from but influenced by its environment. Also, a society was viewed as having processes similar to biological processes by which an organism's structure is developed, maintained, and changed.

The organic analogy promulgated an assumption that society is a living system. Since living systems maintain themselves, there are conditions which must be satisfied in order for them to do so. Eventually the conditions were stated as four system problems: (1) adaptation, adjusting to environmental conditions and procuring resources from an environment; (2) goal-attainment, ranking system goals and mobilizing resources for

achieving them; (3) integration, coordinating and organizing relationships among the various parts of a system; and (4) pattern-maintenance
(also called latency and tension-management), stabilizing and maintaining the organization of a system and handling tension among its parts. It
was assumed that since organic systems maintain themselves then four
subsystems concerned with the four problems contribute to system
maintenance.

The problems were extrapolated and generalized from Bales' study of
small groups (*Working Papers in the Theory of Action,* 1953). Their generality was a breakthrough from which Parsons launched studies of analytical systems, such as the human condition and the cognitive complex,
and descriptions of empirical systems, such as society and personality.

A society was defined as one type of social system which persists for a
long duration of time. In explaining processes which maintain a society,
Parsons used analogies from biology, economics, and cybernetics. L. J.
Henderson's ideas about relationships between organic systems and
their environments, his interpretation of Pareto's concept of equilibrium, and W. B. Cannon's concept of homeostatis were used to define a
society as a boundary-maintaining and self-subsistent system.

Cybernetic theory states that information can be used to control energy. For example, as a source of programmed information a thermostat
can control a furnace which is a source of energy. Parsons used this idea
to account for internal control processes which maintain systems in organized states. In Parsons' adaptation, an individual is a bundle of motivational energy controlled by information, symbolically communicated
as belief, knowledge, and values. Social institutions are reservoirs of
information. They control organizations, groups, and individuals.

Some of the last developments in Parsons' theory were based on the
assumption that societies have internal control mechanisms. The four
symbolic media of exchange — money, influence, power, and value
-commitments — are defined as symbols through which units of a society communicate and exercise some degree of internal control of a society. The equilibrium of a society is a by-product of these internal control
processes. The equilibrium postulate can be traced to the principle of
static mechanics that all the forces acting on a body balance so that a
body is in equilibrium. Parsons extrapolated the idea to society and
argued that control strategies balance forces fomenting change with
forces opposing change.

Parsons' Approach to Theory

After 1956 Parsons was primarily concerned with describing structures and processes of a variety of social action systems. For Parsons, the word "system" means more than the strategy of analyzing society as a system. It appears throughout his writings and it has a general methodological significance. After the specification, with Bales, of the four system problems, it assumed a concrete reference in the analysis of society, the economy, personality, and the political system. In other, non-concrete references the word "system" has been used as a descriptive term designating myriad phenomena. Such a use of the word leaves the reader in a quandary because the empirical referents are not specified. In these instances Parsons used the word to refer to a theoretical perspective.

In *The Structure of Social Action* (pp. 3-42) his methodology was described as based on the view that "system" is a master construct from which to view social phenomena. In that book he conceived of both theories and objects as being systems. A system is made up of units which are interrelated. A theory's units are its concepts; the concepts are related to each other in the theory's propositions; ergo, the system, which Parsons referred to as a "theoretical system." Likewise, an object has units, that is, parts, qualities, and characteristics. Relationships between these make the object what it is; hence, objects are systems, too.

Parsons was committed to the idea that a theory should be an interpretative guide. It should direct attention to those attributes of objects which are considered relevant to a particular theory. He used a theory as a guide to empirical observations, instead of collecting observations and then arriving at a theory as a result of the observations. His disregard of concrete empirical evidence as a base from which to arrive at theoretical statements can be surmised from the scarcity of his communications about specific research findings which might corroborate his theory. He not only wrote about theory, he also wrote commentaries on empirical social issues. The commentaries on social issues hardly ever specify how the issues can be related to the concepts of his theory. Besides, some of his theoretical papers were written as a result of his collaborating with colleagues on empirical research projects. Those papers do not give references to empirical evidence which could have been used as empirical grounds for his theory.

Reminding the reader that it is not necessary that a theory describe or explain an object in its totality, Parsons demonstrated his preference for abstract theory. By abstract theory, he meant that certain attributes of an object are abstracted or selected for study in accordance with a theory's concepts. From time to time, Parsons reaffirmed his preference for abstract theory. One of his more concise statements on the topic was made in 1961: "There is an ambiguity in the common use of 'theory' — the term is often used to designate what I have above called the solution of a problem, e.g., a 'theory of juvenile delinquency.' By 'theory' in the present context I mean a logical system of abstract propositions which as such have no direct empirical content at all. A prototype is the system of differential equations constituting the theory of classical mechanics." *Theories of Society,* vol. II, p. 966, footnote 4.)

We can demonstrate the abstract nature of his theory by using one of the pattern variables, affectivity—affective neutrality. Affectivity describes a situation in which an actor seeks immediate gratification; affective neutrality indicates a situation in which an actor decides to defer gratification, perhaps in order to consider the consequences of his potential action. Using the dichotomy to analyze a situation in which a person is considering going to a movie, if he decides to go to a movie, according to the theory, he has chosen affectivity; if he decides not to go, affective neutrality categorizes his action. In this example the theory directs us to abstract, or select information about gratification and to ignore other information. The act of going to the movie is not of interest except in that our theory describes the affectivity—affective neutrality of the act. We have no interest in the title of the movie, the price of admission, the availability of transportation, or anything else about the decision. The abstract nature of this example is indicated by the fact that the theory has selected out of the empirical event (going or not going to a movie) an aspect of the decision which has been decided by the theoretical concept of affectivity—affective neutrality.

Emphasizing the abstract nature of scientific study is not an unusual perspective. Indeed, abstract thought is not the sole province of academicians or scientists. Abstraction occurs when events are lifted out of their context or when a quality or element of an object is observed as separated from the object of which it is a part. We would find it most difficult to deal with everyday affairs if we did not use abstraction. An example of the ordinary use of abstraction is the manner in which a public discusses "violence in society." It is discussed as though it were an entity separated from the situations in which it occurs and from the persons involved in violent acts. Again, when evaluating individuals, abstract categories such as beauty, truthfulness, or character are used.

Since his theory was presumed to be about organic objects, the abstraction entailed in the study of organic systems was discussed. He used Aristotle's judgment that a hand separated from a living body is no longer a hand to demonstrate the point that a part of an organic whole is different after it has been separated from the thing to which it belongs (*The Structure of Social Action*, p. 32). Although a part cannot be removed from an organic entity, Parsons directed attention to the fact that the part can be analytically removed from the object to which it belongs and it can be analyzed as if it were a separate thing. Since he categorized all of the systems with which his theory dealt as organic systems and since parts of an organic system must be analytically abstracted, Parsons' theory uses analytical abstractions.

Another type of abstraction occurs when a quality of an object is observed apart from the object to which it belongs, such as the color or weight of an object. Here again Parsons directed attention to the fact that such qualities must also be analytically "removed" from the object to which they belong for purposes of studying them. He characterized his theory as being analytically abstract because it designated attributes of behavior which had to be analytically abstracted out of behavior and analyzed as though the attributes were separate entities.

Since there can be more than one theoretical explanation of facts, he cautioned that the theorist should not confuse theoretical statements about objects with the objects themselves. All of these perspectives — the systems postulate, abstraction as an analytical strategy, and the distinction between theoretical concepts and empirical entities — Parsons has attributed to the influence of A. N. Whitehead's conception of science ("An Approach to Psychological Theory in Terms of the Theory of Action," 1959, p.624.)

One of Parsons more important contributions to sociological theory has been his answer to the problem of reductionism. Reduction involves the boiling down of general terms to particulars, such as describing a society by listing the personality characteristics of its members or describing social motivations by listing instincts. Parsons was opposed to this type of explanation because there is not a one to one correspondence between drives and social motives. He would argue, for example, that if we want to study religion, we can study it from the perspective of a society or from the perspective of an individual. We can speak of a person's religious faith; however, society does not have faith; it has religious organizations. Any person's particular religious faith is a result of socialization processes, not of biological drives. These considerations led Parsons to oppose reductionism and he tells us that we must be very careful that we do not attribute to one type of system attributes which are only applicable to a different type of system.

There are many types of social action systems. For instance, both a family and a society are social action systems, but they are different from each other. Since a society is more complex than a family, the contextual meaning of action is very different in a society than it is in a family. Recognizing differences in the complexity of each, Parsons said there could be properties of a society relevant to a study of a society but not relevant to a study of a less complex system such as a family. He concluded that at each level of complexity there may be properties of systems significant to that particular level of complexity which are not relevant to a less complex system.

The attempt to solve the problem of reduction has been one source of the apparent complexity of Parsons' theory. His core theory of social action systems is an analytical system. When its concepts are used to study empirical systems, different words are used to designate the empirical referents of the theoretical concepts. For instance, in the theory of general action systems, values are maintained by a cultural subsystem. In an analysis of a society, a fiduciary subsystem deals with values. In an analysis of a personality, a personal identity is concerned with values; in a cultural system, values are maintained by constitutive symbols or a civil religion. This example demonstrates that after learning the concepts of the theory of general action systems in Chapters 2 and 3, one must also learn different words which denote these concepts for each system to which the theory is applied, in Chapters 4 and 7.

References and Suggestions for Further Study

Parsons' reports of influences on his thought are stated in:
    "A Short Account of My Intellectual Development (1959)
    "An Approach to Psychological Theory in Terms of the Theory of Action" (1959)
    "On Building Systems Theory" (1970)

Martel's "Talcott Parsons" (1979) is a biographical sketch of Parsons' academic career.

Sociological Inquiry (vol. 51, 1981) contains articles by some of Parsons' students and colleagues about their associations with Parsons. In that issue see the articles by Dean Gerstein, Harry M. Johnson, Gerald Platt, and Neil Smelser.

See also: Chapter 3 of Hamilton's *Talcott Parsons* (1983);
    the memorative statements in: ASA Footnotes, August, 1979, and *The American Sociologist* 15:2 (1980)

For comments on some aspects of the academic political environments of Parsons' career see:

Mullins and Mullins, "Standard American Sociology" (1973)

Wiley, Norbert, "The Rise and Fall of Dominating Theories in American Sociology," (1979)

Martindale, Don, "Titans of American Sociology: Talcott Parsons and C. Wright Mills," (1982)

The Structure of Social Action (1937), Chaps. 1, 2, 18, and 19, contains Parsons' philosophy about action, systems, abstraction, and norms.

Chapter 2

The General Theory of Action

Introduction

Action theory differs from a theory of behavior in that it takes into account values, norms, and motivations which guide, direct, and control behavior. Parsons' theory of action explains this control of behavior as relationships between organic energy, personality, society, and culture. Although only individuals act, the theory was generalized to describe the conduct of collectivities, institutions, and societies. He also applied it to nonaction situations, such as the conditions for human action.

So far as individuals are concerned, Parsons was primarily interested in their role performances. According to him, there are four analytical ingredients involved in a role performance:

(1) a culture supplies values, symbols, and knowledge;
(2) a society provides the normative regulation of behavior;
(3) a personality supplies motivations; and
(4) a behavioral organism supplies energy.

He categorized each of these as a subsystem of action.

Each subsystem gives meaning to behavior. When a person acts, his behavior has meaning for him and action theory describes four types of meaning: meaning from the perspective of culture, from the perspective of society, from the perspective of personality, and from the perspective of organism. As will be apparent in the following chapters, action theory emphasizes the importance of the cultural meaning of action.

When any individual acts, the four aspects of meaning are expressed by an actor's evaluations of his motivations and the situation in which action is anticipated. The evaluations are made from the four perspectives. Parsons hypothesized that the evaluations include four dilemmas and the pattern variables classify the dilemmas.

This chapter contains the assumptions of action theory, definitions of the four subsystems, relationships between them, and definitions of the pattern variables. Action theory is described from two perspectives: firstly, from a perspective of one who is an outside observer describing behavior according to the theory (observer); secondly, from a perspective of the person who is acting (actor) and who is behaving in accordance with the postulates of action theory.

Assumptions of Action Theory

There are seven assumptions of the theory:
(1) Action takes place in situations.
(2) It involves a release of motivational energy.
(3) Action is directed to the attainment of ends.
(4) Actors use means to bring about ends.
(5) They have available to them alternatives from which they can choose means and ends.
(6) Situations, motivations, and choices of means and ends are regulated by norms.
(7) There are conditions for action. If an actor has control over things which affect his behavior, they are means; if he cannot control them, they are conditions.

Situations are made up of physical, cultural, social, and nonsocial objects, and an actor's evaluations of these objects define a situation. If actors want to bring about an end, or a future state of affairs, they must evaluate the potential use of objects as means or ends and organize their energy so that means and ends are attained. Therefore, action theory describes an actor's evaluations prior to engaging in activity. The theory assumes that an actor maps a plan from four different but related perspectives: from the perspectives of values (culture), norms and roles (society); motivations (personality), and energy (behavioral organism). Each of these four perspectives is referred to as a subsystem of action and each also includes four dimensions, as set forth in the following section.

Definitions of the Subsystems of Action

From the Parsonian perspective, an organism does not act. It provides energy for an actor's motivations, for speech, perception, muscular coordination, etc. The other subsystems — culture, society, and personality — control and mold an organism's energy into behavioral tendencies.

Culture is made up of (1) knowledge or beliefs about reality, (2) expressive symbols which elicit emotions and feelings, and (3) values which are used to judge morality. Each of these has four levels of generality: Knowledge is composed of facts, statements, theories, and assumptions. Facts are at the lowest level of generality. A higher level of generality is attained by organizing and combining facts into statements as solutions to problems. Greater generality is then produced by integrating these statements into theories, and, finally, the most general level of knowledge is that of the assumptions on which the theories are based.

Expressive symbols indicate the cathectic meanings of objects. Their lowest level of generality is given by symbolizing that objects are appropriate for means. On a second level, objects are identified as appropriate for ends. A third level defines objects in a relationship with an actor, such as my family, my friend. Finally, a most general symbolic level defines an object as warranting general respect; for example, an object of worship.

Values also have four levels of generality. The lowest level evaluates objects for their utility as means; secondly, for their desirability as goals or ends. A third level provides standards for ranking goals. Finally, the most general level provides standards for evaluating different spheres of activity.

A fourth component of culture, constitutive symbols or a world view, does not enter action directly; it supports and legitimates the other cultural components. The lowest level of a world view defines the meaning of activity; secondly, the meaning of different spheres of life; thirdly, the concept of natural order; and, finally, a most general level, conceptions about ultimate concerns which Parsons said were religious beliefs.

Beliefs, symbols, and values guide and direct action and are grounds for shared meanings between actors. An example: knowledge defines the kinds of substances appropriate for food and the kinds of materials to be used to build houses. Shapes and forms of buildings and art objects are expressive symbols which elicit emotional feelings and attitudes. Body language, literature, music, and historial objects are also expressive symbols in that they are capable of eliciting feelings and attitudes. Values are inferred from standards of evaluation which are used to rank the relative importance of alternative activities. A case to the point is Americans' valuing free speech, free press, and equality of opportunity. There are standards for evaluating whether or not specific activities conform to these values. Usually the standards are implied in the decisions of a federal court.

Society is analytically separate from but related to culture and personality. It is made up of collectivities, norms, and roles. Collectivities are groups in which there is a common basis for persons' associations. Interest groups, work organizations, families, friendship and social clubs are examples of collectivities. Norms regulate interactions between roles, as well as rights, obligations, privileges, and duties. According to Parsons, a society is not a collection of individuals; it is an organization of roles. If we wish to study individuals, we should study personalities.

Personality is composed of needs, performance capacities, sentiments, attitudes, and roles. Needs are biological, physiological, and social. Performance capacities are traits, such as physical strength, general health, muscle coordination, and general intelligence; they manifest themselves in styles of role performance.

The biological nature of a *behavioral organism,* its genetic material, metabolic mechanism, regulatory processes, and complex organization, provides energy for action.

Relationships between the Subsystems of Action

Social processes maintain relationships between the subsystems. Institutionalization maintains relationships between culture and society. Integration processes maintain relationships between society and personality, and socialization processes maintain relationships between personality and behavioral organism.

Institutions are collections of roles organized and bound together by cultural values. Roles involving similar activities are institutionalized when they are legitimated by values which are shared by role incumbents. Instances are role performances in families in that most of the time on occasions which are similar, the members of many families behave in a similar way. Parsons' action theory accounts for the similarity by assuming that persons having similar roles in different families use the same cultural values to justify:

(1)Styles and contents of role performances in similar situations;
(2)Coordination of their roles with others' roles in a family;
(3)Family group activities;
(4)Expectations for normative conformity; and
(5)Positive and negative sanctions of role performances.

Institutionalization is a process whereby a pattern of behavior is legitimated by cultural values and beliefs. An example of a legitimation process which contributes to institutionalization may be demonstrated by considering the relationship between the value of success and the manner in which persons attempt to bring about their own success. Not only does American culture place a high positive value on success as an end, it also encourages individuals to believe that a good job is a symbol of success and that an education is a means to a good job.

As students are studying, listening to lectures, taking tests, and complying with norms of an educational organization they justify their activities by saying that they will get a college degree so that they can get a good job, and eventually they will be successful. Perhaps in planning their activities they think of an expressive symbol - money - as an indicator of success. Of course, the kind of job they have in mind and the meaning they attach to success can be unique for each of them, but there is a similarity to the values and beliefs they use to justify their activities. Furthermore, in educational organizations throughout the society, professors, teachers, and deans justify their support of rules, regulations, and academic standards by referring to the same values as does the student. These officials say that they enforce the norms to bring about situations in which students will get good educations and that a quality education is a valued means for a student's success. Many organizations throughout the society are doing the same things, in the same way, using the same values.

Going about our ordinary activities, guided by our own beliefs and values, we fulfill our personal needs and goals. Simultaneously by obeying the norms of a collectivity and by using the values of a collectivity to justify our activities, we perpetuate a pattern of role expectations, norms, and cultural values. In this way the value placed on education by the society is reinforced and a pattern of behavior is infused with value, that is, institutionalized. From the Parsonian perspective, values are the warf and weft of meaning, culturally, socially, and personally.

Although socialization processes contribute to maintaining relationships between culture and society, their most direct effect is controlling and molding organic energy into social motivations for role performances. Socialization is accomplished by internalization and identification. Identification occurs when an individual wants to be like another person. He behaves in accordance with the other person's wishes in order to receive approval. Internalization occurs when social learning has been so thorough that cultural beliefs, values, and norms become personality traits or psychological dispositions of our own personality.

We think our desire for success, education, and a good job are our own goals; we acquired them by internalizing the values of our families, and the values are shared with others in the society. When we are role performing, for example, mothering, studying, fathering, dating, working, we routinely and often without giving much thought to the style or content of our behavior, express in our behavior and attitudes the traditional norms associated with those roles. This is an indication of our having internalized values and norms.

From the Parsonian perspective, institutional and integrative links between values, norms, and behavior provide actors with subjective meanings of their behavior. Actors are also aware that others in similar roles express themselves in very much the same way as they do. To the extent that most persons in a particular society manifest similar styles and contents of behavior and share similar values, a society is said to be integrated. A society is integrated to the extent that members of its population have internalized values, beliefs, and norms relevant to their roles.

The processes of socialization, integration, and institutionalization produce mutual understandings and expectations between persons and they maintain a society's organization. These processes are schematically summarized in Figure 2-1.

Figure 2-1

Processes and Relationships Between Subsystems of Action

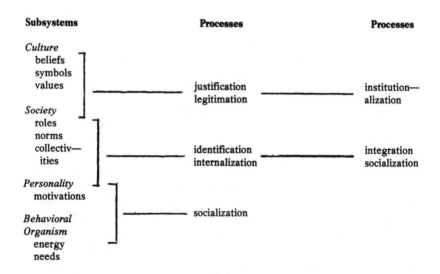

In Figure 2-1 the subsystems are culture, society, personality, and behavioral organism. Each subsystem's elements are listed under each subsystem. Two columns labelled processes list the processes which maintain relationships between the subsystems. The processes occur at two levels. The most general level is designated by institutionalization, integration, and socialization. Institutionalization maintains relationships between culture and society; integration and socialization maintain relationships between society and personality. The more specific processes of justification, legitimation, identification, internalization, and socialization are experienced by individuals in their role performances. In everyday life situations, an individual justifies his role performances by using values (culture) to legitimize his actions. He has internalized the norms of his roles (society) to the extent that these norms are experienced as motivations (personality) to behave in prescribed ways. His learning of his roles (society) included the internalization and identification processes. And socialization also resulted in the direction and channeling of energy (behavioral organism) so that eventually there is motivation (personality) to perform various roles. All of these processes were explained above in the example of the relationship between the value of success in the American culture and individuals' role performances in educational organizations.

Hierarchies of Information and Energy between Culture, Society, Personality, and Behavioral Organism

Different amounts of information and energy are contributed to action by each subsystem. Through its information about beliefs, symbols, and values culture has greatest control over action. The norms of a society have the next most information and control; personality has less control than society. Although behavioral organism contributes the least amount of control and information, it supplies action with the greatest amount of energy. Personality ranks second in the amount of energy supplied, then society, and culture supplies the least amount of energy (See Figure 2-2).

Cultural control of action occurs by groups using values to legitimate activities. By organizing action so that it complies with a group's cultural values, members of a group control their role performances. Control is implemented by group norms (society) being stated as guidelines for role performances (personality). Control or information also enters action when performances are sanctioned according to whether or not they comply with the norms. Not only does normative regulation control individuals' behaviors, it also supplies information about how to act and information about which values are relevant to role performances. Persons are socialized to comply with society's norms. By having internalized norms associated with their many roles, personalities satisfy their needs and exercise self-discipline by conforming to normative expectations. As a result, personality controls and organizes the drives of an organism into patterns compatible with normative role expectations. Thus, the hierarchy of control is from culture (values) to society (norms) to personality (roles) to behavioral organism (energy).

Biological and physiological processes of an organism supply energy for a personality's motivations. Personality's role performances contribute energy for group activity. In the example of an educational organization discussed above, each of us brings to a university or school the proper motivations and sentiments which give its organization zest, meaning, and purpose. Our activities provide energy for the organization, and it uses our work as energy. The products of our labors are used to justify its existence. Its representatives justify educational activities by appealing to the cultural belief that education is valuable. In the long run, the ongoing affairs of an educational organization can be thought of as a type of energy which maintains the cultural value of education.

The directions of control and energy are summarized in Figure 2-2 below:

Figure 2-2

Hierarchies of Information (Control) and Energy Among Subsystems

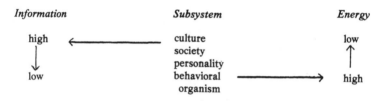

Information	*Subsystem*	*Energy*
high	culture	low
↓	society	↑
	personality	
low	behavioral	high
	organism	

Adapted from Tables 1 and 2, *Societies: Evolutionary and Comparative Perspectives* (1966), p. 28.

The following section describes how an actor uses values to analyze situations. In describing action from the perspective of an actor behaving in accordance with the postulates of action theory, Parsons described how an actor must evaluate his motivations and use values to make judgments about objects in a situation. These evaluations are: (1) value orientations and (2) motivational orientations.

Actor's Orientations

An actor may approach any situation with three types of motivational orientations and three types of value orientations. All of them may not be used in an action but they are available if the situation warrants. Elements of the cultural subsystem, empirical beliefs, expressive symbols, and values, are used as *value orientations*. Empirical beliefs provide an actor with cognitive standards for intellectual thought processes and definitions of reality. Expressive symbols indicate appreciative standards for judging the desirability of situations or objects. Values are implied in standards of morality for making decisions about what is right and wrong and for evaluating conflicts between cognitive and appreciative standards.

We can demonstrate the use of the three standards by applying them to shopping for a refrigerator. According to Parsons, evaluations of situations always involve the use of cognitive and appreciative standards. When we examine the characteristics of a refrigerator we use cognitive standards to obtain information about the size of the motor, the materials from which it is made, its size, and the amount of electricity it uses. Some appreciative standards for judging the desirability of a refrigerator deal with colors which coordinate with a decor, the amount of noise it makes, and the manner in which the doors open. The locations of shelves and freezing compartment also are evaluated. Normally, its purchase will not involve moral standards about issues of right and wrong. However, if cognitive standards instruct us that the refrigerator we like best because it is pretty is of inferior quality, there may be conflict between cognitive and appreciative standards. This is a dilemma and we will have to use moral standards to resolve it.

Three types of *motivational orientations* are described by words similar to those used to describe the value orientations. A cognitive motivation is an actor's interest in obtaining information about objects. A cathectic motivation is an interest in determining the desirability of an object. An evaluative motivation is an interest in utilizing moral standards as a basis for making choices resulting from conflicts between a cognitive motivation and a cathectic motivation.

According to Parsons, all evaluation involves cognitive and cathectic motivations. We cannot desire (cathect) an object unless we know (cognition) something about it. And all objects of which we are aware cognitively are also positively, neutrally, or negatively cathected. An evaluative motivation, concerned with solving some dilemma of choice, always triggers a cognitive motivation because a cognitive motivation is capable of arriving at evaluative judgments. A cathectic motivation is concerned with satisfaction of needs and gratifications; it cannot judge the consequences of actions. A cognitive motivation can make these judgments. It provides a capacity to appraise situations, to obtain information necessary to make decisions about conflicts, and the ability to assess the consequences of alternative courses of action. Therefore, decisions always entail cognitive orientations. Nevertheless, the decisions may result in satisfactions of either cathectic or cognitive motivations. An evaluative motivation is a desire to use moral standards to make choices between alternatives. However, even if one goes after one's desires (cathectic motivation) the decision to do so is cognitively decided. In the example of whether to buy the refrigerator we like or the one of superior quality, if we decide, as a result of an evaluative motivation using moral standards, to choose the one we like we will use cathectic motivation and appreciative standards to evaluate the refrigerator we like; then, we will use a cognitive motivation to decide to buy it.

Conflicts between cognitive and cathectic motivations are common experiences. Something as routine as selecting food at the market can cause conflict between cathectic and cognitive motivations. If we are very hungry when we shop, desiring food which is immediately satisfying, we can be cathectically motivated and consider purchases of snack food. On the other hand, our cognitive motivations urge us to choose food with greater nutritional value than snack foods. That's the conflict! Using an evaluative motivation we can resolve the dilemma by choosing one type of motivation, the cathectic or the cognitive. We will then use the appropriate cultural standards of evaluation, cognitive or appreciative standards to evaluate our choice. However, a cognitive motivation will actually be used to make the choice.

Different aspects of culture appear in each of three subsystems, as depicted in Figure 2-3. They are elements of a culture; in a society they are standards of evaluation; in a personality they are motivational and value orientations.

Figure 2-3

Cultural Elements in Three Subsystems

Culture	Society	Personality	
	standards of	*orientations*	
elements	*evaluation*	*value*	*motivational*
empirical beliefs	cognitive	cognitive	cognitive
expressive symbols	appreciative	appreciative	cathectic
values	moral	moral	evaluative

Adapted from *Toward a General Theory of Action* (1951), pp. 3-29; 53-76.

The Pattern Variables

The pattern variables are categories which describe cultural elements, standards of evaluation, actors' values and motives, habits of choice and definitions of roles. They present a series of dilemmas which any actor confronts and about which he must make decisions in order to act.

Four sets of pattern variables describe actors' motivational and value orientations. They are presented as two sides of four dilemmas. Three of them are always used to evaluate social situations. Perhaps there are other kinds of decisions made by actors, but from the Parsonian perspective, the four are the minimum number needed to describe an actor's evaluations of situations in which action is anticipated. Two sets of the pattern variables describe motivations: affectivity-affective neutrality and specificity-diffuseness. Two sets describe values used to evaluate objects: universalism-particularism and quality-performance. Quality has also been referred to as ascription and performance has been referred to as achievement.

Affectivity-affective neutrality describes an actor's motivational orientation. It designates the dilemma of whether or not one chooses to satisfy his desires immediately. If affectivity is chosen the actor decides to seek immediate gratification. If affective neutrality is chosen gratification is postponed or renounced. All action involves this decision.

The affectivity-affective neutrality dilemma involves the issue of choosing between cognitive and cathectic motivations, on the one hand, and an evaluative motivation, on the other. As explained above, cathectic and cognitive motivations are inextricably bound together. Thus, the issue of affectivity-affective neutrality involves the issue of using them together, on the one hand (affectivity), and, on the other hand, whether to use an evaluative motivation (affective neutrality). If affectivity is chosen, the choice has been to adopt a cognitive/cathectic motivation and to seek immediate gratification; an evaluative motivation is not relevant. If affective neutrality is chosen, an evaluative motivation has been chosen; gratification is postponed or renounced and further evaluation ensues. The further evaluation entails the dilemma of universalism-particularism.

Universalism-particularism is the dilemma of whether to use cognitive standards or appreciative standards. If cognitive standards are chosen, universalism describes the choice; if appreciative standards are chosen, particularism applies. This dilemma does not arise in all action; its arousal depends on whether or not gratification is deferred or renounced (affective neutrality).

When cognitive standards are chosen, objects are evaluated by using standards intended to apply to a general category or class of objects. For

instance, if professors use cognitive standards (universalism) to evaluate students, they use the same standards to evaluate all students in
the class and these are the standards considered appropriate for judging
students by the culture of the university. If appreciative standards
(particularism) are used, students are evaluated in accordance with the
professor's relationship to each of them or according to some unique
emotional response aroused in him by each. In such a case, the evaluator
is the central focus. Evaluations are based on an interest in his relationship to the object being evaluated.

Specificity-diffuseness describes the scope of significance an object has
for an actor. If interest in an object is narrow in scope, specificity describes the interest; if it is broad, diffuseness describes the interest. All
action involves this evaluation. The most obvious use of a specific
-diffuse evaluation occurs in our relationships with friends. Some of
them have broad significance for us because they influence many dimensions of our lives; therefore, they have a diffuse significance for us.
Others have narrow significance; for example, we may associate with
them merely because they play a good game of golf or tennis, and we are
not much interested in or affected by other aspects of their life activities
or personal characteristics. Parsons suggested that fleeting relationships are usually characterized by specificity, long-term ones by diffuseness. Specificity-diffuseness does not designate characteristics of actors
nor inherent qualities of objects. Describing a motivational orientation,
it describes an actor's range of interest in an object.

Quality-performance (also called ascription-achievement) is used to
describe a situation in which innate characteristics of an object are
evaluated (quality) or an object's performance is evaluated by considering what an object does or can do. Quality-performance is especially
appropriate for evaluations of relationships between individuals because
such relationships involve choices of whether to judge others' innate
characteristics, such as race, age, or sex. The pattern variable becomes
relevant in employment situations when persons are hired or promoted.
If employees are evaluated by considering their age, sex, or race, they
are being evaluated for their qualities, or ascriptive traits. If they are
evaluated according to how well they can do a job, they are evaluated for
their performance or achievement. Parsons stated that this variable is
not appropriate for judging physical objects because physical objects do
not perform.

All action involves choices between affectivity or affective neutrality. If
immediate gratification (affectivity) is chosen, an actor must also make
decisions about the scope of his interest in objects (specificity
-diffuseness). If the situation is such that the actor must be oriented to
another person, he must make decisions about whether to evaluate the

other's qualities or performances. Hence, all action involving another person requires decisions about: affectivity-affective neutrality, specificity-diffuseness, and quality-performance.

If gratification is postponed or renounced (affective neutrality), further evaluation is necessary and attention focuses on cultural standards of evaluation (universalism-particularism). This is the dilemma of whether to use cognitive (universalism) or appreciative (particularism) standards.

The dilemmas described by the pattern variables pertain to issues related to one situation at one time. Obviously, the same issues may arise again. For instance, having postponed gratification at one time, an actor may confront the same issue in the same situation at another time. Deciding not to go to a movie on Tuesday does not preclude considering the issue again on Wednesday.

Parsons' initial statement of the pattern variables included a fifth one, a self-collectivity issue which describes the dilemma of whether one's own interest or a group's interest should be satisfied. If the choice is to satisfy a personal interest, self is chosen; if a group interest is satisfied, collectivity is chosen. Parsons dropped this pattern variable, stating that there are only four basic dilemmas involved in an action; that the issue of the self-collectivity dilemma does not arise in all action. It is only an issue when an individual is acting for a group. An instance of its relevancy might occur when an individual is representing a group. An office manager might be purchasing equipment for his staff. Acting as a representative of a company which has a policy that the least expensive products adequate for the job should be purchased, he could be confronted with the dilemma that he likes expensive equipment. In such a situation, his dilemma is whether to buy the equipment he (self) likes or that which company policy (collectivity) recommends.

The pattern variables are not continua; they are dichotomous choices which any actor must make in evaluations, either implicitly or explicitly, consciously or unconsciously, as preliminary conditions for action. Preliminary conditions for action require an actor to evaluate and make choices about his motivational orientations, described by affectivity-affective neutrality, and an evaluation about his relationship to objects, specificity-diffuseness. Further, an actor evaluates the objects which are available for the satisfaction of his motivations. For that purpose he uses: quality (ascription)-performance (achievement) and universalism-particularism.

Cross-classification of affectivity-affective neutrality and specificity-diffuseness describe four types of attitudes, as shown in Figure 2-4 on the following page:

Figure 2-4

Types of Attitudes

	affectivity	*neutrality*
specificity	segmental gratification: seeking gratification in a limited relational context	approval: use of appropriate standard to evaluate an object in a limited perspective
diffuseness	love: seeking gratification in a broad relational context	esteem: use of appropriate standard to evaluate an object in a broad relational context

Adapted from *The Social System* (1951), p. 108; *Toward a General Theory of Action* (1951), Figure 3.

Universalism-particularism and quality-performance are cross-classified to describe four ways persons, as social objects, can be evaluated in interactive situations, as shown in Figure 2-5 below:

Figure 2-5

Types of Evaluations of Objects

	universalism	*particularism*
quality	expectation for conformity to a general standard for evaluating qualities	expectation for conformity to standards for evaluating qualities in a limited relationship to the evaluator
performance	expectation for achievement in accordance with a general standard for evaluating performances	expectation for achievement in accordance with a standard for evaluating performances of members of a group taking into account their relationship to the evaluator

Adapted from Figure 2A in *The Social System* (1951), p. 102, and Figure 4 of *Toward a General Theory of Action* (1951).

The attitudes in Figure 2-4 and the evaluations in Figure 2-5 can be used to analyze a two-person-interaction situation. In Figure 2-4 pattern variables describe an actor's attitudes about his desires for gratifications and the scope of significance of his relationship with the other person. The cells designated by affectivity indicate that the actor desires gratification in a relationship which has broad (diffuseness) significance or a relationship which has a limited (specificity) significance. A case of a desire for gratification in a broad relationship (love) might be desiring a response from a close family member, a spouse or a child. In any number of friendship situations actors have relationships which are limited (segmental gratification). An actor could seek gratification from a friend in a game of tennis or golf and limit the relationship to those activities.

In Figure 2-4 the cells designated by neutrality indicate that the actor has deferred or renounced gratification in a relationship and has chosen to evaluate the other person. Specificity-diffuseness describes the scope of significance relevant to the evaluation. In the case of specificity the other person is evaluated in a limited context; for instance, is he a good tennis player? In the case of diffuseness, the other person is evaluated in a broad context; for instance, in evaluating family members we take into account our understanding and knowledge of their personalities, abilities, our years of associations with them, our memories of shared experiences, and many other aspects of our relationships with them.

The evaluations in Figure 2-5 categorize normative expectations which an actor has for another person. When two persons are interacting each evaluates the other person with whom he is interacting. Parsons refers to such evaluations as expectations that the other person will conform to some standards of behavior. In the cells categorized by universalism the person is expected to conform to some general standard appropriate for a class of objects. An example of this is a professor's expectations that a student conform to a university's general academic standards. In the cells categorized by particularism there is an expectation that the other person conform to some standard which takes into account relationships between the two persons. An example might be a professor's expecting a student who is his friend to conform to exceptionally high standards because of his personal interest in the student's accomplishments; or a supervisor in a work situation might show favoritism for a friend who works for him by having less strict expectations for him than for workers who are not his friends.

The cells categorized by quality and performance indicate the aspect of the other person which is evaluated. Quality or inherent characteristics, such as age, race or sex, can be evaluated; or the other person's performance or achievement can be evaluated. The other person is expected to conform to standards for evaluating qualities or achievements.

In the example of a professor's expectations of a student, usually students are expected to conform to general (universalism) performance standards; however, it is possible that a student might be expected to conform to general (universalism) standards appropriate to his age or sex (quality). The generality of the standards defines the universalism of the expectation. That which is evaluated defines the quality or performance of the evaluation.

An expectation for a person to conform to particularistic standards for evaluating qualities occurs when a parent expects his child to exhibit age-appropriate behavior and emphasizes the importance of the relationship such as, "my son." An expectation for a person to conform to particularistic standards for evaluating performances occurs when an individual's work is expected to be similar to that of others in a work group. If two persons belong to the same work group in their interactions each may use the group as a base for a particularistic standard, judging that the other's performance should conform to the group's standards. The considerations of the relationships between the two persons, in a family and in a work group, are the bases for considerations of relationships in the evaluations (particularism). The parent's expectations for age-appropriate behavior is a concern for a quality of his child. Expectations about another's work is a concern for his performance.

Parsons used the types of evaluations of objects in Figure 2-5 to classify different societies' cultural values. That topic is discussed in Chapter 6 in the section on Four Types of Social Structures. Empirical studies of social relationships have used the evaluations and attitudes. Some of these studies are reported in the next section of this chapter.

The foregoing definitions of the pattern variables have been presented as ways of categorizing an individual actor's definitions of situations. Parsons did not intend such a limited use of the pattern variables. They appear throughout his works and are used to categorize values and motivations in several types of systems. They define a society's values. Personality theory (Chap. 7) explains socialization processes through which they are internalized as actors' motivations. Parsons' theory of social change (Chap. 5) explains their evolution as a historical process. Also, they have been used to classify types of societies, and their importance to a society is one of the bases for the social prestige of individuals (Chap. 6).

Analyses and Research Using the Pattern Variables

A review of studies which have used the pattern variables indicates that when they were first stated, the four sets were included in research projects. Recently the two object variables, ascription-achievement (quality-performance) and universalism-particularism, have been given greater attention than the two motivational variables. The object variables have been useful in describing values of organizations and societies. They have also been applied to the analysis of the values of societies at different stages of industrialization.

There are numerous studies of stratification which compare the relative weights of ascriptive and achievement characteristics in assignments of status and prestige. A novel research design was used by Nock and Rossi (1978) to determine the relative weights of ascription and achievement in persons' assignments of social status. Nock and Rossi had a sample of 536 adults in the United States rate 50 vignettes about households. The vignettes were statements about achievements, occupational and educational attainments of the husband and wife in a household. Also included in the vignette were statements about the husband and wife's families, their fathers' occupations, educational attainments, and ethnicity. These were viewed as ascriptive characteristics. The various vignettes were made up of ascriptive and achievement traits of the households. In the vignettes, the characteristics were somewhat randomly varied. Subjects rated the vignettes on a nine-point scale.

Results of the analysis indicated that, although ascriptive characteristics were related to assignments of status to the household with which they were associated in the vignette, the most important characteristics affecting assignments of status were the achievements of the husband and wife. The occupational prestige of the husband was more important than the occupational prestige of the wife.

Tartar (1969) developed operational definitions of the pattern variables and used them in a study designed to predict discrepancy between attitudes and action. Forty subjects were asked about their anti-Negro attitudes and their willingness to be photographed with a Negro. Tartar's experiment was contrived to activate attitudes in a situation in which there was social opposition to the attitudes. Subjects were induced to behave in opposition to their attitudes. The study reported the number of persons who changed their actions in violation of a previously expressed attitude. The pattern variables were used to measure attitudes in an attempt to determine whether or not they could be used to predict which subjects would exhibit behavior in violation of a previously expressed attitude. Specificity-diffuseness had some predictive power, but the other variables were nonsignificant.

Maniha (1975) studied universalism and particularism in the promotions of the higher officers in the St. Louis Police Department between 1869 and 1947. The research reported on the history of the organization of the department with respect to its depoliticization and bureaucratization. The social mobility of officers in different stages of the organization's development was analyzed. Findings indicated that merit and seniority (achievement) were important in an officer's getting promoted; that the effects of merit and seniority varied depending on the stages of the organization's development. In early stages, the ascriptive factor of ethnicity was important in recruitment but not in promotions.

In *The First New Nation* (1963) Lipset compared the values of four English-speaking democracies (Australia, Canada, Great Britain, and United States). He concluded that the United States emphasized achievement, universalism, and specificity.

Several studies have used the pattern variables to explain types of interpersonal relationships. Stouffer and Toby (1951) examined a type of role conflict experienced when one's obligations to friends (particularism) are in conflict with obligations to institutionalized group norms of universalism. They hypothesized that when this type of conflict is experienced some persons are more likely than others to resolve the conflict by acting on particularistic obligations.

Stouffer and Toby assumed that friendship obligations were characterized by affectivity, diffuseness, and particularism, and that loyalty to group norms involved neutrality, specificity, and universalism. A sample of 648 undergraduates were given descriptions of several situations in which conflict existed. They were asked to evaluate their obligations to a friend or to a group. Some of the situations described were: If you were grading exams for a class in which a friend was enrolled, would you give the friend a break. If you were working in a library and a friend needed a much-used book would you hide it for him. If you proctored an exam, saw a friend cheating, would you turn him in. Subjects evaluated the last situation under varying conditions. The study permitted the conclusion that obligations to friends were more likely to be honored when it was unlikely that students would be observed violating group norms.

Scarr (1964) analyzed the Stouffer-Toby data. The analysis permitted a conclusion that particularistic orientations decreased when risk of detection was present, and willingness to recognize a particularistic obligation depended on the situation being evaluated. Using different methods of analysis and adding more situations to the study, Scarr's evidence suggested that a particularistic orientation is made up of: a willingness to accept particularistic obligations and a willingness to act particularistically. Since a willingness to act depends on a situation and the amount of intimacy in a friendship, willingness to accept a particularistic obligation is appropriately viewed as a personality attribute.

Toby (1953) asked male and female high school seniors to name students of the same sex who were their closest friends, the best students, most popular, and most poised. Students were expected to use universalistic criteria to evaluate the best students. However, the evidence indicated religious loyalties affected the choices. The effects of religious loyalties were interpreted as a use of particularistic standards. For instance, Jews were more likely to name other Jews as best students than they were to name Christians; Christians were more likely to name other Christians than they were Jews.

The study concluded that the best students received many votes from both Christians and Jews, and that those who received most of their votes from others of the same religion were not actually the best students. It was argued that universalistic standards were used to judge students whose statuses were nonambiguous; however, when evaluators were uncertain that a student was actually the best student, particularistic standards (religious affiliations) were used.

Evidence was suggested that some persons will be more likely to use particularistic than universalistic standards. Thus, the conditions under which a preferred evaluation may be changed has been investigated. Research has suggested that group discussions can bring about changes in a preferred standard. Whether the change moves from particularism to universalism or from universalism to particularism depends on the relationships between discussants, whether they are from the same ingroup or are strangers to each other. Data supported an inference that ingroup discussions promote particularistic standards and discussions among strangers promote universalistic standards. (Alker and Kogan, 1968; Horne and Long, 1972.)

Loomis and McKinney (1956) studied relationships between superiors and subordinates in two types of communities in Costa Rica. One was a large estate community; the other was a community of family-size farms. Social science specialists in Latin American studies were asked to evaluate the way superiors in the two types of communities would relate to subordinates. In the large-estate community, an administrator's relations with a subordinate supervisor were evaluated; in the family-size farm community, an informal community leader's relationships with his assistant were evaluated. The experts used scales for affectivity-affective neutrality, universalism-particularism, ascription-achievement, and diffuseness-specificity. In the large-estate community, the relationships were characterized as moderate neutrality, universalism, achievement, and specificity. In the family-farm community, the relationships were characterized as relatively high affectivity, particularistic, ascriptive, and diffuse.

Williams (1959) used the pattern variables to study two types of social relationships. Type I friendships were characterized by affectivity, diffuseness, and collectivity. Type II friendships were characterized by neutrality, specificity, and self. Two hundred ninety-seven individuals and 103 of their best friends gave information about their relationships. The study reported that women and young persons were more likely than men and older persons to have type I friendships. Type I friendships were also more likely than type II to have had a long history, to have originated in social or home environments, and prior to the friendship to have had a common acquaintance with a third party. These type I friends were also inclined to perceive that they shared common beliefs and values, similar social backgrounds, and empathy.

Zurcher, et al., (1965) studied universalistic-particularistic role orientations of employees in Mexican and American banks. There were 38 Mexican, 43 Mexican-American, and 148 Anglo-American employees studied. By using the Stouffer-Toby scale, the Mexicans were observed to have more particularistic orientations than either of the other two groups, and the Mexican-Americans were more particularistic than the Anglo-Americans. The study suggested that because the Mexican bank used universalistic norms in employee relationships, the Mexican employees, with particularistic orientations, were alienated from their work.

References and Suggestions for Further Study

Action theory and the pattern variables in Parsons' early writings can be found in:
  Chap. 1. "Categories of the Orientation and Organization of Action" and in Figures 1-11 accompanying Pt. II, in *Toward a General Theory of Action* (1951);
  Chap. 1."The Action Frame of Reference and the General Theory of Action Systems: Culture, Personality, and the Place of Social Systems," in *The Social System* (1951);
  "Some Comments on the State of the General Theory of Action" (1953);
  Introduction to "An Approach to Psychological Theory in Terms of the Theory of Action" (1959).

Parsons answered some of the critics of action theory in "The Point of View of the Author" (1961).

Dubin's "Parsons' Actor: Continuities in Social Theory" (1960) stimulated Parsons' clarification of the multiple frames of references of action theory; see also Parsons' "Pattern Variables Revisited: A response to Robert Dubin" (1960).

Cross-classifications of the pattern variables can be found in *The Social System* (1951), especially the last part of Chapter III on "Types of Social Value-Orientation."

Loubser, *et. al., Explorations in General Theory in Social Sciences* (1976), vol. I, contains several papers on action theory.

Sources for Parsons' views about the importance of the cultural subsystem in action theory are:
  "The Place of Ultimate Values in Sociological Theory" (1935);
  The Social System (1951), especially Chap. 8 on "Belief Systems and the Social System: The Problem of the 'role of ideas';" and Chap. 9 on "Expressive Symbols and the Social System; The Communication of Affect";
  Theories of Society (1961), vol. II, "Introduction (to Part Four, Culture and the Social System)" and the editorial foreword to Section B (Belief Patterns) and Section C (Expressive Symbolism);
  "The Concepts of Culture and of Social System" (1958).

An early discussion of the cultural subsystem's components can be found in *Theories of Society* (1961), vol. II, Introduction to Part Four on Culture and the Social System.

Parsons had much to say about the values of American culture.
His essays about empirical issues, such as ethnicity and religion, contain his thoughts on that topic.
In "The Link Between Character and Society" (1961) he (with White) responded to David Riesman's view of the American character.

For some operational definitions of the pattern variables, see Blau (1962); Dean (1961); and Scarr (1964).

The following discuss action theory in a general historical context: Hinkle (1963), Lazarsfeld (1972), and Rubinstein (1977).

Chapter 3

Systems Theory

Introduction

Parsons' systems theory is based on assumptions about three types of systems: organic systems, action systems, and social action systems.

1. *Organic systems* are: (a) self-regulating; (b) maintain themselves distinct from their environments; (c) made up of units which contribute to system maintenance; and (d) integrated, that is, their units' activities are coordinated. All of the systems with which his theory deals were defined as living organic systems. From such a perspective, his theory focused on describing the structures and processes which contribute to integration and maintenance of organic systems.

2. An *action system* is one type of organic system. It is a human being with a culture who is symbolically oriented to at least one object. After stating the components of action, as described in Chapter 2 herein, Parsons treated action as a system and referred to it as a general action system. The definition of that system is given below.

3. A *social action system* is a subcategory of action systems. It includes at least two humans interacting in the context of a socio-cultural definition of a situation. Parsons' works which describe activities involving more than one person were concerned with the analysis of social action systems. Although he frequently referred to societies as "social systems," the action frame of reference was always an integral part of his theory of social systems; hence, in his writings, "social system" can be assumed to be equivalent to social action system.

As a result of socialization, as an organism (organic system), a person develops into a personality with a culture. Thereafter, cultural objects and symbols having been internalized, a person relates his activities to cultural values and social norms. Consequently, the person is an action

39

system in that when the person acts he uses values and norms to evaluate situations and objects. When an individual is interacting with another person they share cultural definitions of situations and they comprise a social action system. Parsons has also referred to this type of system as a system of interaction between ego (the actor) and alter (the other).

Very complex social action systems have also been analyzed, for example, an economy, a family, the American university, a political system, and society. The primary focus of analyses of these complex social action systems is the socio-cultural integration of the many actors within the systems. Although Parsons' theory is based on the assumptions of action theory, he has stated that technically individuals or collectivities act in situations and social systems function in environments. Nevertheless, he analyzed non-action systems as though they were action systems, for instance, his analysis of the conditions for human action, described in this chapter.

Assumptions of Systems Theory

Parsons' social action systems function in the same way organic systems function. Therefore, the following characteristics of organisms are assumptions of his systems theory. A living organism is made up of units which are interrelated and, taken together, the units form a boundary-maintaining entity. Its parts or units are in contact with each other, but any one unit is not necessarily in direct contact with all of the other units. An organism exists in some kind of environment and its units have some contact with the environment, although not necessarily direct contact with all of the environment. Before stating Parsons' approach to the study of action systems, an illustration of a systems analysis of a family is presented for the purpose of demonstrating the overall perspective of systems theory.

When we look at something as a system the first thing we are interested in is identifying the units of the system. The units of a family are its members: parents of one or more generations and children. Let us assume we are interested in the study of interaction within a family and, further, that we operationally define interaction as verbal communication. In this example, the focus is on communication, but other types of interactions could be used to define the family as a system. If we are observing verbal communications we want to know whether or not family members talk to each other, indirectly or directly: Do their verbal communications influence each other? If the mother, father, and children talk to each other, either directly or indirectly, and if they mutually influence each other, their interactions define the boundaries of a family as a system. If they do not talk to each other or influence each other, the family is not a system. From the perspective of systems theory, the major interest is the family. We are only interested in its members insofar as their activities affect the family; their activities which do not affect the family are not relevant to the system analysis of the family.

There are several types of analyses subsumed within systems theory and the most important of these are: an analysis of system processes, functional analysis, and structural analysis.

After a system's units have been identified, an analysis of processes describes activities of the units. The following are identified: interactions and exchanges between units, modes of communication, styles and contents of interactions. In analyzing a family, we could include the study of socialization, observe consumption patterns, health and nutritional practices, and recreational activities.

A functional analysis identifies the processes which maintain a system, processes which maintain the boundary between a system and its external environments, as well as environmental conditions which affect a system's stability or instability. The crucial question is: What does a process do for the particular system? In answering the question, Parsons classified the answers according to whether a process focused on internal workings of a system or a system's relationship with its external environment.

Parsons thought that a functional analysis is more analytical and less easily referenced to concrete empirical phenomenon than the other types of analyses subsumed under systems theory. Referring to a family as a system, in a traditional family, an adult male usually contributes economic resources and members share love and emotional support. Also, family members contribute knowledge and information about how to solve problems. This kind of analysis provokes an interest in identifying the kinds of things a family needs in order to keep the family together as a unit, needs for the family to maintain itself as a working unit and to maintain its boundaries. All of these issues, concerned with how the family is sustained as an entity, comprise a functional analysis. Furthermore, after a family's needs have been identified, its units are examined to determine how each unit contributes to the satisfaction of those needs and to the maintenance of a family in a particular environment.

Structural analysis is a third concern of systems theory. The study of stable, enduring relationships among the units of a system is a structural analysis. Using our example of the family again, let us consider the structure of power in a family. While there are many kinds of power, for the purposes of discussion, let us assume that power is the control over decisions. A person who makes all of the decisions which affect a family has the most power; a person who makes no decisions affecting the family has the least power. If we find that the female adult makes most of the decisions, that the child makes none, and the male adult makes some, we have defined one type of power structure. We might be interested in comparing this structure with one in which power is more equalitarian: All members of the family participate equally in decision-making processes. The study of how each of these power structures affects the family as a whole is, therefore, a structural analysis.

Finally, the theory includes a study of structural change. An analysis of structural change explains changes in relationships between system units and how such changes affect a system. In the above example of the two types of power structures in a family, if in one family we found that the power structure changed from the one in which the female adult had the most power to the equalitarian structure, an identification of the change and an analysis of its effects on the family would be an analysis of structural change.

By way of summary, the requirements for analyzing something from the perspective of Parsons' systems theory are:

1. A system is defined by identifying units which are interrelated, either directly or indirectly. This identifies a system and locates its boundaries so that we know what is inside of it and what is outside of it.

2. Activities of units are identified and defined as system processes.

3. A functional analysis describes the processes which maintain a system, specifies a system's needs, describes how processes contribute to the needs, and, coincidentally, to the survival of a system.

4. Structures are delineated by identifying stable continuous relationships between units.

5. A structural analysis explains how a particular structure, as in 4 above, affects a system, its maintenance, and self-regulation.

6. Changes in a system's structure are identified. The source of change is identified as being internal to the system or external to it. Changes in structure are analyzed for the purpose of determining how they affect a system.

Processes are presumed to maintain any organic system in equilibrium. There are four corollaries to this general assumption:

1. A principle of inertia states that the rate and direction of a system's action will be unchanged unless it is met by opposing forces.

2. A principle of action and reaction states that if there is a directional change it will be balanced by opposition of force equal to the force of the change.

3. A principle of effort states that changes in rates of actions are proportionate to their motivational forces.

4. A principle of integration states that a unit which is central and im-

portant to a system's pattern of organization is maintained in a system's organization.

Parsons proposed that systems should be analyzed by determining which processes are concerned with matters external or internal to a system, as well as those which are primarily concerned with means and ends. From these perspectives, four system problems were identified as a result of Bales' studies of the interactions of members of small groups as set forth below.

Bales' Interaction Process Analysis

Robert F. Bales observed the discussions of members of small, task-oriented experimental groups. The groups evaluated a situation in which an employee had difficulty with workers above and below him in a status hierarchy. Members of the experimental groups were asked to decide, as a group, why the person had the problem and what he should do about it. Discussions of the problem were recorded and the 12 categories used to record types of interactions in groups have become familiar as categories for interaction process analysis.

As a group discussed the problem, members' statements were classified as handling the following problems: (1) task-directed problems of orientation, evaluation, and decision, and (2) group-directed problems of social control, integrating members into the group, and handling tension between members. These were then further specified as four types of problems that a group, as a system, had to solve: (1) orientations and evaluations of the problem were categorized as adaptation to the situation; (2) arriving at a decision was said to be attaining the group's goal; (3) holding the group together by handling feelings of hostility created by the discussions was referred to as managing tension; and (4) keeping the group together until a decision was reached was designated as integrating the group. Bales and Parsons generalized these as four problems which all systems must solve: *adaptation* (to the situation), *goal-attainment* (solving the problem), *integration* (keeping the group together), and a *latency problem* (handling tensions among members).

Four Problems for All Social Action Systems

The four system problems became an integral part of Parsons' theory. Justification for their importance follows from the assumptions of his theory of action systems:

1. Since all action is directed to the attainment of ends or goals, an action system must be concerned with *goal-attainment*. The goal-attainment problem includes a need to rank goals.

2. Since the theory assumes that an organic system maintains itself as a system, a system must adapt to its environments by obtaining resources and facilities for handling all of its problems, thereby contributing to its self-maintenance, hence, the problem of *adaptation*.

3. *Integration* refers to a need to regulate and coordinate units of a system so that they contribute to system maintenance, as well as a need to regulate units so that conflict between units does not destroy a system. The integration problem follows from the assumption that organic systems are self-regulating.

4. *Latency,* also called tension-management, and most frequently pattern-maintenance, denotes a need to motivate and stimulate units to provide necessary services and support for a system and its goals. In the case of the group discussions, communications which contributed to and maintained group solidarity were used. Parsons assumed that values, beliefs, and symbols are used to solve this problem.

The pattern-maintenance-tension management problem is designated as the latency problem because cultural values and beliefs are not always manifest in action; some of them are latent. In a group, for instance, from a reservoir of commitments to values, individuals can tap the group's latent values in order to motivate others in the group. The pattern-maintenance aspect of the latency problem refers to a need for a stable pattern of values within the group. The tension-management aspect refers to a need for containing disruptions to group processes. The last resort for handling disruptions is a group's beliefs, values, and symbols. If these cultural elements are continually in a state of flux, appealing to them in order to resolve conflict or in order to legitimate activities is ineffective, hence, the importance of maintaining a pattern of values and beliefs, designated as pattern-maintenance.

Parsons classified the four problems as to their points of concentration. Adaptation and goal-attainment have a focus external to a system. The adaptation problem is concerned with adjustments to external and internal conditions and the procurement of resources for such adjustments. Goal-attainment processes define and rank system goals and allocate resources among conflicting goals. Both must be concerned with the external environment.

The problems of latency or pattern-maintenance and integration have focus to internal aspects of a system. Latency is directed to intra-unit integration. Values, beliefs, and symbols are anchored in the various units of an action system. Activities directed to pattern-maintenance nurture and guard the integrity of the various units by maintaining their values and relating the values to their legitimate depositories. Integration focuses on inter-unit relationships. Such activity includes defining units' rights, duties, normative regulations, as well as enforcing rules and regulations which resolve conflicts between units.

Parsons assumed that actions require judgments about whether objects should be used as means or as ends. Actions concerned with the problems of adaptation and latency treat objects as means. Actions directed to the problems of goal-attainment and integration view objects as ends. The means-ends issue identifies the instrumental-consummatory dimension of action, and together with the external-internal distinction, classifies the focus of each problem, as shown in Figure 3-1.

Figure 3-1

System Problems

Types of Needs

	Instrumental (means)	*Consummatory* (ends)
Environmental Referent		
External	Adaptation	Goal-attainment
Internal	Latency (pattern-maintenance)	Integration

Adapted from Figure 1.1, *The American University* (1973), p. 12.

Stinchcombe's Application of the Four Problems

Stinchcombe (1975) analyzed traffic as a system, defining four problem areas. His analysis provides a good example of an analytical use of the four problems. Modes of transportation must adjust to the geography of the physical environment (adaptation) by securing places to route paths for traffic so that vehicles have a monopoly on the continuous use of routes. The routes must be constructed to interconnect so persons and motor vehicles can get on and off a route and do not end up in the middle of nowhere. The main goal (attainment) of a traffic system is finding out where people want to go and their points of origin. Since many people move in the same direction at the same time, the information must be communicated to those who handle the adaptation problem so that routes can be designed with adequate capacity to handle the flow of traffic. Integration is handled by the control and regulation of rights to operate vehicles and to use traffic routes and by erecting signs and symbols which coordinate pedestrian and motor vehicles' movements. The integration problem is also addressed by traffic laws, their enforcement, and the licensing of drivers. Drivers must understand these signs, symbols, and laws and be committed to the value of safe travel. Driver education courses train them to know, support, and value motor vehicle and traffic laws, thereby addressing the pattern-maintenance problem.

Relationships between Motivations and System Problems

Bales, Parsons, and Shils hypothesized that the four system problems could be thought of as four different phases of action. Action is in a particular phase when activity is focused on one of the four problems. Thus, there are adaptation, goal-attainment, integration, and latency phases of action. The pattern variables were then used to describe actors' orientations in each of the four phases of action.

It will be recalled from Chapter 2 that all action involves actors' evaluations of objects and their attitudes about the gratificational potentiality of objects. Four sets of pattern variables describe these: First, actors' attitudes are defined by affectivity—affective neutrality and specificity-diffuseness; evaluations of objects are defined by universalism-particularism and quality-performance. From a perspective of a group as a social action system, all action involves evaluations described by combinations of these variables.

Prior to working with Bales on the system problems, Parsons viewed the pattern variables as ways of categorizing an individual actor's evaluations of situations. The pattern variables were used to classify action from the perspective of an actor. After working with Bales on the system problems, he viewed them as ways of describing individuals' actions from the perspective of a social system, in this case, a group, in which an individual is interacting with others. In the previous sections of this book, as the pattern variables were defined, the examples given were stated from the perspective of an actor who was evaluating a situation. After working with Bales on the four system problems, Parsons became aware of the multiple perspectives from which action could be viewed. Although he considered one actor in a situation, evaluating objects from the perspective of his cultural beliefs and values as an action system, he formulated the four system problems from the perspective of the group as a social action system. The problems of adaptation, goal-attainment, integration, and pattern-maintenance were conceived as problems, not of individuals, but as problems of a group. The pattern variables were then used to classify actors' attitudes and evaluations appropriate for solving a group's problems from the perspective of the group as a system. He postulated that when the pattern variables are used to describe action from the perspective of a system within which an actor is acting, an object variable must be matched with an attitudinal variable. Each phase of action was then described by a combination of pattern variables, using one object variable (universalism-particularism or quality-performance) and one attitudinal variable (affectivity—affective neutrality or specificity-diffuseness).

From the perspective of a group, the nature of each problem provides a frame of reference within which actors' behaviors are evaluated. For instance, when individuals in a group are working on the problem of goal-attainment for the group, norms regulate an individual's behavior so that it is viewed by the group as consistent with the objective of attaining group goals. Actors are expected to evaluate objects as to their potentiality for attaining group goals, thus affective motivations indicating desires for gratificaton of goal-attainment are countenanced. Similarly, with each of the other three problems, group members are expected to adopt perspectives appropriate to solutions to the problems. The perspectives appropriate to each problem are described by combinations of the pattern variables set forth in Figure 3-2.

Figure 3-2

Relationships of System Problems to Evaluations of and Attitudes Toward Objects

System Problems	Evaluations	Attitudes
adaptation	universalism	specificity
goal-attainment	performance	affectivity
integration	particularism	diffuseness
latency	quality	affective
(pattern		neutrality
maintenance)		

Adapted from *Economy and Society* (1956), p. 36.

Adaptation and latency problems direct attention to a concern with the means of action; goal-attainment and integration issues direct attention to the ends of action. When objects are treated as means, they are evaluated in a more general frame of reference than when they are evaluated as ends. In Figure 3-2 universalism and quality describe such a general evaluative perspective concerned with the general purposes for which objects can be used. On the other hand, the goal-attainment and integration phases of action require a more limited interest; objects are evaluated as ends or as being appropriate for consumption or gratification. The issue is, what can the objects do for the group? Performance and particularism direct attention to that issue.

In Figure 3-2, with regard to adaptation, the universalism orientation of adaptation designates a need to cognitively evaluate objects. After cognitively evaluating them, objects need to be seen as useful for the group. Specificity denotes a group's expectation that in solving the problem of adaptation members of the group will have attitudes toward objects which are concerned with objects' usefulness for the objectives of the group.

Whatever the purpose of action, a goal-attainment phase of action indicates the purpose has been accomplished. It is the end state of action. Affectivity describes members' attitudes toward objects as indicating that they recognize that objects have been gratifying. Evaluations of objects as to their performance potential have been required in order to attain the group's goals.

Activities directed to the integration problem must be concerned with maintaining a group as a system until its purpose is accomplished. The diffuseness of actors' attitudes refers to the requirement that they have a concern for the group as a whole. Particularism denotes that relationships among group members are emphasized.

Latency or pattern-maintenance problems are directed to maintaining the group's values. In solving this problem, attitudes cannot be concerned with special interests. Attitudes of neutrality signify an interest in the general culture of the group and the need for a generalized commitment to the group's values. The latency or pattern-maintenance problem directs attention not as much to concrete objectives, such as accomplishing a goal or making rules, rather there is concern for the loyalty and support among group members. The objects which are evaluated are the units of the group, in this case, the members of the group. If attitudes among the group members are affectively loaded, either negatively or positively, tension can increase, not decrease. Therefore, neutrality is appropriate for describing the appropriate attitudes for handling the latency problem. Moreover, if members' performances are emphasized and related to their contributions toward the group's efforts, tension or conflict might ensue. Consequently, members' evaluating each other for their qualities rather than their performances lessens tension or conflict among members of the group.

Integration of an Action System

An action system is composed of a lot of acts strung out over time. When activity is focused on a particular problem, there is an interval when it is directed toward planning an attack on the problem, and there is an interval when the problem is being solved or has been solved. Therefore, for each phase of problem-solving, action includes an initiating and a culminating phase. In Figure 3-3, combinations of the pattern variables are rearranged to categorize action at the beginning and at the end of each problem phase.

Figure 3-3

Pattern Variable Shifts in Phases of Action

System Problem	Phase	Pattern Variables
adaptation	initiating culminating	universalism-specificity performance-neutrality
goal-attainment	initiating culminating	specificity-performance affectivity-particularism
integration	initiating culminating	affectivity-particularism diffuseness-quality
latency	initiating culminating	diffuseness-quality neutrality-universalism

Adapted from *Working Papers in the Theory of Action* (1953), pp. 183-187.

Phases of action are interrelated and coordinated as a result of their having the same values. Common values between the phases can be read off of Figure 3-3. Referring to that figure, specificity-performance values are relevant to both adaptation and goal-attainment activities. Goal-attainment and integration are both guided by affectivity and particularism; integration and latency, by quality and diffuseness; and latency and adaptation have universalism and neutrality in common. The sharing of the same values in problems of action indicate that the values underlying each phase of action are connected and interrelated to values in adjoining phases. Such sharing of values among the phases provides

what Parsons called links between object and attitudinal values and between the four phases of action. The links in the values of the four
phases of action contribute to the equilibrium of an action system. They
coordinate activities directed to the system problems.

Each phase of action also has performance and sanction norms. From
an actor's perspective, the normative prescriptions are communicated to
him as others' expectations about how he should behave (performance
norms) and as their attitudes toward him (sanction values). The actor is
expected to behave so as to show achievement, appreciation, cultural responsibility, and solidarity. As a result of compliance with these expectations, the actor can expect to receive the following attitudes from
others: approval, response, esteem, and acceptance. These norms and
the pattern variables categorizing them are depicted in Figure 3-4.

Parsons' writings on socialization explained an actor's internalization
of the sanction values and performance norms. Chapter 7 herein, Personality and Social Interaction, explains the internalization process and
the use of sanctions and expectations in interactions.

Figure 3-4

Performance and Sanction Norms Appropriate for Each Phase of Action

Adaptation		*Goal-Attainment*
	universalism	*affectivity*
	neutrality	*particularism*
specificity	P achievement	P appreciation
performance	S approval	S response
quality	P cultural	P solidarity
diffuseness	responsibility	S acceptance
	S esteem	
Latency		*Integration*

P= performance norms
S= sanction values

Adapted from *Working Papers in the Theory of Action* (1953), p. 203; *Family,
Socialization and Interaction Process* (1955), pp. 172-173.

A group is integrated because all of its members are guided by the performance and sanction norms set forth in Figure 3-4. For each phase of action, actors' behaviors are regulated by the appropriate norms. For instance, in adapting to a situation, members of a group are all expected to conduct themselves so that the group's goals are achieved. Each member tries to contribute to the achievement of group goals, and each communicates to others that they are expected to do likewise. Also, actors use approval to sanction each other's behavior, either giving approval for contributing to the group effort or withholding approval when contributions are not forthcoming. In activities directed to goal-attainment actors are expected to show appreciation for a group's goals. If they do, they receive response from others in the group. In attempting to contribute to integration of the group they are expected to demonstrate that they support the group, thereby increasing group solidarity. If they do this they will receive the group's acceptance. In handling the latency, tension-management, pattern-maintenance problem they are expected to demonstrate that they subscribe to the group's values. Their behavior is expected to symbolize their commitment to the culture of the group. If they conform to these expectations they can expect to have the esteem of other members of the group. These normative regulations of action coordinate members' activities, guiding and directing them to solutions of the four problems.

A great deal of Parsons' work was devoted to explanations of the processes which integrate social action systems and how system integration is maintained. According to him, the patterns given in Figures 3-2, 3-3, and 3-4 are used by persons who belong to the same social action system. Interactions between members of a system are coordinated and interrelated as a result of the members' orienting their activities to the same four system problems and as a result of their adopting the same perspectives described by the pattern variables as presented in Figures 3-2, 3-3 and 3-4.

The General Action System

By combining the theory of action (Chapter 2) and the theory of systems, Parsons arrived at a general theory of action systems. In his general theory, the four components of action, described in Chapter 2, were referred to as: a cultural subsystem, a social subsystem, a personality subsystem, and a behavioral subsystem. As does all organic systems, the general action system solves each of the four problems. Accordingly, activities of each subsystem are categorized as being involved in solutions to one of the problems.

The theory of action systems is presented here as a description of an individual actor. Since the goals of action are those of an actor's personality, goal-attainment is the province of personality. As a source of energy for personality's motivation, the behavioral aspects of an organism (behavioral subsystem) are primarily concerned with adapting action to an environment; they are focused on the problem of adaptation. A culture (cultural subsystem) provides values, beliefs, and symbols for evaluating and defining situations. Values, beliefs, and symbols are used to solve the latency problem. Social systems (groups) provide norms for an actor's self-control and sanctions from others with whom he interacts. Such normative regulation is addressed to the problem of integration in that norms which control an actor's behavior coordinate his behavior with that of persons with whom he interacts.

Symbolic Media in the General Action System

Relationships between the four subsystems of action are maintained by four media: intelligence, performance capacity, definitions of situations, and affect. Each of the media is anchored in one of the subsystems of the general action system.

Intelligence is anchored in a behavioral subsystem; performance capacity in personality subsystem. Definitions of situations are anchored in a cultural subsystem, and affect, in a social subsystem. The media are not concrete; they are symbolic; their form varies. They maintain and integrate relationships between the four dimensions of action. Figure 3-5 is a schematic presentation of the subsystems of the general action system, the media of the system, and the relationships between the subsystems.

Intelligence is not a genetic characteristic: it is produced by socialization processes. It is a capacity to solve cognitive problems and to obtain knowledge about objects and their usefulness. Most action occurs in situations in which others are present. Affect symbolically communicates about the bonds between actors and their loyalties to groups. All action is premised on some definition of a situation. Behaviors as ordinary as laughing, speaking, waving, ignoring others, and showing displeasure are premised on definitions of situations in which those behaviors are appropriate. Values, beliefs, and symbols are rooted in a shared culture and form the bases for actors' definitions of situations. Any action requires some capacity to perform the action. Although we might think of capacities as abilities to do certain specific things, capacities can be communicated indirectly or inferred symbolically by styles of performances.

Relationships between Subsystems of Action

In Figure 3-5 intelligence provides an actor with the means to appraise situations, to use and respond to language, etc. Performance capacities permit the organization of information about environmental conditions within which action occurs. A personality relates information about the environment to motivations. It coordinates information about the environment, definition of a situation, and capacities. It harnesses action consistent with a personality's performance capacity and values in order to attain goals. Identity and style of action are affected by the cultural

Figure 3-5

**Relationships Among the Four Subsystems of General Action
and the Symbolic Media of Action**

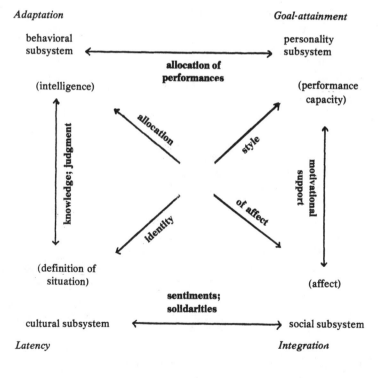

Adapted from *The American University* (1973), p. 435, 439, and "Some Problems in General Theory in Sociology" (1970).

subsystem's values and beliefs which are communicated to a personality in myriad social relationships. Groups and individuals who influence a personality are components of the social subsystem. The social subsystem is composed of others who influence action by positive and negative sanctions. The behavioral subsystem uses intelligence to distribute positive and negative evaluations among personality's relationships in many situations and groups. It also evaluates and appraises the relative importance or influence of others.

In the following explanation of Figure 3-5, relationships between the subsystems of action are abbreviated by the first letter of the two subsystem problems between which a relationship is depicted; e.g., L-G refers to the line between the lower left corner (latency) and the upper right corner (goal-attainment). The relationships are illustrated by using the example of action used in Chapter 2 - evaluating a refrigerator.

Allocation of performances between A-G refers to the use of intelligence to appraise situations for opportunities for action and to organize competencies in order to attain a goal. The searching for information about refrigerators, exploratory shopping for one, and calculations of costs of various makes and models are examples of allocations of performances.

Values are used by actors to arrive at frames of references and definitions of situations. The knowledge-judgment relationship between L-A refers to using intelligence to define a situation. In the case of buying a refrigerator, one person's definition of the situation might be concerned with a refrigerator's utility; another's might be a judgment that the kind of refrigerator one buys is symbolic of one's social status. The two points of view indicate two different definitions of the situation.

Actors belong to many different groups which are located in the social subsystem. An actor's relationships in groups influence his values and, therefore, the manner in which he defines situations. All of this is indicated by the solidarities and sentiments relationships between L-I. In the example of evaluating a refrigerator, if one belongs to groups in which others view refrigerators for their utility, the actor, too, is likely to define the situation in a similar way. On the other hand, if the actor belongs to groups in which others think of refrigerators as symbols of social status, then he is likely to view them in the same way, defining the situation of shopping for a refrigerator as a search for a status-enhancing appliance.

Values of a group and the affect which an actor expects to receive as a result of complying with the sentiments of a group can reinforce the actor's use of his capacity to perform. Furthermore, merely by anticipating affect from a significant group, an actor can become motivated to harness his capacities to bring about some type of action. If our shopper expects to receive positive evaluations or affect from groups because of his abilities to locate and acquire a desirable type of refrigerator, then these anticipations motivate him. Thus, the G-I relationship is defined as motivational support.

An actor's identity and style (L-G) involves a blending of his behavioral capacities and his values and beliefs. Some persons have no patience; others do. And here, patience is used as an example of a performance capacity. If we think about the styles of persons with and without patience with similar definitions of a situation, we would expect their styles of action to differ. If they both viewed selecting a refrigerator as a status-enhancing activity, we would expect the one with patience to spend considerable time shopping and investigating types, colors, models, makes, etc. On the other hand, the impatient person would probably order by a telephone call to a reputable dealer and later boast about the store from which the purchase was made, thus, two different styles of action.

Finally, the allocation of affect (A-I) refers to the use of intelligence to judge and rank and actor's loyalties to various groups which are significant to him. When there is conflict between groups for the actor's support, he uses intelligence to evaluate their demands. Assuming our shopper has two groups of friends, as mentioned above, one group concerned with status, another with utility, in making a decision about which group's norms to follow, the shopper will have to evaluate his loyalties to these groups and their importance to him.

The media assume diverse forms and they symbolize value standards and meanings. The pattern variables define the media's perspectives: affectivity-quality underly affect; specificity-particularism, performance capacity. Intelligence is characterized as neutrality-performance; definition of situation, as universalism-diffuseness.

A hierarchy of control exists among the media. Definition of situation orients action and has greatest control; then, affect; thirdly, performance capacity; and intelligence has least control over an action system. In controlling action the media's potency is consistent with the hierarchy of control given in Chapter 2 (Figure 2-2) in which culture (equivalent to the cultural subsystem of the general action system) was depicted as having greatest control; society (equivalent to the social subsystem in Figure 3-5) has the next greatest control; thirdly, personality and behavioral subsystem have least control of action. As was stated in Chapter 2, the potency of energy is in the direction opposite to potency of control, from behavioral subsystem (intelligence) to personality (performance capacity) to social subsystem (affect) to cultural subsystem (definition of situation).

The General Action System from the Perspective of an Actor

The perspective of an actor within the system is different from the perspective of an outsider who is standing outside the system of action and describing it. Previous discussions, as depicted in Figure 3-1, were from a point of view of an outside observer. From that point of view adaptation and goal-attainment are oriented to external conditions; latency and integration to internal conditions, as depicted in Figure 3-1. The point of view of an actor engaged in action within a system of action is presented in Figure 3-6.

The meaning of the content of the 16 cells and all of the interchanges between them is beyond the scope of this book. However, the significance of the differences in the perspectives of an outsider looking in on action, as depicted in Figure 3-1, and that of an actor confronting the situation within which action is planned, as set forth in Figure 3-6, contains significant insights about the hierarchy of control. Also, Parsons' distinguishing the two perspectives was an important refinement of his theory. The discussion of Figure 3-6, therefore, is limited to a comparison of the locations of the subsystems of subsystems.

Figure 3-6 depicts subsystems of action and each subsystem has four subsystems which are concerned with the four system problems. The contents of the cells of the personality and social subsystems of Figure 3-6 and relationships between the cells are discussed in Chapters 4 and 7; they need not be discussed here. The components of a behavioral subsystem have not been discussed in detail by Parsons, but the elements of that subsystem appear self-evident and not particularly relevant to a sociological explanation of action. The components of the cultural subsystem were discussed in Chapter 2 as knowledge, expressive symbols, values, and constitutive symbols.

By comparing Figures 3-1 and 3-6, differences in the relationships within an action system can be inferred by noting the environmental reference of the subsystems of the subsystems of action. In Figure 3-1, which describes action from the perspective of an observer looking in on action, the adaptation and goal-attainment subsystems are defined as having external reference. In Figure 3-6, viewing action from a perspective of an actor, these subsystems (adaptation and goal-attainment), indicated by "a" and "g," are placed so that they are internal to the schema, and latency and integration are in external positions. This change describes action as it is constrained by the hierarchy of control. From the perspective of an actor, latency subsystems have most control over action; integration ranks second with respect to amount of control.

Figure 3-6

Structure of the General Action System from the Perspective of an Actor[1]

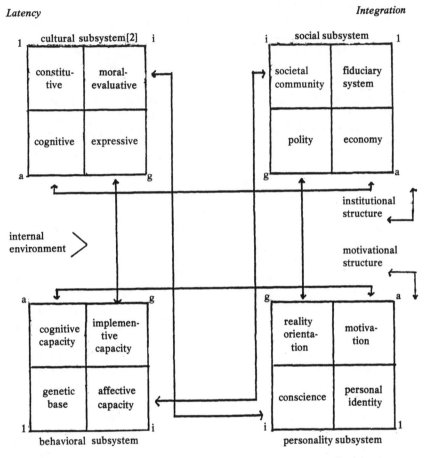

[1] Lines indicate relationships between subsystems of subsystems.
[2] After each word denoting a subsystem add "symbols."

Adapted from *The American University* (1973), Figure A.6.

Goal-attainment and adaptation subsystems have least control over action. In Figure 3-6 each subsystem of the general action system has its own four subsystems. The locations of the subsystems of the subsystems are of interest with regard to latency's control of action and the environmental reference of the subsystems.

The locations of the latency ("l") cells of the subsystems in the most external positions in each subsystem indicate that they have the greatest control of their respective systems. In Figure 3-6, the most general references of each subsystem ("l"), the genetic base of an organism, the identity of a personality, the fiduciary system, and the constitutive symbols of culture are located at the far outside corners of the figure. This location was intended to represent figuratively the idea that these elements do not enter directly into action but that they are the grounds for it. They have greatest control of their respective subsystems, and they focus on maintaining each subsystem's boundary so that it does not become embedded within the general action system's reference.

The meaning of the autonomy of the latency cell of a personality, as depicted in Figure 3-6, is intuitively sensible if we relate it to an individual's sense of his own identity and alternative identities offered by groups in the social subsystem. Many have wondered at the logic and meaning of Irish people who willingly starved for the purpose of legitimating their statuses as political prisoners. From the perspective of the theory discussed here, this can be viewed as an example of the disintegration of a personal identity (pattern-maintenance or latency of a personality) and the failure of a personality to maintain its autonomy. Eric Hoffer has discussed this process as the condition for revolutionary zeal by which persons with weak personal identities identify with social movements, and their memberships in such movements then become the source of their sense of personal identity.

In Figure 3-6, by placing the adaptation subsystems in a position contiguous to the internal environment of the action system and also in a location indicating contact external to the system, Parsons signified that from the internal perspective of the action system adaptive functions in each subsystem must adapt to the other subsystems. It will be remembered that adaptation means not only survival of a particular system, hence, a concern for the external environment; it also designates the capacity of a system to behave independently of its environment. In Figure 3-6 each subsystem must adapt to the other subsystems. Adaptive functions use resources from the external environment and direct the resources to a system's needs and goals. The external-internal focus is represented by locating adaptive subsystems in positions of external and internal contact within the general system of action.

The goal-attainment functions are more specific than adaptive functions. They have short-run significance; consequently, they are internal to the system. In Figure 3-6 the locations of the goal-attainment functions in the innermost corners of the schema are intended to depict the focus of goal-attainment as being internal to the action system.

Parsons designated integrative functions as being concerned with coordinating and maintaining relationships between system units. Integrative actions must be concerned with a broad range of issues dealing with the internal workings of each of the subsystems. Activities directed to the problem of integration have a broader, more general reference than issues dealing with goal-attainment. To the extent that issues external to each subsystem affect its own system's integration, then the integration problems of each subsystem must focus on external environmental conditions which affect its processes. Hence, integration functions ("i" in Figure 3-6) occupy the cells with internal and external references within the general action system.

Conditions for Human Action

Any action is circumscribed by physical conditions of an environment and transcendental non-empirical conditions. The physical environment is made up of matter and energy, the chemical elements, such as oxygen, hydrogen, nitrogen, and matter. The transcendental environment, or the telic system, is a postulated religious entity which is an ultimate basis for cultural beliefs and values. Action is also affected by the general action system and human organic systems.

These circumstances (the physical environment, the transcendental environment, action system, and organic system) are categorized according to the system problems. They define the conditions for human action. Each condition is a system: (1) the physical environment is a physical-chemical system, (2) the human organic system, (3) the transcendental environment is the telic system, and (4) the action system (culture, society, personality, and behavioral organism). The symbolic media of the human condition are: transcendental ordering, symbolic meaning, health, and empirical ordering. Each media is anchored in one of the systems of the human condition, as presented in Figure 3-7. The action system integrates the human condition; thus, it handles the problem of integration. Since the telic system maintains a base for cultural beliefs it is focused on latency. The physical-chemical system is the external environment and it is categorized as adaptation. Goal-attainment is the primary concern of a human organic system.

The system of the human condition has not been an integral part of Parsons' explanations of social behavior or analysis of social systems. It is, however, presented as an example of his view of the generality and utility of the four system problems. After postulating the four system problems, he used them to classify not only action systems, but, as indicated by his use of them in the classification of the human condition, they were also used to postulate the existence of non-action types of systems.

Parsons' theory of social action systems was used to analyze processes and structures of social systems. The remaining chapters discuss his applications of the theory to analyses of society and personality. Society is a social action system and personality is an action system. The Parsonian analysis of these systems follows the general theoretical perspectives outlined in Chapters 2 and 3.

Each system must solve the four problems of adaptation, goal-attainment, pattern-maintenance, and integration. In applying the theory to an analysis of personality and society, Parsons specified the types of activities which specialize in handling each problem. The cultural primacy thesis, that is, the postulate that values have greater control of actions than any other aspect of action, was used to explain the normative control of action. Following the cultural primacy thesis, each system's hierarchy of control was stated so that it was consistent with the hierarchy of control in action theory.

Although society and personality are empirically different, when they are described as systems of action, there are several similarities. In the first place, the system problems categorize stages of development in both systems. Secondly, as units in each are differentiated they become specialized in handling system problems. Thirdly, structural changes are defined as changes in values and the pattern variables describe values of both systems. These processes are specified in Chapters 5, 6, and 7. Finally, the socialization of children describes personalities' internalization of the norms of interaction as given in Figure 3-4.

Figure 3-7

The Systems and Media of the Human Condition[1]

Adaptation   *Goal-Attainment*

Types of Needs

Instrumental   *Consummatory*
[*means*]   [*ends*]

**Environmental
Referent**

External   physical-chemical   human organic
                    empirical ordering   health

                    transendental   symbolic
Internal   ordering   meaning
                    telic   action

Latency   *Integration*

[1] Each cell is a system.

Adapted from Figures 1 and 4, *Action Theory and the Human Condition* (1978),
   p. 361, p.·393.

References and Suggestions for Further Study

The summary treatment of the human condition in this book can be supplemented by a reading of Parsons' "A Paradigm of the Human Condition" (1978). That essay is one of Parsons' last writings and it is an excellent example of his style of theory construction. In it he demonstrates the range of disciplines from which he obtained ideas, recasting them into his own conceptual frame of reference.

The conceptualization of the four system problems and the pattern variables has been documented in *Working Papers in the Theory of Action* (with Bales and Shils, 1953).

The four system problems are also discussed in "An Outline of the Social System" in *Theories of Society,* Vol. I (1961).

The media of the general action system are discussed in "Some Problems of General Theory in Sociology" (1970).

"System" is Parsons' master concept and *The Structure of Social Action* (1937, 1949), especially Chap. 1, was a first statement of the importance of systems theory. Since a theory of organic systems as the foundation of all of his theoretical writings encompasses an implied methodology, his methodology is rooted in his view of the world as made up of systems. Some of his publications which might further elucidate implied methodological strategies embedded in the systems perspective are:

"The Role of Ideas in Social Action" (1938)
"The Present Position and Prospects of Systematic Theory in Sociology" (1945)
"Conclusion: The Place of Sociological Theory Among the Analytical Sciences of Action" in *The Social System,* Chap. 12 (1951)
"The Prospects of Sociological Theory" (1950)
"Order as a Sociological Problem" (1968)
"Systems Analysis: Social Systems" (1968)
"The Present Status of 'Structural-Functional' Theory in Sociology" (1975)
"The Relations Between Biological and Socio-Cultural Theory" (1976)

The assumption that any social action system has control mechanisms which maintain a system's equilibrium has been more frequently debated than researched. One of Parsons more concise statements about the assumption is contained in "The Dynamics of Social Equilibrium" (Part III of "An Outline of the Social System" in *Theories of Society,* Vol. I)(1961).

The following are also recommended:
Bales' "The Equilibrium Problem in Small Groups" (Chap. 4), and Parsons, Bales and Shils' "Phase Movement in Relation to Motivation, Symbol Formation, and Role Structure" (Chap. 5) in *Working Papers in the Theory of Action* (1953).
Zelditch, "A Note on the Analysis of Equilibrium Systems" in *Family, Socialization, and Interaction Process,* Appendix B (1955).
Parsons, "'Voting' and the Equilibrium of the American Political System (1955).
Parsons' "Commentary" in Turk and Simpson, *Institutions & Social Exchange,* Chap. 22 (1971).
Russet, Cynthia Eagle, *The Concept of Equilibrium in American Social Thought* (1966).

For an analysis of the economy as a system, see Parsons and Smelser, *Economy and Society* (1956).

For an analysis of the political system, see:
Parsons, *Politics and Social Structure* (1969);
Rocher, Guy, *Talcott Parsons and American Sociology* (1975).

In *The American University* (1973), Parsons and Gerald M. Platt, with Neil J. Smelser, used system theory to analyze higher education in America and its relationship to American culture.

"Technical Appendix" to *The American University* (1973) contains Parsons' discussion of the action system from the perspective of an actor.

Muench (1981) discusses relationships between subsystems of the general action system.

Chapter 4

Society

Introduction

A society has: (1) a definable membership, (2) control over a territorial area, and (3) a cultural heritage. It is made up of a multitude of interactions between roles. Since its members interact in the context of a sociocultural environment, a society is one type of social action system. Parsons used the theory of social action systems to analyze society. He categorized social processes as involving:

(1) Activities specialized in each of the four system problems,

(2) Relationships between subsystems of a society, and

(3) Processes through which patterned relationships between subsystems are maintained.

Societies vary with regard to their complexity. Those with organizations specializing in each of the four system problems are more complex than those which do not have specialized organizations. According to Parsons, a highly complex society has greater self-sufficiency and internal control processes than a less complex society. The information in this chapter is applicable to complex societies.

A society's most important environments are: (1) its physical environment, (2) other societies, (3) a cultural environment, (4) personalities, and (5) behavioral organisms. As is characteristic of all living systems, a society has processes of interchange with its environments. However, contact with the physical environment is not direct; it is mediated through the behavioral characteristics of a society's population.

Parsons provides us with a view of a society as hemmed in between its cultural environment and the motivations and genetic traits of personalities in its population. Its population is viewed as a multitude of persons who are goal-oriented and who have many social roles. Individuals' achieved goals are energy and facilities for a society. Indeed, the very core of a society, a societal community, exists as a result of persons' normative performances of roles. Although representatives of a society may attempt to influence individuals' goals and although normative controls regulate behaviors, there is sufficient individuality to warrant treating the personality and biological characteristics of a population as environmental contingencies of a society. All societies have to contend with such things as genetic causes of illness, the uneducated, the very young, the elderly. Persons must have the abilities and motivations to perform the functions needed by a society. These abilities or lack of them are environmental conditions to which a society must adapt.

A cultural environment is distinguished from the culture of a society. The former is more general than the specific patterns of institutionalized beliefs and values which comprise the culture of a particular society. For instance, the cultural environment of many societies includes Christian values. However, the culture of any one society institutionalizes the values in different types of organizational arrangements, such as churches, sects, social movements, schools, and administrative offices. Any one society's culture has its own variants of such organizations; nevertheless, Christian values are aspects of the cultural environments of many societies.

Four Subsystems of a Society

A society is organized around solutions to the problems of goal-attainment, adaptation, latency, and integration. Activities directed to handling these problems define four subsystems: An *economy* handles problems of adaptation. A *polity* is concerned with goal-attainment. A *societal community* integrates society. Concerned with problems of latency, pattern-maintenance, and tension-management, a *fiduciary subsystem* maintains the culture of society.

The subsystems are not concrete organizations; they denote analytical dimensions of actions. Different aspects of any one activity may be addressed to each of the four problems. Suppose a person is signing a contract to have a firm build a house for him. In the contract, he agrees to pay money to the builder; money is one aspect of the economy (adaptation). Laws defining the terms which must be in the contract are a part of the normative regulation in a societal community (integration). The type of house which the builder is expected to build is indicative of a style of life. A style of life is influenced by values and values are lodged in a fiduciary subsystem (pattern-maintenance). If it is assumed that the two

parties to the contract are associated with other people who are concerned with the political interests of consumer groups and the building
trades, the political activities of these groups are manifested in polity
(goal-attainment).

Each subsystem can be analyzed as an autonomous system, and in the
chapter on social change (Chapter 5 to follow), the importance of treating them as autonomous systems becomes apparent; however, in this
chapter they are viewed as subsystems of society. They are defined and
relationships between them are described.

Handling the adaptation problem, an economy includes not only business activity but all resource and wealth producing activities throughout
a society. It provides a society with markets, products, facilities, services, and other types of resources. The money and resources resulting
from such activity can be used by a polity as a means for attaining society's goals.

A polity is concerned with goal-attainment. Political activities define
and rank goals of many interest groups. Although Parsons did not view
governmental activity as the only activity of the polity, he said that in
modern societies governmental activity is the core of the polity. Actions
such as voting, petitioning, legislating, and policy decisions of a government are designed to allocate and mobilize resources for attaining goals
of society and to rank the importance of goals and procure resources for
them. A polity's actions also include uses of power to obtain compliance
with its policies. Political power may be used as a base from which to
create opportunities for the effective actions of others; it can be used to
enhance a leader's effectiveness; and it can be used to direct resources
to those projects which are considered necessary for a society. Since a
polity has a monopoly on the control of and use of force, as an extreme
form of power, force can be used to bring about attainment of goals.

The problem of latency is handled by a fiduciary subsystem. A fiduciary subsystem is composed of individuals' motivations and commitments to values. Values and motivations, lodged in a fiduciary, provide a
reservoir which can be used to support and justify the activities of the
other three subsystems of society. Since the normative controls of a societal community will usually be favorably judged if they are viewed as
implementations of values, the reservoir can be tapped in order to obtain
justifications for normative compliance. Sectors of society can communicate commitments to values by justifying a polity's decisions, its use of
power, or as reasons for obeying rules and regulations.

Normative control, such as federal, state, and local laws, professional
and business rules and regulations are categorized as a societal
community. A societal community is concerned with the integration of a

society. Its normative order regulates a division of labor, social interaction, and addresses all types of conflicting interests. Enforcement of regulations is also part of the societal community. These types of activities coordinate relationships between a society's units and contribute influence to the system. Influence can be used to obtain resources, to mobilize support for enforcement of norms, and to instigate actions which create regulations and controls.

From the perspective of society, an individual's learning of values involves activities in a fiduciary subsystem. The collectivities to which he belongs are viewed as a part of a polity; norms regulating role performances have focus in a societal community; and an occupational role is viewed as facilities and resources for an economy.

Relationships Between Subsystems of Society

Parsons defined a vertical structure among the subsystems as a hierarchy of control. It will be recalled that action theory postulated that values have the highest degree of control of action. Since a fiduciary subsystem is the locus of society's values, it has the greatest amount of control over the actions of society. The rank order of the other subsystems' control is: a societal community ranks second, then polity, and an economy has the least control of social processes. The rank order of energy contributed is opposite to control, an economy contributes the most energy; a fiduciary subsystem, the least.

Processes maintain relationships between the four subsystems. There are six types of relationships between the subsystems, depicted in Figure 4-1.

A *market relationship* consists of exchanges of goods and services between an economy and households in the fiduciary subsystem. Values from a fiduciary subsystem underlie consumer demands on an economy. Individuals' values, lodged in the fiduciary, are articulated through their consumer and occupational roles in an economy. On the other hand, an economy, through its advertising, distribution of goods and services, and pricing policies, influences the kinds of things which are valued. Also economic activities appropriate production processes to different types of demands, wants, and needs; they create markets, employment opportunities, and expand or contract them.

The *resource mobilization relationship* between economy and polity denotes the effect which political policies have on the amounts and kinds of goods and services produced as well as the resources created by the

Figure 4-1

Six Relationships Among Subsystems of Society

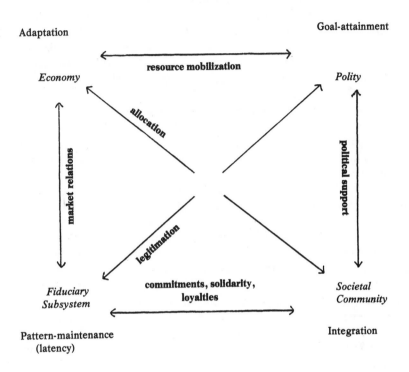

Adaptation   Goal-attainment

Economy ←— resource mobilization —→ *Polity*

allocation

market relations   political support

legitimation

*Fiduciary   commitments, solidarity,   Societal
Subsystem*   loyalties   Community*

Pattern-maintenance   Integration
(latency)

Adapted from Figure 1 of Technical Note to "On the Concept of Political Power" (1963); *The American University* (1973), Figure A.1.

economy which can be used for system goals. Products, facilities, resources, and services resulting from economic activities are channeled to different purposes and destinations as a result of political activities. Policies of a polity can distribute resources to system goals. One instance of a resource mobilization relationship between polity and economy is the way governments' monetary and taxation policies expand or limit money, credit, goods, and services available to an economy. By taxation of profits and wages there is less money for the economy and more for government to allocate to system goals. On the other hand, economic activity, by reducing production, can decrease the amount of resources available to the system. However, political activity can be used to mobilize individuals and groups to do the kinds of jobs and to supply the resources which are deemed desirable or necessary by political units. Examples of such activities have been trade agreements with other societies which increased or decreased domestic production, or the offering of scholarships or tuition grants and loans in order to induce persons to learn new technologies which political leaders judge necessary in order to provide the manpower necessary to develop resources for meeting the needs of American society. An instance was scholarships and grants offered to university students in the early stages of space explorations in the United States which were intended to provide technical competencies required for space explorations.

The *commitment relationship* between a fiduciary subsystem and a societal community refers to values and beliefs which are bases for a societal community's normative regulations. When individuals support social norms they do so because of their commitment to values which are perceived to be foundations for the norms. The norms are rooted in a societal community. The values are rooted in a fiduciary subsystem. Although a fiduciary subsystem is a relatively stable pattern of values, its values are differentiated so that they are related to different units of a society. Thus, there are religious values, political, economic, legal values, and many other kinds of values. The fiduciary subsystem relates these values to their proper units and binds the diversity of the values together into a pattern. Its most important functions are keeping the values referenced to the proper social units and relating values and motivations to the normative regulations of a societal community.

On the other hand, the integrative processes of a societal community regulate behavior keeping it in line with the differentiated values. It uses the pattern of values from the fiduciary subsystem to justify its regulations which maintain cohesion among the various value-interest groups. A part of the fiduciary subsystem of American society includes a belief in the freedom of religion and the separation of church and state. One example of regulation of activity to implement those values to "appropriate" units occurred when the Federal Supreme Court outlawed the use of prayer in public schools. That law became a foundation for normative regulations in schools - prayers were viewed as inappropriate.

The *support relationship* between polity and societal community involves decisions and policies of a polity which support the social control carried out in the societal community. Agents of social control, in the societal community, influence decision-makers to make laws and regulations which are needed in order to meet the demands of other system units. An example of this has been the ways in which collectivities in the American polity, concerned with public health, have mobilized agencies in the societal community to make and enforce laws regulating disposal of wastes. After laws specified procedures for handling harmful substances, the polity set up boards and commissions which were empowered to make further regulations as required by the society's goal of creating a more healthful environment.

The societal community includes norms which are bases for persons' organizational affiliations. For example, the norms of the American Medical Association are a focus for the associational ties of physicians in the United States. In their associations they share norms, loyalties, and solidarities. Principles developed over the years in union contracts, such as workers' rights to organize, to safe working conditions, and grievance procedures are norms regulating conditions of work which bind workers together. The norms underlying these ties are a part of the societal community; the work activities of the individuals are located in the economy; the values underlying their commitments to their work and work groups are components of a fiduciary subsystem. The collective political interests are a part of the polity. Interests, rooted in shared norms, are expressed to a polity as demands for policy decisions. If we think of a polity as politicians seeking votes, when such demands are communicated to them, they probably perceive the demands as contingent support; that is, they will get votes if they support an association's interests.

A *legitimation relationship* between a fiduciary subsystem and a polity refers to values (fiduciary subsystem) which are used to authenticate and justify political decisions. The legitimation process from a fiduciary subsystem is associated with demands that political leaders assume moral responsibility for the consequences of their actions. The legitimation relationship is easily understood by considering the way women promised to vote for politicians who advocated passage of the Equal Rights Amendment to the United States' Constitution. Demands for an Equal Rights Amendment were based on an American belief in the desirability of providing equal opportunities for all citizens. Believing that they espoused that value, pressure groups encouraged politicians to vote for the amendment as an indication of their commitment to the value of equality of opportunities. No doubt politicians committed to the amendment viewed their commitments as legitimated by the value of equality. Of course, from the pressure groups' viewpoints, nonsupport of the Amendment by politicians entailed a moral irresponsibility, a consequence of which might be losing in future elections.

The *allocative relationship* between an economy and a societal community involves an exchange of organizational procedures and needs. Illustrating the relationship, the regulations and laws from the societal community includes the licensing and accreditation of classes of workers, enforcement of labor laws, and regulations of workers and businesses. Such regulations allocate workers and activities to the various enterprises within an economy. When economic conditions change so that there are new types of workers and regulations needed, information is communicated to the societal community as claims to regulatory service. A societal community uses an economy's demands and claims to justify changes in laws, norms, and enforcements. A societal community's laws can be changed and reorganized as a result of changes in economic activity, as has happened in America as a result of changes from agricultural production to industrial production. As industrialization was accompanied by interstate distribution of products there was an increase in the number of federal laws regulating interstate transportation and rights of workers employed in interstate commerce. In a wartime economy there were laws regulating the use of scarce raw materials needed for production of instruments of war. Also, the economic organizations can adapt to changing demands from a societal community, converting a factory from manufacturing cars to tanks.

Integration of Society

The foregoing relationships between a society's subsystems integrate a society so that it is maintained in accordance with the postulates of the general theory of action. With respect to integration, the six relationships set forth in Figure 4-1 have different types of significance for a society. Horizontal relationships define means-ends relationships. Vertical relationships have goal-attainment significance, and the diagonal relationships have integrative significance for a society. According to Parsons, integrative processes are most important to maintaining a society as a system because the degree of a society's patterned and functional integration affects its ability to maintain its structure, boundaries, and equilibrium.

Patterned integration exists when the values of a fiduciary subsystem are threaded throughout a society so that persons' value-commitments are used to legitimate social processes. A society has mechanisms for appealing to its values in order to do such things as resolve conflict, mobilize support for system goals, legitimize laws and the use of power. An example of legitimations of conflict resolution occurs when court decisions and arbitration procedures resolving conflicts are justified by judges and arbitrators as being consistent with values.

A complex society has many values related to many different types of activities. Parsons assumed that in order for a society to maintain itself, its diverse values must be organized into a pattern, that is, patterned integrated. He did not specify exactly what the relationships between the values should be, but he did state that values must be differentiated and specific enough to legitimize the many activities in a complex society, and that values of different sectors of society must be bound together by general abstract values. Furthermore, the general values must be broad in scope so as to tie the specific values together.

Maintaining a pattern of values and incorporating new values into a pre-existing pattern is the province of a fiduciary subsystem. A fiduciary subsystem, the locus of a society's culture, concentrates its integrative functions on intra-unit integration. Intra-unit integration requires that persons be socialized so that they become committed to the values of the groups to which they belong. The patterned integration function of the fiduciary subsystem relates values, beliefs, and symbols to the units to which they belong and maintains the value-integrity of the units. To the extent that the intra-unit integration concentrates on shared values within a unit and preserves a unit's value-integrity, it results in what Durkheim designated as mechanical solidarity for members of the unit.

Much of the normative regulation of a societal community includes rules and regulations about who can do what, when, and where. Not the least of the inter-unit integration is the coordination of activities of persons and organizations. Much of it is worked out informally, such as the cooperative relationships between food producers and distributors of food, cooperation between prosecuting attorneys and police, between owners of parking lots and businesses. Parsons called this type of regulation and control functional integration.

Functional integration includes a society's myriad organizational arrangements which provide capacities and facilities for implementing actions which satisfy needs at all levels of social life. By way of illustration, when there was a need for health services in the United States different from those which could be provided by pre-existing hospitals and medical technicians, interest groups were formed to define the needs. Social workers, public health officers, citizens' groups, legislators, and others participated. Laws and regulations were formulated to permit some pre-existing organizations to take on new activities designed to deliver health care. Private homes, designated as board and care homes, were permitted to provide care for the elderly who could no longer live alone. Physician's assistants were recruited, trained, and certified to provide health care at an intermediate level between that provided by nurses and physicians. A need for rapid emergency care required a selection of some organization which was highly mobile. Fire departments had capacities for fast delivery. Paramedics were trained, licensed, and located within fire departments. Trauma centers became specialized in handling serious emergency medical problems. In the foregoing example, the regulation, coordination, and enforcement of laws and rules for these services are carried out in a societal community.

Also, the rights, duties, and limitations of providers of the services are enforced and administered by agencies in the societal community.

If new types of activities require that other units in a society cooperate or provide facilities for the new functions, coordinated arrangements are made. Of course, a lot of the regulation and coordination of inter-unit integration is done informally and cooperatively without rules actually specifying the arrangements. In the example of medical care, physicians acknowledge the limited skills of physicians' assistants and paramedics. They coordinate their own professional expertise with the service of the assistants and the medics. Hospitals absorb trauma centers into the routine of their organizations.

Along with handling the problem of inter-unit integration, a societal community is also concerned with the autonomy of units in a society so that specialized functions of the subsystems are carried out. The outcome is a type of functional integration of a society similar to Durkheim's organic solidarity. This aspect of integration, for example, precludes functional disorganization. By allowing only physicians to treat illness and only teachers to teach and sanctioning them if they do not, there is the assurance that those activities are performed and that there are persons who do them well.

The Structure of Society from the Perspective of a System (Society) as Actor

The structure of society from the perspective of the acting system is presented in Figure 4-2. The logic of the relationships in this figure is the same as that for Figure 3-6 in Chapter 3; therefore, it is not repeated here. The subsystems of the societal community refer to the associational bonds between persons, as in the previous example of members of professional and workers' associations. Explanations of a polity and an economy are beyond the scope of this book; students who require further explanations of these two subsystems are referred to *Economy and Society* (1956) and *Politics and Social Structure* (1969); see also Mitchell's *Sociological Analysis and Politics: The Theories of Talcott Parsons* (1967). The definitions of the cultural subsystem given in Chapter 2 are depicted in Figure 4-2 as symbolic representations of cultural elements in a fiduciary subsystem. Cognitive elements comprise a rationality system; expressive elements are categorized as a telic system; moral standards are denoted as a moral community, and ultimate meaning or a world view is referred to as a civil religion. As was previously explained in the discussion of Figure 3-6, in Figure 4-2 the four subsystems of the

subsystems are depicted to show that latency has the most general control of action; that integration and adaptation have internal-external reference; and goal-attainment has internal reference.

Figure 4-2

Structure of Society from the Perspective of a System (Society) as an Actor[1]

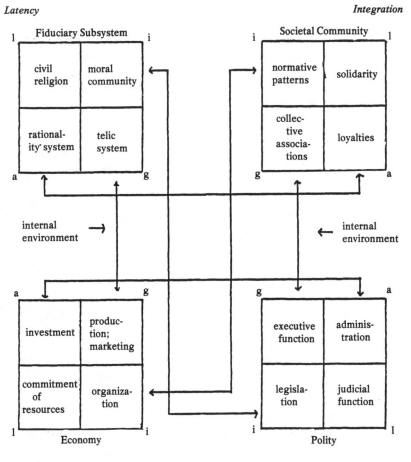

[1] The lines indicate relations between subsystems of subsystems.

Adapted from *The American University* (1973), Figure A.2.

The Symbolic Media of Exchange in Society

Exchanges between a society's subsystems are channeled through the following symbolic media: money, power, influence, and value-commitments. Although the media circulate throughout a society, each is anchored in a subsystem. Money is anchored in economy; power in polity; value-commitments in a fiduciary subsystem, and influence is anchored in a societal community.

The media have the following characteristics and functions:

1. They are symbolic.
2. They communicate institutionalized meanings.
3. They circulate throughout a society.
4. They do not have a zero-sum quality. Not having a zero-sum quality means that if one unit has power, money, influence, or commitment, the unit's possession of the medium does not decrease the amount of the medium available to or possessed by other units.
5. The media can be inflated or deflated.
6. Their quantity can be increased or decreased.

Each of these characteristics is explained in the following paragraphs.

Each medium is a type of language. It communicates a message according to rules for its interpretation. An example can be stated as money's message which is communicated by the numbers on coins and paper. Institutions define the symbolic meaning of the media and their messages. For instance, in legal transactions one dollar has symbolic meaning which differs from its monetary value. When writing wills for clients, lawyers attempt to discourage potential heirs from contesting wills by including in a will a provision that the testator leaves a potential contestant the sum of one dollar. By including the bequest of one dollar in a will, a message is communicated that the testator recognized his relationship to the potential contestant and chose to bequeath him the pittance of a dollar, further symbolizing that the omission of a larger sum was intentional. The symbolic one dollar is also used in contracts. When two parties enter into a contract, each must receive something. The sum of one dollar is used as a sum exchanged for some service when there is a reason for not stating the actual sum exchanged or for the purpose of satisfying the legal requirements for a contract.

The media are not of a definite invariable form. They are used symbolically throughout society, and their form varies depending on the context within which they are used. For instance, power is not merely the use of force to gain compliance; it symbolically underlies leadership authority and decisions. It may merely be implied in activities, symbolically communicated even though it is not used. A policeman does not have to use power; his uniform, authority, gun, and radio equipment are enough to communicate to others that they should comply with the officer's instructions. Power may be created, as when governments dispense power to administrative agencies as authority to regulate and control activities. When agencies are empowered to accomplish goals of a government, the granting of the power to the agency does not take power away from a governmental office which created the agency. Indeed, it may increase its power.

Symbolically, power can be used to manipulate resources, organizations, and values, and it may be exchanged for other valuable resources such as money, loyalty, support, and legitimation. A use of power is not always associated with force; however, there is always the implication that if compliance with demands is not forthcoming, force can be applied to elicit compliance. According to Parsons, power should be used in a collective context; it is the capacity to make decisions which are binding on a collectivity. Power is an ability to direct an organization's activities and to implement its goals. Persons who have power can take action or make decisions which are binding on a collectivity. If one has the ability to accomplish only one action, he does not have power. Those who have power have a capacity to accomplish a general range of collective actions.

Power is the primary medium of exchange used by a polity for goal-attainment. In a polity, a reservoir of power is especially important as a legitimating factor in the regulatory activity of an integration subsystem. In a societal community, if use of force is required to bring about compliance, its use may be challenged. If so, appeals to a polity may gain support for its use. Such an event is important to Parsons' theory of the structure and integration of society. According to him, a subsystem cannot legitimate itself and its activities; it must appeal to or rely on a different source for legitimation. The logic and consequence of this is contained in his theory of evolutionary change.

As a common measure of value, money is an enabling factor. It is a resource for obtaining other valued objects. For example, if an unemployed person can pay for transportation, he can look for a job and, perhaps, he can make some money. If a craftsperson can buy tools they can be used to make things to sell to get money. The amount of money paid for services symbolizes the value of the services. Since money can be used as a manipulative device for inducing others to comply with one's wishes, it is a means of control and communication. Of course, it is the major medium of exchange in an economy.

Money is, of course, purely symbolic, except in the rare case when gold or tangible objects of value are used. Usually it is only a piece of paper or an electronic bookkeeping entry that symbolizes a commitment of persons to transfer property rights. Similarly money is not merely valued for itself. It is symbolic of other valued things and is exchanged for commitments, influence, or power.

Influence is anchored in a societal community. It is a capacity to achieve consensus in a group. More subtle than power, influence does not rely on an assumption that force can or will be used to bring about conformity, nor does its use suggest that negative sanctions will result from nonconformity. When influence is used it may not be necessary to communicate reasons for compliance. Its effectiveness may be based on the prestige of its source. Persuasion is probably the most frequent use of influence.

Influence is linked to membership or reference groups. Persons using influence tap the value-commitments of members of a group in order to persuade others to follow their suggestions. Influence can be increased by a transference of influence in one group to influence in a different group. Hence, the influence of a person is increased. Of course, the reverse can occur. If one has influence in many groups, loss of influence in one group can entail loss of influence in other groups; consequently, influence is decreased.

Value-commitments are capacities, pledges or implied promises to implement values or to fulfill one's obligations to the values of a group. The use of value-commitments relies on an assumption that persons in a group are committed to the values of the group to which they belong or with which they identify. Commitments may be formal or informal, explicit or implicit. And they may indicate the existence of implied contractual obligations and loyalties between individuals. Within any organization, persons may be stimulated to comply with an organization's needs by having someone suggest to them that they have an obligation to perform some needed task. "Cashing in" on obligations can be viewed as an attempt to make latent commitments manifest. Sometimes if we do not perform as expected, someone will say that we have let them down. They attempt to persuade us to implement values shared with them, implying that we have an obligation to them personally and to values which we share with them. We may comply and do as they ask. Commitments may also be given as rewards for past performances. If a worker has received a raise in pay he thinks he deserved, he is more likely to be committed to the values of the organization for which he works. If politicians received votes or money from an interest group, they are likely to support policies which implement the values of the supporting groups. Commitments to values are the outcomes of socialization processes. They are the dominant media of a fiduciary subsystem.

Some of the interesting characteristics of the media are the mechanisms by which they can be expanded. The more highly developed the media, the greater the potentiality for their expansion. Expanding the media provides a society with opportunities for exchanges between subsystems and increases alternatives and potentialities for actions.

Loans and credits expand money. Power can be increased by obtaining support for its applications in new arenas, and it can be decreased by withdrawal of support or narrowing the range of its applications. Using the name of an organization to which one belongs as a base of prestige from which to influence members of other organizations increases influence. On the other hand, influence is decreased when the membership of an organization does not support the area of influence or silences the person exercising influence from the organizational base. When charismatic leaders articulate values which later become institutionalized, there is an increase of value-commitments. Furthermore, expanding the range of activity governed by values or increasing the generality of values underlying commitments may increase value-commitments. A decrease of value-commitments can result from a decrease in the number of persons in a collectivity espousing a value, a decrease in the range of activities governed by the commitments, or by increasing the specificity of the values so that the situations to which they relate are very limited.

The importance of the media follows the hierarchy of control. Value-commitments have greatest control of social processes, then influence, power, and money has least control. The potency of any of the media can be increased or decreased by exchanges among them in the hierarchy. A political candidate may infer value-commitments by making policy statements which he does not have the power or authority to carry out. However, the proposal may be instrumental in his being elected to an office, and once elected, he acquires the power to make policy decisions which implement the inferred values. Perhaps one of the most easily recognized exchanges between money, power, influence, and value-commitments occurs in a downward spiraling of political power. If a politician cannot implement the value-commitments of his constituency, his influence may decline, and thereafter, political and monetary support may disappear. Also, media low in the hierarchy may be expanded by mobilizing those higher in the hierarchy. One fact of political life is that money or power in any area of activity may be used to acquire influence or control of value-commitments.

The Institutional Bases of Symbolic Media

The media are rooted in social institutions. Money is exchanged through the institution of property or rights to possession of objects, services, and other assets. Power is exercised through institutionalized authority. Influence is exercised in the context of institutionalized prestige. Commitments are exchanged in a multitude of institutionalized value patterns throughout a society. The institutionalized bases of property, authority, prestige, and values organize the use of the media by setting forth rules which define areas of their legitimate use and regulate the social relationships in which the media are used. Values in fiduciary subsystem govern the use of the media and define the legitimacy of relationships in which they can be used.

It will be remembered from Chapter 2 that an institution is a complex of norms regulating behavior. An institution, such as property or authority, has societal-wide significance because its rules apply to many actors who are engaged in similar behavior in similar situations.

Underlying the use of money, the institution of property is composed of laws which define rights to possession of such things as material goods, services, equities, securities, bank accounts, etc. There are also established procedures for transferring these rights, encumbering them, and exchanging them for other things. These rules and regulations are what Parsons means by the institution of property being a context within which money is used.

Authority on which power is based is the legitimate right to make decisions which are binding on a collectivity. All organizations have implicit or explicit rules which specify the offices or persons who can make decisions on behalf of the organization. Such rules govern the use of power. As a base from which power is exercised, authority defines the range of activities over which an office or a person's power can be effective.

Groups and organizations institutionalize prestige. Stable organizations and groups have norms which define important accomplishments of their members. Members receive prestige as a result of accomplishments or performances which a group deems worthy of recognition and prestige. It is from such a base of institutionalized prestige that persons have influence. The amount of influence which they have is always relative to their prestige. Furthermore, societal-wide influence is evaluated according to the prestige of the group from which influence flows.

As previously explained in Chapter 2, all complex societies have institutionalized values. One function of a fiduciary subsystem is maintaining the values in such a way that they are referenced to their institutional contexts. This results in implicit and explicit rules about the range of applicability of values and commitments. For instance, humanistic values have a broader range of applicability than do economic or political values. Values appropriate to relationships within a family are not appropriate to relationships with strangers. Judgments about the situations in which values are applicable and the organizations to which values are referenced are important factors in determining the effectiveness of any specific value-commitment.

The media can be inflated or deflated. Inflation results in a medium's losing value relative to the value of the objects for which it is exchanged. Deflationary processes increase the value of a medium relative to the values of objects for which it is exchanged. If either process occurs in most of any medium's exchange rates, the medium becomes unstable. Instability is especially likely in the case of frequent alternation of inflationary and deflationary processes.

In a complex integrated society, when the media are highly developed, strains and tensions are communicated through them. Focusing strain or conflict on the media can result in a decrease of a public's trust and confidence in them. The greater the variety of alternative modes of using the media, and the greater and the more widespread the inflationary or deflationary processes, the greater the likelihood that system strains will focus on the media and their institutionalized bases.

Whereas in the previous discussions, increases or decreases in the media dealt with the amount or quantity of the media in a society. In discussing the inflation or deflation of the media, the emphasis is on the value of the media in exchange; how much money does it take to harness influence; how much influence must be expended to gain control of commitments to values. Of course, oversupply of a medium decreases its value; undersupply increases its value.

Inflationary and deflationary processes which affect the exchange value of money are common and ordinary. Some of the processes affecting the relative value of the other media are briefly summarized:

Generally, processes which increase or decrease the value of only one of the media cause deflationary and inflationary processes. Use of a medium outside the range of its institutionalized base can decrease its value and thereby inflate it. One of the differences between strong leadership and weak leadership may be that the strong leader knows that the judicious use of power retains power's effectiveness. On the other hand, a leader using power too frequently or in areas in which he does not have authority eventually experiences a loss of effectiveness.

Similar examples can be given for influence and commitments. Both are effective within limited ranges. A prestige base is never all encompassing and a particular value on which commitments is based is only applicable to certain aspects of life experiences. Attempts to use influence beyond its base of prestige or to implement values in areas outside the scope of others' value-commitments decrease the value or effectiveness of influence and value-commitments. It is a case of a medium's becoming inflated because of the weakness or illegitimacy of its base. If the base is weak, a medium is less valued in exchange and a lot of it must be expended to procure other things of value. On the other hand, deflation can result from processes opposite to those given above. Using a medium within too narrow a context of its institutionalized base deflates it in exchange. For instance, one's influence is most effective when it is directed to members of a group in which one's prestige is anchored. In this instance, it takes less of it to get the results one wishes than in instances when it is used in groups in which one's prestige is nonexistent or weak.

The Pattern Variables and the Symbolic Media

The pattern variables are used to characterize th evaluative context within which the media are used. Money is used as a means for procuring other things. The generality of its usefulness is characterized by affective neutrality. Performance characterizes its instrumentality. Since power is always directed to some collectivity, it is used in a relational context designated by particularism. Specificity categorizes its being directed to identifiable ends. Influence is directed to members of some collectivity, and the qualitative (quality) aspects of the collectivity are important to its use. It is effective because of members' loyalties (affectivity) to the collectivity. Hence, it is categorized by quality and affectivity. Commitments tap a value frame of reference within a collectivity, values which are general to the collectivity, as designated by diffuseness. The collective values are not limited to special goals or interests; therefore, universalism is appropriate.

This chapter has stated Parsons' application of his theory of social action systems to an analysis of society as a system. In describing relationships between subsystems of a society, Parsons emphasized the stable integrative relationships which maintain a society. Also, the media were proposed as channels through which relationships between subsystems contributed to a society's integration. The following chapter sets forth Parsons' use of a theory of social action systems and evolutionary theory to describe processes which change the structure of a society.

References and Suggestions for Further Study

The interrelationships between subsystems of a society and especially a schema more detailed than the one in Figure 4-1 appear in:
   Chap. II of *Economy and Society* (1956);
   Technical Note to "Voting and the Equilibrium of the American Political System" (1959);
   Technical Note to "On the Concept of Political Power" (1963).
The view of a society from the perspective of an actor can be found in:
   The Technical Appendix to *The American University* (1973).

Sources which contain concise statements about a general perspective of society as a system and the four problems are:
   "An Outline of the Social System" in *Theories of Society*, Vol. I (1961);
   "Systems Analysis: Social Systems" (1968);
   "The Concept of Society: The Components and Their Interrelations" in *Societies: Evolutionary and Comparative Perspectives* (1966);
   "Theoretical Orientations on Modern Societies" in *The System of Modern Societies* (1971).

An early statement of the hierarchy of control can be found in:
   Subsection: in 'A Paradigm for the Analysis of Social Systems" in "An Outline of the Social System," *Theories of Society*, Vol. I (1961); also
   "The Concept of Society: the Components and Their Interrelations" in *Societies: Evolutionary and Comparative Perspectives* (1966).

Symbolic media are discussed in:
   Economy and Society (1956)
   "On the Concept of Influence" (1963)
   "On the Concept of Political Power" (1963)
   The Political Aspect of Social Structure and Process" (1966)
   "On the Concept of Value-Commitments" (1968)
   "Postscript to Chap. 15" ("On the Concept of Influence") in *Politics and Social Structure*, Chap. 15 (1969)
   "Dynamic Process in the University System: The Nature of the Crisis" in *The American University*, Chap. 7 (1973)
   "Social Structure and the Symbolic Media of Interchange" (1975)

For some general discussions and extrapolations on the media, see a series of articles in:
   Part IV. "Generalized Media in Action" in Loubser, *et al.*, *Explorations in General Theory in Social Science*, Vol. II (1976).

Parsons discussed inflationary and deflationary processes of media related to the cognitive complex of American educational institutions, and especially their transmission through the hierarchy of control among different types of action systems in:
   The American University, Chap. 7 (1973).

An early statement of structural differentiation of social systems can be found in:
   The Social System (1951), especially Chap. IV on "The Structure of the Social System, II. Invariant Points of Reference for the Structural Differentiation of Societies."

For some of Parsons' statements about subsystems of society and interchanges between subsystems, see:

"The Economy as a Social System: Its Internal Structure and External Boundaries," in *Economy and Society,* Chap. II (1956)

"An Outline of the Social System" in *Theories of Society,* Vol. I (1961)

Technical Note to "Some Principal Characteristics of Industrial Societies" (1961)

"The Political Aspect of Social Structure and Process" (1966)

"Polity and Society: Some General Considerations" (1969)

The American University, (1973), especially the

"Introduction;" "Appendix" to Chap. 1; Chap. 2 on "The Cognitive Complex;" "Appendix" to Chap. 2; and "Technical Appendix: Some General Theoretical Paradigms."

Although not written in the context of Parsons' theory, but addressing some of the consequences of instabilities of institutions in western civilizations in the twentieth century which can be considered as resulting from what Parsons described as instabilities in the media and their institutionalized bases, see:

Nisbet, Robert A., *Twilight of Authority* (1975).

Chapter 5

Social Change

Introduction

Parsons used biological analogies to account for social change. In doing so, he discussed two types of processes. Those which maintain a society and those which change the structure of society.

Integrative and control processes maintain a society. A society's integrative processes provide mechanisms through which conflict, tension, stress, or change in one area of activity can become dissipated so that forces for change can be put asunder between the interstices of a society's many units. When a society's equilibrium is disturbed there are internal control processes which can return it to a state of equilibrium. These integrative and control processes are similar to the physiological processes by which an organism adapts to its environment.

The second type of process is similar to biological processes which change the genetic structure of a species. With regard to society, similar processes change the structure of society. Parsons treated a society's pattern of values as analogous to the genetic structure of an organism, defining social change as a change in a society's values.

Parsons thought that there are a lot of change processes which do not affect a society's structure, that is, its values; that such changes have short-run effects, usually resulting in a society's increased adaptability. Complex societies increase their adaptability by institutionalizing processes which bring about change in an orderly and nondisruptive manner. Mechanisms designed to contain and control disruptive forces are also institutionalized. For example, socialization of the young always involves anticipations of potential conflicts between generations. Anticipating changes in roles and norms, parents and educators socialize the young to conform to expectations which are different from those which the adults were exposed to in their youth. All societies have institutions, such as churches, schools, and families, which maintain relations between generations, integrating them into the social structure. Resocialization incorporates change at the most elementary level of adult life and most adults have opportunities for resocialization. Institutionalized electoral processes which routinely change the holders of political offices is a type of institutionalized change. Also, by communicating about deviant cultures and legitimating them, the arts and the mass media mobilize support for change which results from deviancy.

When serious violations of a normative order threaten, institutionalized methods of control contain disruptive influences. The institutionalized media of exchange may be used for that purpose. They can be used to instigate, direct, or contain change so that it is kept within acceptable limits. At all levels of society, influence and power are used to control excessive deviancy which has the potentiality of disrupting a society's equilibrium. Interdependencies among organizations provoke vested interests in mutual assistance, and the media are utilized to communicate information about crises in any one area and to direct resources to problems arising therefrom.

A looseness between the layers of the hierarchy of control permits a release of tension and stress created by disequilibrium. It will be remembered that information and control move from values, through collectivities to role performances and motivations of actors. Since values and norms are abstract, general and vague, they permit a relatively wide range of role performances and organizational arrangements. Their vagueness permits some degree of deviancy. Besides, controls exercised by cultural and normative orders are seldom extremely rigid or explicit enough to bring about a revolt because of repressive social control. Indeed, the nonexplicitness of cultural values contributes to their effectiveness as mechanisms of control by permitting behavioral variations; their generality integrates a variety of contents and styles of action, and at the same time, provides escape valves for the release of tension and stress in the normative order.

A great deal of control is carried out at the interpersonal level between persons who influence each other in supportive ways. Extracting compliance to the normative order is more easily accomplished at the interpersonal level than at the organizational or societal level. Such myriad interpersonal controls contribute to a state of equilibrium for the normative structure of a society. In summary, abstactness of values, nonspecificity of norms, and interpersonal controls preclude some challenges to the legitimacy of values, norms, and institutions, thereby forestalling disequilibrium.

We have discussed some of the ways in which institutionalized social arrangements bring about orderly transitions between states of disequilibrium and equilibrium. Alternation. between the two states does not preclude conflict and strain between system units. If one observes a society in disequilibrium it may appear that there is a lot of disorganization; however, after controls are operative, the society may return to equilibrium. The theorist's problem is to identify how these cyclic processes affect a society and identify the kinds of changes, if any.

According to Parsons, structural change is a change in values controlling relationships between system units. The potentiality for change of the cultural order of a society is related to the stability and integration of its values. The more stable and integrated, the less the potential for change.

Changes in values can be initiated by charismatic leaders. To be successful, a movement proposing changes in values must provide a new meaning of life for the individual and society. Leaders of movements must be autonomously independent of the power structure of the old order; yet, they must be strategically located in the power structure of a society.

Forces tending toward change can vary according to: (1) the amount of change advocated;(2)the number of societal units affected;(3)the organizational level of the units affected (values, norms, collectivities, or roles); (4) the importance to a society of the units affected; and (5) the strength and effectiveness of forces resisting change.

Stimuli for change may be external or internal to a society. Some of the most common external sources are genetic changes in organisms or their distributions in a population, changes in the physical environment, and changes in other societies. Exogenous factors which result in a change of society may also be provoked by changes in a society's relationships to its cultural environment, such as new knowledge and definitions of situations. Historically, changes in beliefs have been a consequence of scientific knowledge about the cosmic order of planets in the universe, the heliocentric theory of the universe, and knowledge about other societies.

There are many sources of endogenous change. Deviant role performances can result in structural change. Mass movements and charismatic leaders can also create organizations which foment structural change.

Parsons' most explicit theory of social change has been stated as the evolutionary development of societies. He also suggested that change can be explained by tracing strains in relationships throughout a society in order to determine whether or not strains are significant enough to change the structure of society and its institutions. A strain is a pressure between two units to alter their relationship in such a way that its equilibrium is disrupted. Change resulting from strains will be discussed first.

Structural Change as a Result of Strains

Actors expect others to behave in accordance with normative expectations, and when they do not, there are strains in relationships because of
the deviant behavior. If deviancy is widespread throughout a society it
may change a society's structure. To do so, strains must satisfy the
following conditions: (1) resistance to change must be overcome; (2) a
new structure and a model of the new order must be proposed; (3) there
must be widespread motivation to abandon the old structure and to support the new one; and (4) action complying with the new order must be
rewarded and action complying with the old order must not be.

Parsons and Smelser analyzed structural change in the American economy and summarized a seven-stage model of institutional change in an
economy. The change cycle was used to describe the transition from
owner-controlled corporations to businesses in which ownership is separated from management. Although the model was applied to economic
institutions, it was viewed by Parsons and Smelser as a general model of
change appropriate to any type of structural change of a social system. It
is an example of the above four conditions.

The change process began with (1) a dissatisfaction with the productiv-
ity of the economy and employees' dissatisfaction with a situation in
which they had responsibilities but had no control over policy decisions.
The dissatisfaction received enough support that it could not be contained. (2) Dissatisfaction was generally expressed as criticism of the ef-
ficiency and effectiveness of owner-controlled corporate enterprises. (3)
Support for a new pattern of organization and for opposition to owner-
controlled industries was mobilized. (4) Proposals for alternative organizational arrangements, such as separation of ownership from management, were tolerated. (5) Proposals for alternative organizational
arrangements were further specified.(6)The proposals were implemented and some were rewarded by profit and some were punished by finan-
cial failure. (7) Those organizational arrangements which were rewarded
were incorporated into the routine of business firms and they became institutionalized as part of the structure of the economy.

Some change of a society occurs because individuals acquire motivations for deviancy. The deviant motivations affect role performances
and, perhaps, the groups to which the deviants belong, but a society's
values are seldom affected. To initiate structural change, deviance must
take certain paths through the normative structure of a society.

According to action theory (see Chapter 2), action is made up of values,
norms, collectivities, and roles. These components form a hierarchy of
control in which values legitimate norms, and norms regulate collectivit-

ies and roles. With respect to structural change of society, each of the foregoing components of action has different strategic importance. Roles, collectivities, and norms are more specific, more replaceable, and therefore, societally less important than values. Deviant role performances alone cannot bring about social change. If deviant role performances change norms regulating specific role relationships, if values change so that new norms are legitimated, and if these changes are widespread throughout a society, then the structure of society changes. If this type of change occurs, its impact will be significant because changes in values and norms will affect role relationships and relationships between institutions.

Relationships between the sexes in American society can be used to demonstrate structural changes which might stem from deviant role performance. Entering the work force, an increasing number of American women have deviated from traditional role performances in which women remained at home to assume major responsibility for the care of children. When changes in sex-role performances result in changes of norms about what males and females are supposed to do in families, when there is a generalized expectation that women should have a career and should be responsible for contributing economic resources to a family by working outside of the home, when males are expected to assume responsibilities for care of children, when children are taught these new sex-roles in families throughout a society, and when the new sex-roles are justified by values, significant structural change in society will have occurred. Changes in norms and values will affect other organizations in society, especially economic and political organizations. This is an example of what Parsons means by changing the structure of society. Structural change must result in changes in a society's institutionalized values and normative patterns.

Smelser's Use of Strain as a Precondition for Collective Behavior

In a *Theory of Collective Behavior* Smelser hypothesized that strains can instigate collective behavior designed to bring about uninstitutionalized social change. A hierarchy similar to the hierarchial structure of the components of action was used to classify types of collective behavior. The hierarchy is composed of: values, norms, mobilizations into organized roles (collectivities), and facilities. Facilities are means which assist or hinder goal-attainment. They are lowest in the hierarchy and values are highest. The lower level components, roles and facilities, are specific to situations and not general to a society. Those at the higher level, values, are general in their effects on a society. Strains can occur at each of the four levels in the hierarchy. Those occurring at the lower levels do not affect the higher level components unless certain conditions are satisfied.

Smelser's value-added theory of collective behavior assumes that strains are most likely to occur at the lowest levels of the hierarchy, and in an attempt to mobilize activity to relieve the strain, there is an attempt to harness the force of values in order to bring about structural change. The theory defines collective behavior as an uninstitutionalized collective action designed to remedy strains by directing attention to the higher level components, values, in the hierarchy.

The logic of Smelser's theory is based on the hierarchy of control of action theory. Changes in values bring about changes in all of the components of action below values on the hierarchy; norms, roles, and facilities. Changes in norms result in changes in the components below them in the hierarchy: roles and facilities; however, values are not affected. Changes in roles and facilities do not entail changes in the components above them - values and norms.

Evolutionary Theory of Social Change

Parsons' theory of the evolution of societies provided historical examples of societies that did and did not contain the ingredients for launching them into a modern era of development. Since the historical examples were selected to demonstrate his theoretical perspective they have been ignored in the following discussion. Instead, the theoretical frame of reference within which he accounted for the evolution of societies is emphasized. In the context of the theory of social action systems and the evolution of the four subsystems of a society the following topics are discussed:

(1) Characteristics of societies at different stages of evolutionary development; (2) relationships between evolutionary processes, system equilibrium, and four subsystems of a society; (3) illustrations of evolutionary processes in western Europe, England, and the United States; and (4) evolutionary processes in modern societies.

Changes in the structure of a society are by-products of its evolutionary development. Parsons' perspective of this type of change has roots in evolutionary theories of living organisms. Although there are several types of evolutionary theories, Parsons' is related to an evolutionary theory which assumes that as a system increases in size or density it becomes more complex. Complexity means that there is an increase in the number of specialized units within a system. When units are specialized they are very good at doing some things, but not very good at doing a lot of things. Hence, as specialization increases, each unit should have some of its own needs met by other units. Consequently, unit's specialization creates a need for system units to cooperate and to coordinate activities so that each unit can maintain itself, carry out its specialized functions, and contribute to the maintenance of a system.

Parsons' theory explains progressive structural change of society, the outcome of which is a more complex, a more adaptive society. Although such a society is sensitive to changes in its environments, it is relatively autonomous and capable of maintaining itself.

Complexity increases a society's adaptability only if its specialized units are integrated into a working whole, into a system. Integration is important because when a society has many specialized units, and if units are integrated into a system, it is quite likely that when a problem arises there will be a unit capable of handling it. Conversely, if units are not coordinated and integrated into a system, it may be difficult to direct a unit's activities to the problems which need handling. As in other theoretical perspectives, we note Parsons' emphasis on system integration.

Parsons used the four ideas central to an evolutionary perspective - differentiation, specialization, integration, and adaptation - to explain how four subsystems of a society become differentiated. He restated the ideas as differentiation, adaptive upgrading (specialization), inclusion (integration), and value-generalization (adaptation).

Differentiation is merely the formation of new units. Parsons postulated a binary principle of differentiation by which one unit divides into two, as in cell division. Differentiation must result in two units which are structurally and functionally different. This excludes from the theory the type of segmentation which results from division of one unit into two units which have the same functions. Differentiation denotes one unit's dividing into two different units each of which has different areas of specialization.

If it is to survive as a distinct unit a newly differentiated unit must become increasingly specialized (adaptively upgraded) in its defined task, and the task must be performed more effectively than it was prior to the formation of the new unit. In order for adaptive upgrading to occur, the new unit needs a degree of autonomy and it must have resources for the performance of its activities. According to Parsons, significant differentiation and adaptive upgrading processes occurred when economic activities became separated from activities of a family. Historically, work was done in the context of family life. A differentiation occurred when the place of work was located outside the family. Occupational roles and familial roles became differentiated, distinct from each other with different norms controlling the roles.

Inclusion refers to the integration of a new unit into a society so that its operations are coordinated with activities of other specialized units. Inclusion may require the passage of new laws or the development of norms to regulate relationships between pre-existing units and the new, recently differentiated unit. Also, agencies of control and regulation may be required to enforce laws and norms which regulate the units. If the newly differentiated unit is to be maintained and if the society experiencing the differentiation is to maintain its stability, the control strategies must allow for autonomy of specialized units, and, at the same time, coordinate units' activities so that conflict between units is not so disruptive as to destroy a society or the units.

Value-generalization is the process of values becoming sufficiently general or broad in scope to support and legitimate a new unit and its activities. Ideally, a unit's activities should be consistent with the values of the society of which it is a part, and the values should legitimate its activities as contributions to a society. Value-generalization is an adaptive process internal to society. In the following discussion of evolutionary stages, the importance of the internal value-generalization process will become clear because of Parsons' assumption that differentiations within a pattern-maintenance subsystem occur as each of the other three societal subsystems is differentiated.

One of Parsons' general and important propositions is that as a society becomes more complex, its values must become more general or abstract in order that the many kinds of specialized activities and interests can be legitimated. If the many types of activities are to be legitimized, values must also become increasingly differentiated. As values are differentiated, a pattern of values should also include values which integrate the diverse values of specialized units. Parsons thought that a general umbrella of religious beliefs accomplished this.

The assumption that value-generalization is important for maintaining society as a system is consistent with Parsons' philosophical point of view that values are of overriding importance because they legitimize the norms which integrate a society. Consequently, in explaining social change Parsons assumed that value and normative elements are more important than material factors. This assumption, of course, is consistent with his cultural primacy thesis.

Although differentiation initiates an evolutionary sequence, evolutionary processes do not occur in any deterministic order. Units are always striving to maintain the legitimacy of their differentiated autonomous character. For example, in the United States, the autonomy of and the relationships among economic, religious, and political institutions have been subjects of ongoing debates. The matters are frequently topics in statements of politicians about what government should or should not do and in decisions of the Federal Supreme Court. Significant historical events have institutionalized increments of differentations of these institutions as exemplified in the outlawing of slavery, passage of anti-trust laws, regulations of interstate commerce, and legal directives for the separation of church and state.

Parsons' evolutionary theory explains the differentiation of each of the four subsystems of society. As each subsystem is differentated, it is adaptively upgraded; if not, the differentiation is only temporary. As a system adjusts to include differentiated units, value-generalization legitimates new units. Differentiation of each of the four subsystems is accompanied by differentiations within each of them. The discussion here is limited to the evolutionary development of the four subsystems of society. Differentiations within the subsystems are ignored, except for differentiations within the pattern-maintenance subsystem. That differentiation is important to the logic of the theory.

Parsons derived a sequential order of differentiations of the subsystems of society as a logical extension of his theory of the hierarachy of control. The sequential order in which the four subsystems of a society are differentiated defines a general direction of social change: (1) the pattern-maintenance subsystem is internally differentated into sacred-secular values; then the other three subsystems are differentied, (2) the goal-attainment, (3) the integration subsystem; and (4) the adaptation sector. After differentiation of a subsystem, if the differentiation is to be maintained, the pattern-maintenance subsystem also undergoes a differentiation process.

Stages of the Evolutionary Development of Societies

Four types of societies are used to depict stages of development: primitive, advanced primitive, intermediate, and modern.

Primitive societies, organized around kinship and religious bonds, do not have differentiated subsystems. The pattern-maintenance subsytem is the dominant organizational unit. They do not have a written language. Social organization is based on ascriptive criteria, family heritage and kinship, within prescribed geographical regions. Controlling economic and political activities, religious beliefs and kinship ties are dominant. Social control is also maintained by religious and kinship restrictions on social interaction, intermarriage and trade between groups.

If a primitive society reaches an advanced stage of development it may become launched for further evolutionary development. The characteristics which are favorable to further evolutionary development are set forth below as attributes of an advanced primitive society.

An *advanced primitive stage* is reached when the pattern-maintenance subsystem commences differentiating so that there are secular values as well as sacred values. The goal-attainment subsystem starts developing when political and religious functions are differentiated. Differentiated political functions can become a foundation for a polity.

Frequently, valuing wealth or prestige is a secular intrusion which fractures kinship ties and kinships groups' exclusive control over geographical areas. Intermarriages between kinship groups may be permitted because they increase a group's wealth or prestige. Such a splintering of the bonds of kinship prepares a foundation for elementary stratification based on factors other than kinship.

Severance of exclusive kinship ties is a precondition for the development of stratification based on nonkinship criteria. It permits prestige rankings of persons based on their control of such things as economic resources, territory, military and political organizations. If sacred and secular functions and kinship status become independently variable there is an increased likelihood that persons will be evaluated for what they can do (achievement or performance) instead of who they are (ascription or quality).

Stratification based on nonkinship and nonreligious functions is important for further evolutionary development. That type of stratification in advanced primitive societies occurs when alignments and intermarriages between kinship units result in advantageous positions of wealth, power, or religious standing. Then, a two-class society develops in which one class has control over economic resources, political power, or religious wisdom. Members of the class with greater prestige begin to engage in political functions that are separate from religious functions, although the same person may perform both functions. Although political power may be linked to kinship, political organization is based on control of territory.

After a softening of religion and kinship's rigidity, stratification based on achievement is more likely if an advanced primitive society is relatively large. Large societies require centralized leadership, and a need for leadership can be used to legitimate the granting of relatively high status to those who fulfill the need. Further differentiations of units are likely if political functions are judged to be important and if political functions, residence, and control of economic resources are fragmented from kinship affiliations. Using social functions of persons to legitimate differences in their social rank is the beginning of a social order distinct from a cultural order. Distinctions between the social and cultural orders may begin when nonreligious achievement criteria, such as political leadership, instead of religious ascriptive criteria, are used to legitimate activities.

In conclusion, in advanced primitive societies, a loosening of religion's monopolistic control of social arrangements is a precondition for a secular-sacred differentiation within a pattern-maintenance subsystem. A complex society cannot solve its numerous problems if it has one dominant belief grounded in conditions which man cannot control and if the belief is not directly concerned with social arrangements. For that reason, further evolutionary complexity requires more than one legitimating belief and a weakening of religion's control. Furthermore, in advanced primitive societies, specialization of political activities, although frequently intertwined with kinship and religion, increases the number of organizations from which further evolutionary differentiations may arise.

Intermediate societies have a higher level of evolutionary development than advanced primitive societies. They have a written language, clearly distinguishable secular and religious functions, and well-defined social strata. The societies are complex enough so that there are three levels of stratification: (1) religious and political rulers and decision-makers (2) middle level administrators, and (3) common people who are agricultural workers, craftsmen, and merchants. In these societies, an internal differentiation of the pattern-maintenance sector and legitimation of political activity are two processes significant for further evolutionary development.

The intermediate stage is crystallized when, in the pattern-maintenance subsystem, the range of behavior legitimated by religious beliefs is narrowed. If religion becomes specialized a society can be said to have changed from a sacred to a secular society. The change does not mean that a society is less religious; it means that the scope of authority and legitimation by religious beliefs is narrowed and specialized and that other values can be used to legitimate nonreligious activities. For example, ethical and pragmatic principles are likely to be used to justify behavior and to give a nonreligious meaning to aspects of life that once were interpreted exclusively in a religious context.

If evolutionary processes are to continue the pattern-maintenance subsystem must begin value-generalization so that religious views become less dominant and secular values are acceptable. Value-generalization of secular beliefs is most effectively accomplished if values and beliefs include cognitive standards of evaluation (universalism) which can be used to justify: (1) granting citizenship to different types of persons, (2) secular prestige rankings of individuals, (3) purely political activity, and (4) a secular legal order. If values are generalized sufficiently to accomplish these tasks, inclusion of different groups and strata will ensue and a society capable of handling its four problems is more likely.

A written language and individuals specialized in scholarly philosophical and artistic expression assist value-generalization. When religious and secular beliefs become differentiated there is a potential for ideological conflict which can create fragmentation of a pattern-maintenance subsystem. There is a need for interest and concern about conflicts and ongoing debates about values and beliefs. Written forms of communication assist such discussions. The outgrowth of philosophical debates between specialists can be a revision of values and beliefs which includes areas of agreement and specifications of the spheres of life governed by principles about which there have been disagreements.

Conflict over values may be resolved in many ways. However, the outcome of the resolution must be an integrated and differentiated value-belief system with certain potentialities as a precondition for development of a more advanced society. In the first place, the power of a goal-attainment sector must be legitimated and take precedence over other types of activities. If this does not occur, goals of a society cannot be accomplished. Norms and social control functions must be legitimated so that a society can be maintained as an integrated whole. Additionally, the kinds of economic activities needed to meet a society's goals must be legitimated. Values and beliefs must be diverse enough to justify different types of economic activities and broad enough to include enough manpower to contribute economic resources to a society. Probably no one overriding value is adequate to legitimize the many activities associated with these functions. Consequently, there are needs for many beliefs and values specific enough to justify a diversity of ordinary everyday activities. Value-generalization is most effective at integrating a society when it can be based on a general moral ethic binding diverse values, activities, and interests together.

Value-generalization is not the only precondition for the integration of a society. The following types of organizations are also important: an effective political leadership capable of handling the goal-attainment problem and legal norms and regulatory agencies that effectively manage social control. In order for integration to occur a population must have some connection to the social order; therefore, requirements for belonging to a political order, or being a citizen, must be broad enough to include them. Specifically, political associations and legal norms must not be so restrictive as to create new ascriptive bases for inclusion in a political community.

A relatively clear demarcation of political activities, separated from economic and kinship interests, permits a greater expertise and specialization in the pursuit of a society's goals; it also creates conditions for conflicts about power and wealth. Despite its potential for arousing conflict, the power inherent in political activities is a resource for the development of a legal order capable of regulating conflict.

Development of a legal system is the initial stage of the creation of a society's integration subsystem. That subsystem can be used to consolidate the autonomy of political institutions. However, such a development will not occur unless it is preceded by the legitimation of the political arena. The legitimation of power in the political arena is the foundation of all legal systems. With political power to back up a legal system, and with a legitimation of the political sector behind that power potential, there is increased probability of an integration subsystem's effectiveness, an increased probability that norms and laws will be obeyed.

Legitimation of the political arena includes the support and loyalty of people within a territorial boundary, control over a geographical area, and protection of the area from outside intruders. If people in a territorial jurisdiction have diverse beliefs, legitimation of political activity is difficult. On the other hand, if there are commonly shared beliefs within the political unit, the legitimation process can be rather successfully and smoothly accomplished. Nevertheless, even under the most favorable circumstances, a differentiation of the political sector is associated with a need for an ideology defining the meaning and symbolic significance of citizenship within the political unit. In primitive societies, political activities are frequently legitimated by beliefs that a ruler is descended from a god or that he has extraordinary powers because of ancestry. Intermediate societies cannot rely on religious beliefs for justifications of political activities. Therefore, an important attribute of societies in the intermediate stage of evolution is a pattern-maintenance subsystem which can effectively legitimize political activity and the concomitant differentiation of a legal order initiating development of a societal community (integration subsystem).The sacred-secular differentiation of the pattern-maintenance subsystem is a foundation from which such legitimation can arise.

In summary, in intermediate societies, sacred-secular differentiations within the pattern-maintenance subsystem continue. A polity becomes increasingly differentiated. Although the integrative and adaptive subsystems are not clearly differentiated, their functions begin to be differentiated, and there is some kind of a legal order which can become a basis for a societal community.

Modern societies have the four system functions differentiated. Their complexity is an impetus for ongoing value-generalizations, continued differentiation of religious and political institutions, and a differentiated economy.

Three types of organizations contribute to the development of an autonomous economy: bureaucratic organization, market relationships using money as a medium of exchange, and democratic associations.

Bureaucratic organizations' use of universalistic standards and emphasis on achievements contribute to the modernization of a society. By emphasizing employees' achievements they are able to remain free from ascriptive-based loyalties so typical of primitive societies. A society with these organizations is a beneficiary because bureaucracies stimulate citizens to acquire motivations for achievements and these motivations assist in the development of a vigorous economy.

As a society's complexity increases so does its need for qualified manpower. Its specialized subsystems need highly competent workers. Bureaucratic organizations can satisfy these needs. In the first place, their recruitment of expertly qualified workers to fill well-defined offices of authority can develop a reservoir of manpower for a society. Secondly, since in a bureaucracy, power is in an office and not a person, bureaucracies assist the differentiation processes of society by subscribing to the princple that a worker's status in a bureaucracy is separate from his status in other types of activities. Finally, the organizational characteristics of bureaucracies can be used by a society to accomplish important tasks. An example has been the use of transportation organizations to engage in economic activity and thereby expand empires.

Market relationships exist when there are people ready and willing to buy and sell goods and services. A society with widespread market relationships can move resources where they are needed and can stimulate economic activity to produce the kinds of facilities needed. An inclusion of many people in market relationships is a precondition for the development of an economy.

The use of money as a medium of exchange in market relationships creates impersonal relationships. In economic relationships using money one does not have to be concerned about whom he does business with, social rank, kinship or religious status. He can negotiate economic exchange with anyone. Consequently, money is a liberating force which permits universalistic relationships, thereby promoting development of univeralistic standards of judgment. It also provides a society with an alternative manipulative device which can be used instead of power. Finally, surely money can also stimulate economic motivation because since it can be easily stored, it is an efficient way to accumulate wealth.

There are four institutialized components of democratic associations: (1)leadership in elective offices, (2)voting rights for members of a political community, (3)rules regulating voting, elections, and political campaigns, and (4)a principle of voluntary membership in a political community. Since these elements of a democracy must be regulated, a universalistic legal system is a precondition for the development of a democracy.

In a very complex society, a broad base of participation in democratic

associations enhances the loyalty and support needed to legitimate political activities of a goal-attainment subsystem. In *Democracy in America,*
Tocqueville phrased it appropriately when he said that in a democracy,
with the common people participating in the governing process, they felt
that they were the government and looked askance at others who criticized what they had done.

In summary, bureaucratic organizations and market relationships using money foster universalistic norms. Since universalistic norms permit
considerable degrees of freedom in allocating persons to work roles they
contribute to a society's economic development. Since democratic associations extend the range of participation in a political community they
may provoke ideologies which can be used to support a polity's goal-
attainment activities.

Industrial revolutions have also assisted the advance of modernization.
The technological developments which accompany industrialization extend the range of markets and commodities. Historically, as industrialization proceeded, labor and services have become differentiated from
kinship affiliations. Whereas, prior to industrialization, familial and
economic functions were performed in one unit as a household economy;
with industrialization, work roles were differentiated from roles in the
family, and labor became mobile. Differentiation of occupational from
familial roles is associated with the development of a nuclear family kinship structure. Norms regulating kinship ties become specialized as a result of an emphasis on nuclear families and the concomitant narrowing
of the range of kinship affiliations. Adaptive upgrading of a societal
community has been a consequence of the specialization in norms
brought about by the prevalence of nuclear families.

Evolutionary Processes, System Equilibrium, and Four Subsystems

Differentiation processes always result in disequilibrium. Disequilibrium continues so long as newly differentiated units have not been integrated into a society. As a disturbance is filtered through a society
there are adjustments which stimulate a reorganization of the structure
of the system.

System equilibrium depends on an inclusion of newly differentiated u-
nits and inclusion depends on value-generalizations. For illustrative purposes, let us consider a society in which children are educated in religious organizations. If schools become differentiated from religious organizations, if secular schools specialize in the education of children, and if
religious organizations no longer educate children, then the secular
schools are deemed a newly differentiated unit. The need for inclusion

means that the secular schools' activities will have to be coordinated with activities of other units in the society, and especially with religious activities. Schools should have cooperative relationships with families, churches, and economic organizations. Also the other units of the society will be required to provide organizational support for the schools. Schools will have to have resources and personnel. The education provided by the secular schools should be viewed as adequate for economic organizations to accept the students as competent to become employees. If a society's values legitimate the schools and if legitimation (value-generalization) precedes the inclusion process, the norms regulating the coordinative-cooperative relationships between the old and new units are likely to be adequate to integrate the new unit into the system.

As inferred by the foregoing example, value-generalization assists the inclusion of newly differentiated units. It involves a differentiation of the values of a society so that there are values and beliefs that support secular education and justify the secular schools' autonomy. And these values should become widely distributed among a society's population, thereby providing widespread support for the secular schools. Some values should also be general and vague enough to relate the more specific values legitimating secular schools to the values of other units of a society. In this case, there should be general values which relate the value of secular education to the value of religion. If value-generalization fails, so will inclusion.

Once a change sequence is initiated by differentiation of units, pattern-maintenance processes lead evolutionary development and integrative processes lag behind. Both processes may stimulate disequilibrium in a society. They may trigger interests which are opposed to the new unit. Long-established units in the society may be threatened. Changes in values may be resisted. Moreover, before newly differentiated units have been included into the system, value-generalization processes can create conflict and demands for further differentiations, or resistance to inclusion can create conflict and can be a condition for revolution. The most effective value-generalization process is one which is associated with value specification by which a unit is legitimated and, simultaneously, both old and new units are legitimated by a common general value.

The highest level of evolutionary development is the modern stage in which the four subsystems have become differentiated. However, evolutionary processes do not cease. After the four subsystems are differentiated, the subsystems themselves become increasingly complex. Their evolutionary development also entails the processes of differentiation, adaptive upgrading, inclusion, and value-generalization. Although not a topic of discussion here, these evolutionary processes can also be sources of disequilibrium.

After the four subsystems have been differentiated, evolutionary processes are articulated through the four subsystems: (1) adaptive upgrading through economy, (2) differentiation through polity, (3) inclusion through a societal community, and (4) value-generalization through a fiduciary subsystem.

The lower the level of value-generalization, that is, the more specific the values of a complex society, the less likely the patterned and functional integration of a society. The more complex the society and the greater its functional and patterned integration, the less susceptible it is to major structural change resulting from narrow or particular circumstances or events. Of the six relationships between the subsystems of modern societies (Figure 4-1, Chapter 4), the greatest potential for conflict and disequilibrium of the system exists in relationships which define the integration of a society; that is, relationships between economy and societal community and relationships between polity and fiduciary subsystem. These potentialities for conflict exist merely because of differences in the concerns of the subsystems. A polity's concern for attaining goals and an economy's concern with the instrumental aspects of action provoke orientations of expediency and practicality. On the other hand, a fiduciary subsystem and a societal community's concerns for organization, stability, and preservation of relationships within a system provoke orientations toward maintenance of established relationships and preservation of pre-existing patterned relationships.

In a complex society, initiation of a structural change cycle is most likely to occur: (1) as a result of needs of a polity or an economy or (2) exchanges between economy and polity. An economy has the greatest potentiality for change and a fiduciary subsystem the least. Differences in subsystems' sensitivities to change are consistent with the hierarchy of control presented in Chapters 2 and 3. The most specific, least socially generalized units are sensitive to environmental changes. These units are the polity and the economy. On the other hand, the most general societal units specialized in maintaining the patterned and functional integration of the system are less capable of adjusting to environmental changes. These units are the societal community and the fiduciary subsystem.

Modernization of Europe, England, and the United States

Parsons applied his evolutionary theory to the analysis of various geographical areas in northwestern Europe, viewing them as comprising a single system of modern societies. Some of his ideas are discussed here for purposes of illustrating his theory.

Development of the modern era in the western world began in the 17th century when religious divisions occurred. In sections of Europe, Protestantism challenged the hegemony of the Roman Catholic church. Thereafter, divisions arose within the Protestant movement. The splitting of both religious organizations provided an environment in which political territorial units developed.

Initially, political units were controlled by landed aristocracy. As conflict between ethnic-religious groups developed, there was a need for leadership to organize groups to engage in conflict and to protect specific geographical regions. The most stable political units were those that were supported by religious orders and with residents who shared common cultural heritages.

Since it had several religious groups, England was able to establish political units which were relatively autonomous and independent of religious organizations; citizenship was defined politically rather than according to religious belief. Legitimation of political activities developed as a general moral commitment and not as a commitment to a religious belief or to any one political belief. Nonreligious philosophies dealing with such questions as the origin of government, the nature of man and his intellect became relatively independent of political and religious organizations. Secular philosophical debates fostered internal differentiation of a pattern-maintenance subsystem which became relatively effective in legitimating political and secular activities.

Democratic revolutions in Europe and England aided the development of specialized governmental and political activity. After these revolutions, participation in political affairs stimulated people to think about collective goals of a society. Eventually citizens subscribed to political ideologies which could be mobilized to gain support for political leaders' objectives. Democratic revolutions also contributed to a strengthening of economic units because, with democracy, there arose political interest groups which articulated economic interests. Some of these economic interests cut across ethnic and religious alliances and allowed for economic interests to become an alternative basis for associations. Differentiations of economic interest groups were foundations for a crystallization of an economic subsystem.

The industrial revolution increased the scope of economic activity and aided its separation from other types of activities. As individuals began working away from their places of residence, they were required to comply with norms pertaining to their workplaces and relationships between fellow workers. As work relationships became widespread throughout a society, exemplified by employee-employer interaction, economic relationships were increasingly differentiated and adaptively upgraded.

Differentiation of an economy was aided by the creation of laws legitimating it, especially those laws which provided a method for entering into and carrying out contracts, the adjudication of disputes, and recording ownership of property. Since enforcement of legal rights entailed the use of political power, political institutions were also legitimated because of their facilitation of legal enforcements regarding economic activity.

Parsons illustrated some of the trends in the evolution of societies by discussing the evolution of American society. The settlers of the country brought with them beliefs which initiated the development of a pattern-maintenance subsystem, beliefs about the importance of freedom, the value of work and achievement, and anti-authoritarian attitudes. There was an inclination to judge individuals according to what they could do rather than according to their family heritage, a consequence of which was that the problem of power and wealth's being associated with kinship or aristocracy was diminished.

With the many religious beliefs in America, no one belief could govern activities in the name of religion. Religious pluralism in the colonies provided a condition for further differentiation of the pattern-maintenance subsystem into secular values. Some of these secular beliefs were set forth in the Declaration of Independence, the Articles of Confederation, the Constitution, and the Bill of Rights. Principles in these documents became the core of the pattern-maintenance subsystem, although not the total of that subsystem. Secular and political values were general enough to be used later in legitimating activities in political, legal, and economic organizations.

As an economy developed, courts legitimated its activities; laws limited economic excesses, and economic organizations were thereby integrated into the society.

Evolutionary Processes in Modern Societies

Parsons thought that the most recent developments in modern societies have been: extending the value placed on universalistic standards of evaluation, increasing participation in political processes by citizens, and expanding economic opportunities. These processes were viewed as resulting from increases in the number of persons who are educated. Increasing the number of persons with higher education adds new beliefs to the pattern-maintenance subsystem, making it receptive to a wider range of motivations.

The educational revolution has adaptively upgraded the fiduciary subsystem by providing the variety of values, beliefs, and motivations necessary for satisfying the many needs of a highly differentiated society. The economy has also been adaptively upgraded as a result of the expertise, skills, and competencies provided it by educational institutions. Educational organizations also aid inclusion by allocating people to occupational specialties. By offering specialized programs and certifying that students have completed technical requirements for jobs, they communicate to economic organizations whether or not persons are qualified to perform certain tasks. The result is an exercise of some control and discretion over the division of labor which is so important to the economy.

Parsons viewed modern, industrialized nations as comprising a single system of modern societies. He thought it inappropriate to characterize them as post-modern societies. Although modern societies have four differentiated subsystems, they have considerable disequilibrium resulting from continuing democratic and educational revolutions. Educational revolutions have brought about increasing pluralization of values and beliefs as well as new technologies resulting from increases in empirical knowledge. Continuance of democratic revolutions, such as the civil rights movements in the United States, calls attention to inadequate inclusions of segments of the population into the political community.

Studies Using Parsons' Perspective of Social Change

None of the studies reported here actually test Parsons' theory of social change. Some of the studies report empirical evidence about issues related to his theory; some use his theory as an analytical tool for describing characteristics of communities or societies at different stages of complexity.

Buck and Jacobson (1968) used one of Parsons' early statements of the evolutionary principles as a basis for selecting several demographic, economic, social, and political characteristics as operational definitions of evolutionary universals. They analyzed the level of development for each of 50 countries. The characteristics analyzed were: communications, kinship organizations, religion, rudimentary technology, stratification, cultural legitimation of stratification, bureaucratic organizations, money markets, universalistic norms, and democratic associations. Several indicators were used for each characteristic; only those for technology are given as an illustrative example. Technology was measured as per capita production of electricity in kilowatt hours, percentage of gross domestic products originating in agriculture, and percentage of labor force in industry and in agriculture. Each country was ranked on a five-point scale on each of the evolutionary principles and countries at the same level of development were grouped together. Levels of development ranked from (I) low to (V) high.

Each of the evolutionary characteristics was evaluated in order to determine whether or not it facilitated social change. Different combinations of the characteristics were found to facilitate social change at different levels of development. One of the more important implications of the data was the inference that there was an uneven development of crucial characteristics. Countries at one level were overdeveloped on an important facilitating characteristic and underdeveloped on others. For example, characteristics which were underdeveloped at one stage and overdeveloped in the next stage were: from stage I to II, money markets; stage II to III, technology. Overdevelopments and balances were observed between the following stages: bureaucracy from stage I to II; money markets from stage II to III; and cultural legitimation from III to IV. The evidence corroborated Parsons' theory that social change proceeds as a series of equilibrium-disequilibrium processes.

Jacobson (1971) reported further findings related to the societies in the social evolution study. Three hypotheses were tested: (1) the degree of conflict is less in the more developed societies; (2) there is a direct relationship between a rate of social change and level of development; and (3) at all stages of modernization there is an inverse relationship between social change and social conflict. Secondary materials were used to search out information about civil strife between 1961 and 1965 in 114 political entities. The amount of civil strife was measured by evaluating the number participating in it, its duration, and estimated number of casualties.

The analysis suggested the following statements: Conflict declined among societies above level IV. Amount of social change, as indicated by economic change, increased slowly in societies below level III and more rapidly in societies at levels IV and V. There was a negative relationship between social change and social conflict.

Dean (1967) used the pattern variables to analyze orientations of leaders in five communities. The communities had different types of economic organizations. Leaders were asked about issues relating to the cold war, race, civil defense, and union-management. The data suggested that in communities which were relatively diverse economically and concerned with large socio-economic units, a relatively large number of leaders' orientations could be characterized by universalism, achievement, and performance, and as involving complexity of thought.

Chalmers Johnson (1982) provided a model of social change within the context of Parsons' general theory. Johnson analyzed revolutationary insurrections as outcomes of relationships between the following: sources of provocation for change, disequilibriated systems, status protestors, and accelerators of social change. He suggested that since rebellions presuppose some agreement about what a society should be and revolutions occur because of disagreements about societal issues, revolutions occur in functionally specific societies and rebellions occur in diffuse societies.

Weinstein and Platt (1969) analyzed changes in values as resulting from personalities' fantasies. If personal fantasy wishes become conscious they provide grounds for demands for value change. If there are weaknesses or instabilities in relationships which bind individuals to traditional values, conscious codification of personal wishes may become a base for organized efforts designed to bring about changes in values.

Freeman and Winch (1957) collected data on 48 societies from the Cross-cultural and Human Relations Area Files and tested a scalogram of eight dimensions of social complexity. The items in the scale were: exogamy, punishment of crimes by authorities or personal avengers, functionally differentiated governments or religions, formal or informal education, money or barter, fertility or beauty as criteria for mate selection, and written language. With the exception of exogamy and criteria for mate selection, the items produced a scale of societal complexity.

References and Suggestions for Further Study

Parsons' evolutionary theory of social change was stated in:
  Societies: Evolutionary and Comparative Perspectives (1966); *The Systems of Modern Societies* (1971).
  Toby edited the above two volumes into one volume: *The Evolution of Societies* (1977). The above publications superseded an earlier statement on the topic: "Evolutionary Universals in Society" (1964).

Some of Parsons' discursive comments on social change can be found in:
  "The Problem of Controlled Institutional Change (1945)
  "The Processes of Change in Social Systems" in *The Social System* (1951)
  "Some Trends of Change in American Society: Their Bearing on Medical Education" (1958)
  "Some Considerations on the Theory of Social Change" (1961)
  "The Problem of Structural Change," Part IV of "An Outline of the Social System" in *Theories of Society*, Vol. I (1961).
  "Comparative Studies and Evolutionary Change" (1971).

Some insightful comments on empirical situations dealing with change can be found in:
  "Social Strains in America: A Postscript (1962)" (1963)
  "Christianity" (1968)
  "The Impact of Technology on Culture and Emerging New Modes of Behavior" (1970)
  "Belief, Unbelief, and Disbelief" (1971)
  "Some Reflections on Post-Industrial America." (1973)
  "Religion in Post-Industrial America: The Problem of Secularization." (1974)

For some examples of uses of perspectives similar to Parsons', see:
  Bellah's "Religious Evolution" (1964)
  Eisenstadt's "Social Change, Differentiation and Evolution" (1964) and *The Political Systems of Empires: The Rise and Fall of the Historical Bureaucratic Societies* (1963).
  Levy's, *The Family Revolution in Modern China* (1949).
  Smelser's, *Social Change in the Industrial Revolution* (1959).

Chapter 6

Stratification

Introduction

A theory of stratification attempts to explain how social positions are differentiated and the criteria used to evaluate positions. Parsons' writings do not contain an organized coherent theory of stratification. He provided several lists of attributes and definitions which he thought relevant to stratification processes. Throughout his writings on the topic, issues related to stratification are discussed, but relationships between the issues are not specified. Perhaps some of the lack of coherency in his ideas about stratification can be attributed to the fact that his thoughts about the topic were stated relatively early in his career and they were not reevaluated in the context of some of his most recent ideas. For instance, he alluded to the significance of the media in stratification, but he did not make definitive statements about how each of them relates to a ranking of social positions. The most explicit statements about stratification are based on the theory of social action systems. The generality of such a point of view admits the complexity of stratification processes but offers few clues to ferreting out relationships between power, prestige, authority, ethnicity, race, wealth, and social class.

This chapter reports on the variety of Parsons' comments about stratification processes. One of his most explicit perspectives views stratification as a by-product of the evolution of societies. Societies at each stage of evolution are characterized as having a particular type of stratification. At the most advanced level of evolution, stratification in modern societies is affected by a society's evaluation of the importance of the four problems.

Since stratification in modern societies is more complex than it is in premodern societies, Parsons listed and defined some of the attributes of social positions which can be evaluated. He commented on some of the characteristics of occupations which could be related to stratification processes. Finally, recognizing some of the strains which result from stratification processes, systems theory was used to explain the institutionalization of equality and inequality in the United States. Each of these issues is discussed in the following sections.

Evolutionary Theory and Stratification

The type and amount of social differentiation in a society are dependent on a society's level of evolutionary development. The higher the level of development, the greater the number of differentiated units. Stratification processes are also dependent on the degree of patterned and functional integration of a society. The less the patterned and functional integration, the greater the number of criteria used to evaluate social positions.

The lower the evolutionary development, the more important are ascriptive characteristics. Consequently, in primitive societies there are relatively few differentiations and evaluations are based on ascriptive criteria. The most common ascriptive characteristics used to evaluate social positions are religion, ethnicity, age, kinship, and territoriality.

In advanced primitive societies, the significance of ascription is lessened, and political status and citizenship become important nonascriptive bases for evaluations.

In intermediate societies, positions are differentiated according to secular functions. Political activities are important to intermediate societies, and activities are judged valuable for political reasons. Usually judgments of that kind initiate processes whereby achievements are viewed as distinguishing characteristics of persons' positions. If a secular culture becomes separated from a sacred culture, pragmatic, practical, political, and economic activities can be valued by appealing to secular values. Hence, social positions are likely to be evaluated in accordance with secular values.

The modern stage of development occurs when each of the four subsystems has become differentiated. In modern societies, if a differentiated economy is valued in economic terms, secularization is enhanced. A modern society's judgment about the importance of the subsystems is a basis for differentiations and evaluations of social positions.

Stratification in Modern Societies

Parsons has discussed the following topics related to stratification processes in modern societies: (1) Evaluations of subsystems affect the prestige of activities within them; (2) Societies' values are used to define four types of social structures; (3) The attributes of social positions which can be evaluated are defined; and (4) A schema for analyzing occupations is proposed. Each topic is discussed below.

There are four assumptions underlying Parsons' theory of stratification in modern societies: that (1) the four sybsystems are differentiated, (2) a society is functionally integrated, (3) a society is integrated with respect to values, and (4) at least one of the four system problems is evaluated as relatively more important than the other three. Based on the foregoing assumptions, evaluations of social positions stem from evaluations of the four subsystems.

Stratification and the Four Subsystems

Since in a modern society the four subsystems can be identified, social positions can also be identified according to their contributions to the activities of the subsystems. The subsystem which is most valued by a particular society will provide greatest prestige to the positions located within it. For example, if goal-attainment is valued more than any of the other problems, positions in a polity will have greater prestige than positions in the other three subsystems. Also, if a society is integrated with respect to its values, rewards, possessions, and qualities associated with activities in a polity should have greater value than those associated with positions in the other three subsystems.

After identifying a society's evaluation of its subsystems, the pattern variables are used to describe the dominant values of the society. Alternative combinations of two sets of pattern variables, universalism-particularism and quality-performance, describe values of each subsystem, in Figure 6-1. From Figure 6-1, if a society evaluates adaptation as its most important problem then the values of universalism-performance are dominant and used throughout a society to evaluate all social positions. If goal-attainment is evaluated as the most important problem, then particularism-performance is used to evaluate social positions.

The same logic is used for the remaining two problems of integration and pattern-maintenance.

Figure 6-1

Values of the Four Subsystems of a Society

Subsystem	Values
adaptation	universalism-performance
goal-attainment	particularism-performance
integration	particularism-quality
latency	universalism-quality
pattern-maintenance	

Adapted from "A Revised Analytical Approach to the Theory of Social Stratification," pp. 386-439 in *Essays in Sociological Theory*, rev. ed. (1954).

After a society's dominant values have been identified, the other three subsystems should be rank ordered. Which subsystem is evaluated as second, third, and fourth in importance? The rank order of the four subsystems results in a descending scale of evaluation. According to Parsons, in order to arrive at such a ranking one must presume a stable state of a society.

The above schema was applied to an analysis of stratification in the United States. It was also used to classify four types of social structures. These topics are covered in the next two sections.

Four Types of Social Structures

1. Universalistic-performance (achievement) structure: If a society places greater importance on the adaptation problem than on any other problem its dominant values are universalism-performance. Evaluations use cognitive standards and positions are evaluated by general principles. What people do, how they perform, and the things they have done are evaluated. An emphasis on performances directs attention to whether or not persons are goal-oriented and whether or not they are achievement oriented. Since activities in an economy are highly valued, occupations in an economy are important. Persons are recruited into occupations with expectations that they are goal-oriented, that they desire success, and their achievements are evaluated by general principles appropriate to the levels of their occupations.

A concern for persons' achievements and the use of universalistic standards in evaluations promote generalized universalistic standards for evaluating goals. An individual's goals are regarded as symbols of an instrumental-achievement orientation. The same goals are not expected of everyone, but each role occupant is expected to accomplish a level of performance appropriate to his occupational role. The same standard (universalism) will be used to evaluate performances of all who occupy similar roles. This type of society, of which the United States is typical, also values individualism, neutrality, and specificity.

2. Universalistic-quality (ascription) structure: If pattern-maintenance is of major value to a society universalism-quality are the dominant values. There is a preference for cognitive evaluations, but persons are not evaluated for what they can do or for their achievements; some of their innate characteristics or attributes are evaluated, and general standards are used in the evaluation. An example of this might be evaluating applicants for a job by judging their sex, nationality, race, age, ancestry. The manner in which race was used to evaluate people universally in Nazi Germany is an example of this type of social structure. With an emphasis on the qualitative status in the Communist Party, communist Russia is an example of this type of structure.

This type of society is rigid because individuals cannot change the qualities which are evaluated. Also, after they are in occupations they are still evaluated according to a qualitative standard and their actual performances are of little consequence.

3. Particularistic-performance (achievement) structure. A major concern for goal-attainment emphasizes performances similar to that discussed as characterizing universalistic-performance structures. However, particularistic standards used to judge performances draws attention to a person's relationship to an evaluator (particularism).

Cathectic evaluations are emphasized. Standards of evaluation are not general; they are special ones, viewed as appropriate for the role occupant because of his belonging to a collectivity. Particularism fosters a collectivistic-diffuse orientation, a concern for relationships with others, and traditionalism. Parsons thought the kinship unit in pre-Communist China was an example of this type of social structure. Individuals' responsibilities to kinship units were emphasized and the two sexes were evaluated in the context of traditional relationships within kinship units.

4. Particularistic-quality (ascription) structure. As a paramount objective of a society, integration fosters a rigid structure. Values emphasizing particularistic standards and evaluating persons according to who they are (quality) rather than what they can do leaves little room for initiating change of one's status. An evaluator uses expressive relational

bases for judgments about others, and occupational roles are filled according to some quality of the candidate. An ability to perform, or actual performance, is not a factor to be considered. The standards used to evaluate persons may be imbued with emotional reactions to them because of their group affiliations. Also, in this type of evaluative frame of reference there is a tendency to assign groups to a stable place in a society. These values foster a collectivistic traditionalism with an emphasis on the sex-age structure. Latin American countries and pre-Nazi Germany, and especially their family sex-age structures, have been examples of this type of structure.

The foregoing classification of types of social structures was used by Parsons to demonstrate that the priorities assigned to system problems influence the rigidity or looseness of the scale of evaluation and the types of authority relationships within a society. In societies in which the external aspects of system functions, goal-attainment and adaptation are valued, ascriptive characteristics are not important; if system integration is valued, so is ascription. If pattern-maintenance is dominant there is an ascriptive focus which creates a system-wide hierarachy of generalized esteem.

Of the four problems, emphasis on adaptation creates conditions in which authority relations are not important. On the other hand, authority relationships are important if there are dominant concerns about goal-attainment or integration. In the case of the importance of goal-attainment, authority associated with positions is viewed as necessary because of a need to attain society's goals. In the case of integration, it is necessary to prevent units from interfering with system integration. If a society has one dominant goal and goal-attainment is emphasized, values associated with those interests can create a system-wide hierarchy of prestige. Universalism-performance values create conditions for looseness in the scale of evaluation, but predominance of any of the other three value patterns creates conditions for a tight evaluative ranking scale.

Stratification in the United States

American society's ranking of the four subsystems is shown in Figure 6-2.

As dominant values, universalism-performance emphasize the use of general cognitive principles in evaluations of performances. Although the society does not value the goal-attainment subsystem, roles which are productive and which contribute to a collectivity's goals are highly

Figure 6-2

Ranking of Subsystems, Their Empirical Referents and Values in the United States

Rank	Subsystem	Empirical Referent	Values
Highest	adaptation	economy, occupations	universalism-performance
	latency	education, family, religion	universalism-quality
	integration	regulatory agencies, laws, licensing, social control	particularism-quality
Lowest	goal-attainment	political offices	particularism-performance

Adapted from "A Revised Analytical Approach to the Theory of Social Stratification" in *Essays in Sociological Theory* (1954), pp. 415-439.

evaluated. Persons are expected to be goal-oriented and engaged in an active pursuit of a goal. In fact, one is presumed to be deviant if he does not have a goal of his own or one he shares with others. Since the primary arena in which goals are pursued is in the economy, money is a symbol of success.

Educational organizations use universalistic standards to evaluate performances, and roles in educational institutions, especially those in universities, are highly valued. Their importance arises from the fact that by training people for occupational roles they contribute services to the economy. Science and technology are important to economic activity, and the importance of educational organizations, as resources for science and technology, derives from the economy's need for science and technology. Because of its socializing functions, the family also contributes to the adaptation and latency subsystems, the two highly valued subsystems.

By enforcing universalistic normative standards, the societal community reinforces the society's dominant values. The integration subsystem adjusts and regulates conflicting interests and rights, and creates the normative environment for the society's recognition of and accomplishment of many goals.

Since there is relatively low value given to any one dominant system goal, positions in the polity are less highly valued than positions in other subsystems. However, Parsons inferred that low evaluations of political positions might change in times of crisis, such as economic depressions or war.

Since executives have responsibility for accomplishing an organization's goals and maintaining the structure of an organization, they have most prestige. Executives in different types of organizations at similar levels of responsibility are further ranked in accordance with the rank order of the importance of their organizations' contributions to the system functions. Generally, executives in economic organizations have the highest social rank; the second rank goes to executives in socializing institutions such as universities; third, to those in agencies of social control and regulation in the integration subsystem; and the lowest rank is attributed to executives in the polity.

Parsons suggested that events in the 1960's and 1970's provided some potentiality for changes in American values. The affirmative action programs designed to integrate women and ethnic groups into the upper social strata of the society emphasized the equality of groups rather than equality of individuals. Social movements attempted to institutionalize an evaluation of persons based on their group (race or sex) affiliations. If they are successful, in the future there may be a tendency to evaluate persons according to particularistic and qualitative (ascriptive) criteria.

Another trend of change has come about because of the increasing importance of science and technology and a need for highly skilled technicians. The economy's need for the skills which educational institutions provide has focused attention on the fiduciary subsystem, the situs of education; consequently, roles in that subsystem have relatively high status.

Discrimination processes affecting ethnic groups modify the statification continuum. Also, the values of some ethnic groups deviate from the dominant cultural values of the society. Understanding stratification in ethnic groups probably requires that they be treated as subsocieties with their own stratification. By doing so, ethnic stratification processes can be compared to the dominant evaluative rankings of American society.

In the United States religion is organized along class lines; therefore, a clergy's status derives from the status of the members of his church.

Generally, America's stratification is not a clear-cut hierarchy of prestige. Each strata is composed of relatively loose components. At the top of the scale are the elite with high earnings, a professional elite, such as. lawyers and engineers and, of course, those who have hereditary wealth based on achievements. Next, the upper middle class is composed of professional and business people, civil servants, and military officers. The best indicator of the line between the upper and lower middle class is the upper-middle-class expectation that children will have a college education as a status right. The previous differentiation of white-collar vs blue-collar work, based on income, is no longer appropriate because blue-collar laborers' earnings have increased, entitling them to middle class status.

Recently, the number of unskilled and semi-skilled workers in the lower class has decreased. The lower class is distinguished by its having values inconsistent with the dominant cultural value of achievement. In the lower class, occupations are not viewed as means for achievement; they are means for securing the necessities of life.

Finally, agricultural activities range from the share-cropper types to the large corporate types of farms. Thus, this occupation can be located along the total range of strata from upper middle class to lower class.

Parsons recognized inadequacies in his descriptions of stratification. Firstly, they were based on an assumption that a modern society is patterned and functionally integrated. If a society is not integrated, multiple dimensions of evaluations can exist. At the very least, there can be an inability to classify status positions as a whole, since logically there could be independent hierarchies of evaluation for each of the four subsystems. Secondly, Parsons inferred that power, authority, performances, possessions, and class statuses are not all positively correlated. Even if a society is integrated, his theory does not explain relationships between these attributes. Thirdly, Parsons has repeatedly stated that all societies contain inherent strains. Not the least of these are the ascriptive bases of stratification, such as stratification by race, sex, or age. Therefore, a further development of Parsons' theory required a showing of the relative impact of secondary values or coexisting dominant values. Recognizing the problem, he proposed a solution by discussing the institutionalization of equality and inequality in the United States.

Institutionalized Equality and Inequality

A modern society's adaptive capacity entails activities which produce freedoms and constraints, equalities and inequalities. There is disequilibrium resulting from such activities. The integration of a highly differentiated society depends on the legitimation and balancing of the equalities and inequalities, freedoms and constraints.

American society was used as an example to demonstrate how modern societies produce equalities and inequalities and balances and legitimizes them. Parsons judged that equalities and inequalities exist in four types of activities: cultural, legal, political, and economic. In the following paragraphs, the manner in which activities of the subsystems of society create inequalities is set forth; then, the balances between equalities and inequalities in each subsystem are described.

Goal-attainment and adaptation subsystems create inequalities; latency and integration subsystems legitimate and justify them. It will be remembered that goal-attainment and adaptation are concerned with a society's relationships to its external environments. Inequalities originating in these spheres of activities arise out of a society's needs to attain goals and to procure facilities necessary for attainment of goals. Integrative functions of pattern-maintenance and integration legitimate inequalities by articulating units' rights, justifying inequities as being for the benefit of the society, or as consistent with a society's values and norms.

Social processes create inequalities when it is necessary to mobilize commitments and obligations to accomplish things a society needs done. From the perspective of a society, activities which are most needed are most valued. The importance of some activities is symbolized by an allocation of greater prestige and influence to those units which are more highly valued because of their important contributions. The higher evaluation of those activities is justified by communicating that they are very important, more important than other activities which are not so needed and which are not highly valued.

Influence is used to motivate persons to be committed to system goals and to legitimate the different statuses which have resulted from differential contributions to system needs. In attempting to arouse such motivation, functionally diffuse influence is most effective because it can tap a broad range of value-commitments. For example, attempting to motivate persons to pay more taxes or join the military or contribute to charity, a politician is more effective if he can persuade members of the business and academic communities as well as other politicians, the young, the old, the white, the black, males and females.

A polity must make decisions affecting collective interests, and in the pursuit of any one goal, only some collectivities' interests will be compatible with a goal. The result is that decisions of the polity create inequality. Merely by making choices between alternative goals, as in the classical case of guns versus butter, all interests cannot be satisfied. Nevertheless, inequalities which result from choices and decisions of a polity are balanced by a principle of equal protection under the law.

In the productive functions of an economy there are needs for resources and performances, all of which cannot be evaluated as equal. Performances are evaluated according to how important they are in the production process at a particular time. Consquently, activities of an economy create inequalities. They are balanced by the principle of equality of opportunity.

Inequalities result from institutionalized fiduciary relationships. A fiduciary relationship exists when power or property, or some other instrumental means, is entrusted to an entity for use on behalf of others. In a modern society there are many areas of very technical, specialized knowledge, inaccessible to all. Lawyers, judges, governmental officials, physicians, and teachers utilize specialized knowledge for the benefit of clients, citizens, patients, and students. These experts are fiduciary agents; they assume positions of power, authority, and control, and their superior positions are legitimized. Thereby, a form of relatively high status is institutionalized, as is a form of relatively low status for the recipients of the services. By the accreditation and licensing of experts, such as physicians, technicians, and other professionals, superior statuses are justified, but the superiority is said to be legitimated by the moral responsibility of the professions. Additionally, the inequalities are offset by the principles of freedom of contract and freedom to choose value-commitments. That is, subordinates are free to choose to enter or not to enter the fiduciary relationship.

Using a principle of one member, one vote, the democratic franchise is a form of equality of political participation. There is the assumption that each person's vote is equal in importance and effect. However, democracy in the United States creates inequalities because after representatives are elected they occupy superior power positions from which they can make binding decisions for the society as a whole. Representatives have greater power and authority than the people who elected them, and inevitably, decisions of the representatives produce differential allocations of rights, power, and facilities within a society.

These inequalities arising in American democracy are legitimated by exchanges between pattern-maintenance and goal-attainment subsystems. Beliefs and values in a fiduciary subsystem legitimate political authority and political decisions which have created inequalities. For example, executive orders of governments (polity) mandating that striking workers return to work have been legitimated by beliefs (fiduciary subsystem) that there are overriding public needs for the services or goods produced by the workers. Or, executive orders declaring that persons in disaster areas are entitled to special funds and services have been legitimated by the belief and value that persons subjected to the disaster are entitled to the necessities of public health, food, and shelter.

Justifications of inequities also come about through exchanges between the adaptation and integration subsystems. A societal community uses moral-legal norms to justify differences in allocations of resources and facilities. For example, administrative agencies in the societal community make laws specifying standards and conditions which individuals and organizations must meet in order to engage in all sorts of economic activities. If the standards and conditions cannot be complied with, one cannot engage in an economic activity. This type of regulation restricts economic activity and can be viewed as creating differences in opportunities. An example occurs in most cities where individuals cannot sell crafts on a street corner without a license from the local government, and a large corporation cannot manufacture household appliances without having been licensed and having complied with appropriate health and safety standards. The regulations and licensing procedures are justified by a need for regulations to maintain public tranquility, health, and welfare of consumers, the regulation of public places, and the safety of workers. Nonetheless, inequalities are counterbalanced by institutionalized individualism. According to that belief, individuals are considered free to pursue their interests and goals and are presumed to be eligible to qualify for access to resources and opportunities. All who can comply with the regulations are free to engage in economic activity. Therefore, the value placed on the right of the individual to pursue his own interests balances the inequalities resulting from differences in outcomes of economic activity.

System functions also involve freedoms and constraints. Freedom is a necessary condition for a society's need to accomplish goals. There is a need for freedom to mobilize resources and to allocate them to the problems which need solving. When attention is focused on alternative means, freedom is greater than when attention is focused on goals. Thus, an instrumental phase of activity permits freedom to choose alternatives. However, once a goal is chosen, pursuing it restricts the choices because only some means are appropriate for attaining a particular goal. The logic underlying the foregoing statements was used by Parsons to categorize subsystem functions according to whether or not they entail freedom or constraint.

Using the means-ends and the internal-external dimensions of action, freedoms and constraints were classified according to their place in the action schema as set forth in Figure 6-3. It will be remembered from Chapter 3 that the adaptation and latency problems are concerned with instrumental action (means); therefore, their activities operate in a context of freedom. Concerned with ends, the consummatory functions of goal-attainment and integration are characterized by constraint.

In Figure 6-3, the institutionalized equalities and inequalities resulting from system functions, previously discussed, are related to the four subsystems. Four types of equality are categorized as: (1) equal opportunity, (2) equal protection of the law, (3) equal citizenship rights, and (4) equal membership status. These equalities are a part of the values and beliefs lodged in the fiduciary subsystem. Since they refer to operations within each of the subsystems, in Figure 6-3 they are located in the subsystem to which they refer. Inequalities are categorized as: (1) unequal achievements, (2) unequal power, (3) inequality from fiduciary relationships, and (4) inequality from individualism.

In Figure 6-3 each subsystem contains inequalities which are balanced by equalities. Within the adaptation subsystem (economy), unequal economic achievements are offset by institutionalized equality of opportunity. Within the goal-attainment subsystem (polity), unequal power resulting from political decisions and the superior power of elected officials is balanced by the principle of equal protection of the law. Within the latency subsystem, inequalities due to the inherent superordinate and subordinate statuses in fiduciary relationships are balanced by the principle of equality of basic rights of citizens.

In the societal community pursuit of individual goals, stated in Figure 6-3 as inequality from institutionalized individualism, results in unequal statuses for individuals. However, individuals belong to collectivities and within a particular collectivity the individuals who are members of the collectivity are presumed to have equal status rights. Consequently, equality of membership status within collectivities balance any inequalities of achievements which result from individuals' pursuing, and in fact, achieving different objectives.

As previously stated, the consummatory nature of the goal-attainment and integration subsystems' activities result in constraints or limitations on freedoms. The polity's decisions limit an exercise of freedom and the normative regulations of the integration subsystem also restrain freedom. These constraints are from the polity, constraints resulting from decisions, and from the societal community, constraints resulting from a community's authority to regulate behavior. The instrumental activities of the economy and the fiduciary subsystem balance the constraints with freedoms. In the case of the economy, constraints are balanced by a principle of individuals' freedom to pursue their own interests. In the case of the fiduciary subsystem, the contraints are balanced by a principle that individuals are free to allocate their value-commitments to whomever or whatever they wish. The institutionalized freedoms of the instrumentally oriented subsystems (economy and fiduciary subsystem) counterbalance the constraints of the consummatory oriented subsystems (polity and societal community).

Figure 6-3

Freedom, Constraint, Equality and Inequality in Subsystem Functions

Adaptation	*Goal-Attainment*
economy	polity
unequal achievements;	unequal power;
equal opportunity	equal protection of law;
freedom to pursue interests	constraint resulting from decisions
inequality from fiduciary relationships;	inequality from institutionalized individualism;
equal citizenship rights;	equal membership status;
freedom to allocate commitments	constraint by authority of the community
fiduciary subsystem	societal community
Latency	*Integration*

Adapted from "Equality and Inequality in Modern Society, or Social Stratification Revisited" (1970).

Multiple Attributes of Positions in Modern Societies

From time to time Parsons commented on the kinds of things he thought relevant to a study of social stratification. He provided some cursory comments on the media's significance in stratification processes. He listed and defined attributes which can be evaluated and presumably rank ordered in a stratification hierarchy. The overriding message of his comments was that the issue is very complex.

When the media of exchange are highly developed they expand action potentialities. The expansion creates new styles and forms of inequalities in the media's distribution in society. Broadening their symbolic meaning allows for them to stand for more types of different things. As the symbolic meaning, the forms, and the styles of the media increase, they become important in stratification hierarchies in modern societies.

What is more, evaluations within a status hierarchy, based on persons or collectivities' control of the media, have become increasingly difficult. Parsons did not communicate definitive statements about that issue, but some of his ideas about the issue are summarized.

Since influence operates from a base of prestige, the amount of influence a position or person can command and expend can be used as an indicator of status in a hierarchy. Individuals are members of many collectivities, and the more memberships they have in high prestige collectivities, the higher their prestige. Influence can be concomitant with power, money, or value-commitments. Parsons hypothesized that in a stable society, influence is likely to be associated with power. In a changing society its base is difficult to determine. He suggested that in relating influence to stratification processes one should consider the scope of the interpenetrating channels within which influence is effective and the bases of prestige from which influence can be drawn.

In modern societies positions can be ranked by evaluating the collectivities with which they are associated. There are at least three types of collectivities: (1) specific function collectivities, such as work groups, (2) diffuse function associations, such as social, political, and church organizations; and (3) diffuse solidarities, such as community, kinship, and ethnic groups. Individuals usually belong to more than one of these types of collectivities, at least, a work unit, a family, a religious unit, and a geographical unit. Roles in these collectivities can be evaluated.

Any work organization is a system with its own four functional problems. A position within an organization can be evaluated according to its contributions to the subsystems of the organization. Within any work organization there are three levels indicating status distinctions: technicians, managers, and executives. Finally, an organization's actions can be classified as belonging to one of the four subsystems in a society. All of these can be viewed as characteristics of one social position and each can be evaluated by the appropriate criterion. Hence, evaluation of a position can be a composite of the evaluations of the many characteristics of the position.

Some of the other characteristics of social positions which can be evaluated are: qualities, performances, and possessions.

Qualities are: memberships in kinship units, authority, qualities of personalities, and units of a society. These are designated as qualities because although they can be modified by learning, they cannot be transferred from the possessor. Qualities and performances are characteristics of a role which is located in a collectivity and a collectivity is located in one of the subsystems of a society. Roles are evaluated by the values of the subsystem in which they are located and according to the importance of subsystems in which they are located. Using the evaluation of a priest of a Catholic church to illustrate the qualitative base of social positions, since religion is an aspect of a pattern-maintenance subsystem, the values of that subsystem are used to evaluate the position. If we assume the priest works in the United States, the dominant values of the society, those of the adaptation subsystems, are also used to evaluate the position. The particular church in which the priest works can be viewed as a collectivity and that collectivity is also evaluated. The priest also belongs to a kinship unit, has a personality, and has authority and each of these is evaluated. Parsons made no definitive statement about how these many evaluations can be put into a single indicator of the prestige or status of the priest.

Performances or achievements cannot be isolated from qualities. Evaluations of performances are always relative to some qualitative base as described in the preceding paragraph.

Possessions are independent of a person or a social position because they can be transferred between actors. They can be used as means or as ends. In a stable integrated society, the allocation of possessions belonging to a social position tends to be consistent with evaluations of the position's qualities and performances.

Authority is an indicator of the relative superiority of different positions. Within a collectivity, authority is the legitimate power to control the actions of other members of the collectivity. The values which are used to evaluate subsystems' functions are also used to legitimate power and to define and rank authority. Parsons suggested that authority is probably most appropriate to the evaluative ranking of the upper ranges of a power structure. It was suggested that authority is more important to evaluations of social positions in societies that value goal-attainment or integration. Since authority is necessary for getting things done, it is especially important in a society which values goal-attainment. It is also important when integration of a society is valued because authority is a base from which support for regulative activities can be legitimated.

Power is a capacity of a unit to attain its goals, facilities, or rewards. It can be used to control other units so they do not interfere with a unit's interests. Power may be institutionalized or noninstitutionalized. It is institutionalized if it is based on a society's values and if control of possessions comes about as a result of their being positively correlated with status derived from compliance with the values of a society. A noninstitutionalized form of power exists when there is deviation from a society's values, and when units of a society are permitted to engage in activities not supported by a society's values. Power is noninstitutionalized if possessions have been attained by deviant means.

One indicator of the degree of patterned integration of a society is the degree of consistency in the evaluative rankings of performances, possessions, and power. The greater the patterned integration and the more stable the society, the more likely are positive correlations between qualities, performances, possessions, and power. The less the patterned integration and the less stable a society, the less likely is this correlation, and the more important the noninstitutionalized aspects of power.

Although Parsons did not specify relationships between the foregoing attributes, he proposed that each channel of status or each attribute evaluated can be presumed to have some degree of independence from other attributes as well as some degree of interdependence with other attributes.

Occupations in Modern Societies

Occupational status is one indicator of prestige. An occupation is task-oriented and its activities have relevancy to a society's economy. Therefore, an individual's occupational status is evaluated by the values of an economy, universalism-performance. The status of an occupation is also evaluated by the values of the subsystem in which an occupational collectivity functions. In America, occupational roles in the economy have the same values as the dominant values of the society as a whole, universalism-performance; however, occupational roles in the polity are affected by at least two types of values; first, the dominant values of the society (universalism-performance), and secondly, within the political subsystem, particularism-performance also apply (Figure 6-1). Differences in the importance of the two sets of values in American society may be one way of explaining differences in the prestige of equivalent occupations in the economy and the polity. The values of the economy are consistent with the values of the society as a whole. However, for occupational roles in the polity, persons are still judged and evaluated by values of the economy or the society as a whole. Because of the situs of the occupations' functions, they are also evaluated by the values of the polity, or goal-attainment subsystem, and the two sets of values are contradictory. Occupations in each of the other subsystems can be subjected to similar analysis.

Several matters related to an occupation can be evaluated: relationships with the recipients of its products or services, its products, and its location in a work organization. The things produced by an occupation are either a means or an end. If means are produced, the occupation serves an adaptive function and is instrumentally oriented. If an end is produced, the occupation serves a nonadaptive function and is expressively oriented.

Two characteristics of the terms of exchange of an occupation's products are important. Terms of exchange may be personal or impersonal. Impersonal exchanges occur when products are dispensed in a manner such that the occupational role is not expected to be concerned with the feelings or attitudes of the recipient. The most typical examples of impersonal exchanges are relationships between buyers and sellers of consumer goods. The seller is not expected to be concerned with a buyer's motivations and attitudes. On the other hand, a case of personal exchange occurs in occupations in the field of human relations, such as physicians and counselors; they are expected to be concerned with or interested in feelings and personal attitudes of the recipients of their services.

The foregoing implies another significant matter, whether or not an occupation and recipients of its goods and services belong to the same collectivity, such as a buyer in a department store buying for other departments within the same store. The buyer will have a collectivity orientation. If an occupation and recipients of its goods and services do not belong to the same collectivity, a self-oriented attitude exists.

An occupation can be classified according to whether its work has a specific or diffuse responsibility in an organization. Does it perform specific tasks for units within the organization (specificity), such as purchasing supplies, or are its tasks carried out for the benefit of the organization as a whole (diffuseness), such as maintaining good relations with employees

Any work organization can be analyzed as a system. Occupations can be located in a subsystem within the organization. The values of each subsystem, set forth in Figure 6-1, are used to evaluate and rank performances of occupations according to the subsystem within which the performance takes place. Actors' performances are also regulated by the performance and santion norms of each subsystem. These performance-sanction norms are the same as those set forth in Chapter 3, Figure 3-4. Since the logic of the evaluations is the same as that explained in Chapter 3, it is not repeated here.

Parsons thought that in the United States the educational revolution and the professionalization of occupations had increased the complexity of stratification processes. Using advanced technologies and scientific information in production and management, organizations use different types of professionals. Professionals and technicians who work for business organizations have affiliations with professional and technical organizations outside their work group. One consequence is that many different types of highly skilled workers are found within the same organization.

Considering the importance of professional affiliations of workers and the increase in the number of different types of professionals within one business enterprise, it was proposed that the study of occupations in modern societies required a consideration of: (1) the organizational base from which professionals work, (2) the subsystem focus of their work, (3) professionals' affiliations in organizations outside of the workplace, and (4) the subsystem focus of these professional affiliations. Such an analysis was called a study of a stratification bundle. A stratification bundle was thought to serve an integrative function for a society. By having loyalties to several groups which subscribe to different values, workers' interests were thought to be less rigidly grounded in one interest group, permitting them to express in value-commitments a wide range of values. Loyalties to several groups with different values were viewed as contributing to the integration of a modern society.

References and Suggestions for Further Study

Parsons' analysis of stratification processes as set forth in this chapter can be found in:
"An Analytical Approach to the Theory of Stratification" (1940)
"A Revised Analytical Approach to the Theory of Social Stratification" (1953)
"The Occupational System" in *Working Papers in the Theory of Action* (1953)
"The University Bundle: A Study of the Balance Between Differentiation and Integration" (1974)
"Empirical Differentiation and Variation in the Structure of Societies" in *The Social System* Chapter V, 1951
"Introduction" to Pt. Two on "Differentiation and Variation in Social Structures," *Theories of Society,* Vol. I, 1961
Societies: Evolutionary and Comparative Perspectives (1966)
"Postscript to Chapter 15" ("On the Concept of Influence") in *Politics and Social Structure* (1969)
"Equality and Inequality in Modern Society, or Social Stratification Revisited" (1970)
"Social Structure and the Symbolic Media of Interchange" (1975).

Specific stratification issues are discussed in:
"The Professions and Social Structure" (1939)
"The Sociology of Modern Anti-Semitism" (1942)
"Age and Sex in the Social Structure of the United States" (1942)
"Democracy and Social Structure in Pre-Nazi Germany" (1942)
"The Kinship System of the Contemporary United States" (1943)
"Racial and Religious Differences as Factors in Group Tensions" (1945)
"Population and Social Structure of Japan" (1946)
"Certain Primary Sources and Patterns of Aggression in the Social Structure of the Western World" (1946)
"Social Classes and Class Conflict in the Light of Recent Sociological Theory" (1949)
"The Distribution of Power in American Society" (1957)
"The Pattern of Religious Organization in the United States" (1958)
"The Role of General Theory in Sociological Analysis: Some Case Material" (1959)
"Some Principle Characteristics of Industrial Societies" (1961)
"Full Citizenship for the Negro American" (1965)
"The Nature of American Pluralism" (1967)
"Some Comments on the Sociology of Karl Marx" in *Sociological Theory and Modern Society* (1967)
"The Problem of Polarization on the Axis of Color" (1968)
"Kinship and the Associational Aspects of Social Structure" (1971)
"Some Theoretical Considerations on the Nature and Trends of Change of Ethnicity" (1975).

Parsons' *Politics and Social Structure* (1969) contains many seminal ideas relevant to stratification processes.

Chapter 7

Personality

Introduction

Parsons' writings about personality deal with four issues: (1) childhood socialization, (2) an analysis of a personality as an action system, (3) the normative control of personalities in interaction situations, and (4) deviancy as it relates to a personality's problems of adaptation and integration. Each of these issues is discussed in the following sections of this chapter.

As the previous chapters have demonstrated, after postulating that action involves the subsystems of culture, society, personality, and behavioral organism, Parsons defined various types of action systems as comprising relationships between these subsystems. He used the same strategy to describe personality as an action system. It will be remembered that action theory (Chapter 2) describes relationships between the subsystems as involving institutionalization and integration. Institutionalization relates culture to society and integration relates personality to society. Parsons' thoughts on childhood socialization provided a detailed analysis of the integration of children into the normative order of a society.

Childhood socialization molds organic energy into social motives and after social motives are acquired a personality is controlled by a societal community. After internalizing dominant values of his society a young person develops a personal culture which is used to justify his social roles. Thereafter, as an action system, his personality is oriented to cultural objects in a variety of social action systems.

Parsons wrote about an infant's socialization as though it occurred exclusively in a nuclear family with a mother as a primary caretaker. In the earliest phases of socialization, motivation is directed to satisfaction of organic drives. The pleasure an infant receives from a mother's care

127

bonds child to mother, creating a foundation from which relationships with others develop. Later, after a child has learned that there are social conditions for the satisfaction of his needs and wishes, organic drives become subordinate to social interests, and an ego develops. An ego is concerned with goal-attainment of a personality and it relates an individual's actions to a variety of social action systems.

Socialization processes create a personal culture which is more or less representative of the culture of the society in which socialization has taken place. The culture of a personality is manifested as a personal identity and an ego ideal. A superego is a foundation from which conscience is experienced. It coordinates and integrates personality as a system. All of this occurs after personality has developed as a system; that is, after the following have been internalized: beliefs about the empirical world, feelings and sentiments, expressive symbols, roles, norms, and values. These are the elements of the cultural and social subsystem defined in Chapter 2.

The logic of socialization was based on five learning processes; therefore, the learning processes are discussed first. After defining the learning processes in the following section, they are illustrated in the sections on socialization and personality as a system.

Learning Processes

Socialization involves five learning processes: (1) cognitive identification of objects; (2) evaluation of the cathectic value of objects; (3) differentiations of organic energy into need-dispositions; (4) generalization of objects; and (5) integration of objects and need-dispositions. These processes are summarized in Figure 7-1.

Objects are cognitively identified when one is aware of them, acquires knowledge about what they are and for what they can be used. They are cathected when clues from the environment establish that they are a source of gratification.

An object has motivational significance when it has been cognitively identified and it has also been a source of gratification or it has been evaluated as a potential source of gratification. Experiencing objects as gratifying creates motivation because thereafter organic energy is directed to the object as a source of gratification. As inferred from the foregoing statements, development of motivation requires the following: (1) organic energy, (2) objects which are cognitively identified, (3) either the experience of pleasure from identified objects or an expectation that identified objects are a potential source of pleasure.

Figure 7-1

Learning Processes

cognitive identification of an object;
cathexis of the identified object;
acquisition of a need-disposition;
generalization: cognitive classifications of the object into general and specific cognitive
    and cathectic categories;
integration: establishment of relationships between cognitive and cathectic categories
    and between objects, categories, and need-dispositions;
cognitive identification of a second object; comparison of cathectic value of first and
    second object;
cathexis of second object;
    cognitive and cathectic differentiation of the first and second object;
differentiation of first need-disposition into two need-dispositions;
generalization: cognitive classifications of old and new objects into general and
    specific cognitive and cathectic categories;
integration: establishment of relationships between old and new categories, objects, and
    need-dispositions, and relationships between each and all of them.

Adapted from *Family, Socialization and Interaction Process* (1955), Ch. IV, pp. 187-257,
    Figure 1, p. 198; Figure 2, p. 217.

In discussing learning processes Parsons was less concerned with generalized motivation than with specific motivation. He preferred to deal with what he called need-dispositions. He used 'motivational energy' to denote generalized drives which are not linked or attached to a particular object. 'Need-disposition' was used to refer to motivational energy which is organized around perceived objects. By 'need-disposition' Parsons directed attention to two aspects of motivation. Need refers to a requirement that an organism accomplish something, satisfy a need; disposition refers to a tendency or disposition to react to an object in such a way that the object satifies a need.

After a person has cognitively identified an object, cathected it, and experienced gratification from it, the object may be internalized. It is internalized if there are perceived relationships between objects and gratifications such that an object is perceived from the following three perspectives: (1) as a cognitively identified object external to a personality, (2) the object is cathected, that is viewed as capable of satisfying a need, and (3) there is a disposition to respond to the object. Such an internalization process creates a need-disposition in that there is a tendency to respond to an object because it is perceived as a source of gratification.

The acquisition of a first need-disposition is important because it becomes the basis for the development of other need-dispositions. It divides into two need-dispositions, and these in turn, divide into four need-dispositons.

Each time a new object is internalized and a new need-disposition is acquired there is a change in the structure of motivation. One type of change results merely from the fact that a new object and a new need have been added. Another type of change is derived from the assumptions of Parsons' theory. Since the theory assumes that all systems are integrated, personality must also be integrated. Hence, the most recently internalized objects and the most recently acquired need-dispositions must be integrated, coordinated, or at least related to old objects and old motivations. Consequently, each time a new object or a new need-disposition is acquired, integration processes relate them to pre-existing objects and need-dispositions, thereby changing the structure of a personality.

Objects are cognitively generalized and classified into hierarchically ordered categories in which some categories are more general and inclusive than others. Using the example of a child's cognitively understanding that he is separate from his mother we can illustrate three levels of generalization. A specific cognitive category exists when he recognizes that he is an 'I' and that his mother is an 'other.' A more general category involves his classification of the two of them as related to each other, designated as 'we.' The idea of 'we' implies a residual category, a 'non-we' or 'they' category which is more general and inclusive than the 'we' of mother and child.

Cathected objects are also generalized and classified into hierarchically ordered categories. For instance, a child cathects his mother because she satisfies his needs. He then generalizes the cathexis of her as a mother to a cathexis of her as a parent. The designation of parent is more general than mother. Thereafter, a father is cognitively included in the category of parent and the cathexis of the mother is generalized to him as a father-parent. Classifying them both as parents is more general than the classification of each of them as a parent.

Generalization of cognition and cathexis permits elements of a situation to be categorized as similar and makes it possible for a personality to understand and respond to a range of objects instead of having to understand and respond to the unique attributes of objects. Therefore, generalization of cognition and cathexis increases the number of elements integrated into a personality. It facilitates flexibility, stability, and consistency of a personality, and contributes to a personality's adaptability.

As in other systems, personality tends to be both functionally and patterned integrated. Integration is a process by which internalized objects and need-dispositions are organized into a relatively stable pattern as a precondition for personal autonomy and for maintenance of the boundaries of a personality. Hence, learning also includes a type of integration in which relationships between objects, between need-dispositions, and between objects and need-dispositions are established.

Socialization: Differentiation of Personality's Subsystems

Inducing him to acquire socially appropriate motives, socializing agents are buffers between a child and his environment. Although any experience may be primarily cognitive or cathectic, learning always involves both. Initially, since satisfaction of his organic drives are important to an infant, cathexis is dominant. Pleasure is derived from his mother's satisfaction of his organic needs and the pleasure bonds mother and infant. Later, the bond becomes a foundation for a child's experiencing reciprocal relationships with the mother, and these reciprocal relationships are foundations for the development of relationships with others.

After an infant's organic needs have been socialized and after he has been sensitized to normative control, his learning about relationships between the sexes and generations in the family is a conduit by which he acquires his first social roles. A father's instrumental functions and a mother's expressive functions facilitate the internalization of appropriate sex roles.

Socialization processes are classified into two stages and eight phases. The stages are defined by the collectivity within which socialization occurs. The first, the preoedipal stage, occurs within the family and culminates with the differentiation of motivations so that there are four need-dispositions. The four need-dispositions define an attitudinal structure (as set forth in Figure 2-4), described by two of the pattern variables: affectivity-affective neutrality and specificity-diffuseness.

The second, the oedipal stage, also occurs within a family, but it has linkages to interactions outside of the family. Experiences in peer groups provide conditions for a child's internalization of values and norms. These values and norms, previously described in Chapter 2, Figure 2-5, are described by the two pattern variables: universalism-particularism and quality-performance (ascription-achievement). Also, in the oedipal stage need-dispositions become increasingly differentiated and integrated, combining and recombining to form constellations of role identities.

The eight phases of socialization are a series of equilibrium and disequilibrium states of a personality system. Each phase begins with a relatively stable equilibrium state. The stability is disturbed by some item of

new information, such as a change in the attitude or behavior of a socializing agent, a withholding of gratification, or increased motivational energy stimulated by a child's growth. Disturbances create disequilibrium
and a child experiences relative deprivation and frustration. Frustration
provokes a change in behavior and attitude. Parents reinforce a preferred behavior by sequentially emphasizing one of four types of control:
permissiveness, support, denial of reciprocity, and manipulation of rewards. Each discipline strategy is emphasized at different phases of the
socialization process. Using one of the control strategies, a socializing
agent encourages a preferred change by arranging situations in which a
child learns new information about the cathectic value of a new object. A
restructuring process begins. The child cognitively and cathectically dis-
crimates new objects and acquires a new need-disposition. Then, the restructuring process is reinforced by a socializing agent's selectively re-
warding or withholding gratification.

Four phases of socialization are stable; four are unstable. The unstable
phases initiate a change in the structure of a personality. The stable
phases consolidate the structure. Each stable phase is characterized by
the objects internalized, the need-dispositions acquired, the type of discipline used, the subsystem differentiated, the cognitive and cathectic
categories acquired, and the pattern variables internalized. The stable
phases are schematically set forth in Figure 7-2. They are: (1) oral-
dependency, (2) love-attachment, (3) latency, and (4) maturity (also called genital). Since they are the equilibrium states in which a structure of
personality is established the discussion in this section will focus on a
description of the structure of each stable phase of development.

The unstable phases are: (1) A birth or oral crisis occurs when an
organism must establish a relationship with a mother in order to receive
gratification. (2) An anal phase is a crisis created by demands that a
child exercise some autonomy and self-control. (3) The oedipal phase is
created by a need to let go of a strong dependency on a mother. (4)
Adolescence is a crisis stimulated by demands that a child become less
attached to a family and orient his activities to a larger collectivity.

In the discussion which follows each stable phase is described by the
objects internalized, the need-dispositions internalized, the differentiation of an id, ego, and superego, and the acquisition of cognitive categories described by the pattern variables. It is assumed that the person
being socialized is a male child with a female sibling.

Oral-dependency: At birth an infant must adjust to a new type of environment. His first crisis, the oral crisis, occurs because of his need to
make a transition from the closed environment of the fetus to an environment which is more open and which is less stable.

Figure 7-2

Stable Phases of Socialization

Phases [subsystems]	Discipline	Object Categories	Need-dispositions; [pattern variables]	Cultural Values [pattern variables]
oral-dependency	permissiveness	mother-child (1 unit)	oral-dependency (self-collectivity)	
love-attachment	support	mother; self (2 units)	dependency; autonomy (specificity-diffuseness)	
latency	denial of reciprocity	family sex-generation roles (4 units): mother, father, male self, female sibling	nurturance conformity security adequacy (affective neutrality)	
(4 subsystems differentiated; motivational structure fully developed)		universalistic-particularistic role types for instrumental-expressive, superior-inferior role types (8 units) extra-family reference		(universalism-particularism)
maturity	manipulation of rewards	quality-performance role types for each of 8 role types of previous stage (16 units); societal reference		(quality-performance)
(latency subsystem fully developed)				

Adapted from *Family, Socialization, and Interaction Process* (1955), pp. 35-54.

In the first stable phase of socialization the exclusiveness of an infant's interest in his mother's satisfaction of his needs fosters a diffuse attachment to her. The constancy of her care-giving activities and the organic focus of his motivations provide a situation in which the two of them, mother and infant, are cognitively identified by the infant as one object. It is this one object which is perceived as a source of gratification, and it is cathected. As the mother-child object is cathected an infant's motivation is structured into a first need-disposition, oral-dependency, which links his motivational energy to the mother-child object.

Although an infant has not internalized them, rules regulate relationships with a mother and permissiveness is used as a disciplinary strategy. When satisfaction of his needs is delayed he confronts his first adaptation problem, whether to insist on gratification or whether to comply passively with the rules requiring him to forgo it. The pattern variable self-collectivity is appropriate for describing the conflict between his interest (self) and the rules of the mother-child relationship (collectivity). Adjusting to the contingency of this situation, he learns to manipulate the situation, himself, and his mother so that he does receive gratification, thereby successfully adjusting to the situation. By learning to adjust to situations over which he does not have total control he exercises some degree of adaptation to his external environment and acquires an ability to maintain the boundary of his person.

Love-attachment phase: The oral-dependency phase is disturbed when, in the anal crisis, there are expectations that a child should become less dependent on a mother and should develop autonomy. Encouraging him to care for himself, his mother manipulates him and situations so that he begins to learn to care for some of his needs by feeding himself and by adjusting to the demands of toilet training. Using support as a disciplinary strategy, she reinforces his caring for himself by communicating love for him. He is rewarded when he does things for himself or when he forgoes gratification. Her behavior provides a situation in which he begins to understand the difference between love and care.

A cognitive differentiation of love and care broadens his perspective about the mother-child relationship. Eventually, he cognitively identifies two functions which his mother performs in his behalf. Her taking care of his needs is an instrumental function; her loving him is an expressive function. The cognitive differentiation of these two types of activities is an occasion for him to begin separating adaptation problems from integration problems. The caring activities are related to his problems of adapting to the environment. The integration problem stems from love and care relationships between mother and child. These objects, love and care, mother and child, are internalized by the child.

Caring for himself provokes a child to think about his needs in specific terms. As his needs are experienced and defined by him with increasing specificity, he orients to his mother for the purpose of receiving clearly defined kinds of gratifications. As a consequence, his formerly diffuse attachment to her becomes specific. The pattern variable specificity-diffuseness describes this differentiation.

As mother and child exchange love and care they develop reciprocal relationships. Their exchange of gratification stimulates a child to differentiate himself from his mother and to take the initiative in interactions with her. A mother reinforces her child's actively loving her and his initiating activities involving both of them. Not only does he acquire abilities to love and care for himself, he learns to love and care for his mother. Thus, he cathects two objects: his mother and himself. Cathecting the two objects is a precondition for a differentiation of the oral-dependency need-disposition into two need-dispositions: autonomy and dependency.

After the need for autonomy has been separated from the need for dependency a first moral dilemma is confronted, that of balancing dependency needs with autonomy needs. In this context, a self develops. The need for autonomy is a base from which an 'I' initiates activity, and mother's evaluations are grounds for a child's understanding himself as an object, as a 'me' which is evaluated.

Latency: The love-attachment phase is disturbed by an oedipal crisis when a child is expected to relinquish some of his attachment to his mother and to seek support from other family members. The expectation frustrates him and disturbs the equilibrium of the love-attachment phase. His father commences supervising him. Father's supervision is supported by the mother, and in concert, they act as a power coalition denying reciprocity to the child. Understanding that the mother supports the father's demands and that she loves the father, the child also cathects his father because his mother does. The cathectic relationship with a father is an occasion for cognitive discrimination of the father's role. Parsons states that this is the first time the child internalizes the father-child role relationship.

A child's understanding of the roles of the sexes and generations in his family is a by-product of his having cognitively and cathectically discriminated his father. In the two previous phases he differentiated his mother's instrumental and expressive roles. In the third phase of socialization these roles are linked to the sex structure of the family. It is learned that in his family females are expressively oriented and males are instrumentally oriented. It is understood that not only the mother, but females generally fulfill expressive functions, and that a male child is expected to emulate his father's instrumental role. Hence, the sex-linked instrumental and expressive roles within the family are generalized.

As a result of numerous experiences of differences of power of two generations within the family, a child begins to understand that all adults have more power than children. There is also a recognition that his sister shares his experience of the greater power of parents. He cognitively discriminates the lesser power of children in the family and generalizes power differences of children and parents: they, the parents, have more power than children and children have less power than parents.

After cognitively discriminating roles of the two sexes and generations within the family, four objects, father, mother, self, and female sibling, are internalized. Generalization is extended to a more abstract level from which the following collectivites are also internalized: they, the parents; we, the children; we, the males; and they, the females.

Although internalization of the roles of the sexes and generations is limited to a perspective within a family, there is a larger communal referent implied. As noted above, a child has already discriminated his mother's expressive role within the family; however, the father's instrumental role is perceived as having a locus external to the family. The extra-family reference is important because a father's instrumental role provides a foundation for understanding extra-familial collectivities and roles. Although previous phases of socialization control the child's satisfaction of his needs in the context of a family, the extra-family reference stimulates a child to become aware of a broader community within which he is expected to exercise autonomy, self-discipline, and sex-appropriate behavior. The pattern variable affective neutrality describes such an extra-family reference for self-discipline. The internalization of that variable is the first control of a superego. With the internalization of the controls of affective neutrality an attitudinal structure is developed and is described by: affectivity-affective neutrality and specificity-diffuseness.

Frustrations resulting from a child's having to comply with normative expectations of persons who are not members of his family provoke him to increase the functions of his ego. Consequently, the previously acquired need-dispositions of dependency and autonomy become instrumentally and expressively differentiated; the oedipal frustration is lessened; and there is a stability of the latency phase.

Dependency differentiates into: (1) an expressive dimension, nurturance, and (2) an instrumental dimension, conformity. Nurturance is a need to experience gratification, and it can be directed to the self, as well as to others. It is the basis for the development of the goal-attainment subsystem of personality. Conformity designates the requirement that a child comply with normative expectations of others. It is a base for differentiation of a pattern-maintenance subsystem of a personality.

Autonomy also differentiates into two need-dispositions: (1) instrumentally, there is a need for adequacy, and (2) expressively, there is a need for security. Security is manifested in a child's receiving and giving love and support in social relationships. It is a base for a differentiation of the integration subsystem of personality. Adequacy denotes a need to perform in accordance with standards appropriate for a child's age and sex. It is a foundation for differentiation of an adaptation subsystem of personality.

After the four need-dispositions are differentiated they are referenced to a personality's subsystems as shown in Figure 7-3.

Figure 7-3

Subsystems of Personality and Need-dispositions

	Adaptation	*Goal-Attainment*
	Instrumental Functions (means)	**Expressive Functions** (ends)
Environmental Focus		
External	Adequacy id	Nurturance ego
Internal	Conformity ego-ideal identity	Security superego conscience
	Latency	*Integration*

Adapted from *Family, Socialization and Interaction Process* (1955), pp. 172-176; *The American University* (1973), Figure A.6.

Id, Ego, and Superego in the Latency Phase

Conditions for the development of a superego are: (1) a child's internalization of the parents as agents controlling motivations; (2) emancipation from the nuclear family; (3) acquisition of an orientation to an extra-family frame of reference for actions; (4) a generalization of the parental control function to a more or less autonomous function within a personality such that self-control operates within the context of a personal conscience; and (5) internalization of social norms and values. After the oedipal crisis, and with the stability of the latency phase, all of these conditions are not satisfied. Although a child's superego functions are differentiated, the pattern-maintenance subsystem from which it receives its grounding is not fully developed, and a child has not been emancipated from the nuclear family. An extra-family reference has been acquired, but the family's influence and control are still dominant.

In the latency phase, a superego, differentiated from an ego, commences coordinating actions by relating an individual's actions to the norms of his society. However, in this phase, grounding for a superego is not in a society's culture because the child has not yet internalized all of the cultural values and has not developed a personal identity which is the core of a personal culture.

Directed to pattern-maintenance problems, an ego-ideal or personal identity is the repository of a personal culture as a reference base for an actor's understanding of the meaning of his roles. It is the most stable aspect of a personality and is the base from which a superego, concerned with personality's integration, interprets a personal culture.

As discussed above, in the first phase of socialization organic needs are the primary goals of an undifferentiated personality. Initially, their decreasing importance is a by-product of an infant's erotic relationship with his mother and her control strategies. Adapting to the environmental conditions controlled by his mother, an infant begins testing the reality of his environment. He is continually subjected to occasions on which he is expected to comply with others' wishes and he is forced to adopt a reality orientation to the conditions which regulate the satisfaction of his drives. Eventually, he acquires a reality orientation which enables him to cognitively appraise situations from a reality perspective rather than solely from a pleasure-seeking perspective. Such a reality-oriented perspective, differentiated from the organic based pleasure-seeking perspective, is an indication that an ego has been differentiated from an id.

An id is a personality's source of motivational energy. It handles the adaptation problem of a personality and mediates personality's use of organic energy. It's mediation provides performance capacities such as movement, physical dexterity, sensory perception, etc.

An ego handles personality's goal-attainment which includes carrying out role performances, appraising social situations, definitions of personality's need-dispositions, and relating personality's roles to social collectivities.

After the equilibrium of a latency phase, pleasure is no longer defined as fulfilment of organic needs; it is defined as fulfilment of social expectations. With a lessening of the importance of organic drives and the pleasure resulting from their satisfaction, functions of the id and functions of the ego become more distinctly separated. Relationships between id and ego become more organized, and ego dominates the id. As a consequence, an id is integrated with the social dimensions of personality. Its energy becomes a facility for an ego to channel and direct.

Internalization of Cultural Values in the Latency Phase

Although superego functions have been differentiated, they are not fully operative because their reference bases of integrity and ego ideal are not fully developed until the dominant cultural values of a society have been internalized. An internalization of these values is a by-product of experiences in peer groups and educational organizations. Cultural values categorized as universalism-particularism are internalized as a result of relationships with peers in the latency phase; ascription (quality)-achievement (performance) are internalized as a result of peer relationships in adolescence.

In the latency phase, relationships with peers and teachers reinforce and generalize the previously internalized familial sex and generation-roles. Children generalize the roles of adults and children as a consequence of experiencing the generational power relationships between teachers and students. Peer groups provide situations within which male instrumental roles and female expressive roles are reinforced, and these roles are further generalized to relationships outside a family. Internalization of the generality of the universal-particular standards by which roles of the sexes and generations are evaluated is reinforced by a child's developing feelings of loyalty to his teachers, school, class, and peer group.

In addition to reinforcing understandings of role relationships previously acquired, in the latency phase peer-group and educational experiences contribute to a child's internalizing the dominant cultural standards for evaluating social objects. Relationships within a family foster and condone evaluations of persons according to their relationships to others (particularism). Hence, children understand particularism in the context of a family; relationships with peers reinforce the understanding in extra-familial situations.

Insofar as relationships in a classroom with a teacher and other students require performances in accordance with general standards appropriate to a child's age, he is introduced to universalistic standards. Teachers evaluate his performances by comparing him with other children. They use general standards appropriate for a particular age group. These are universalistic standards of evaluation. As a result of having been evaluated according to universalistic standards, a child develops an ability to use them himself. Moreover, members of his own family begin to view him as a member of the larger community and commence evaluating his performances according to universalism.

Learning to use universalistic standards contributes to an ability to think logically. Evaluating others particularistically, in terms of their relationship to an evaluator, stresses unions, and utilizes a conjunctive logic. When universalistic standards are applied to age and sex categories, a child must evaluate persons according to differences as well as similarities. Such evaluations require that he stress differences between categories of objects, thereby necessitating the use of disjunctive logic. Objects must be classified into groups and differences between groups must be defined. Then, general (universalism) standards are used to evaluate the groups. Thus, the cognitive discrimination entailed in universalistic standards expands cognitive ability as well as the ability to use abstract categories.

An internalization of abstract categories is assisted by experiences of power relationships within peer-groups. Whereas, in a family power differences are understood relative to relationships between parents and children (particularism), in a peer-group, power is less stable; it is determined by multiple criteria which vary from situation to situation. Young persons must learn to scrutinize the bases of power in a multitude of relationships, such as power based on popularity, academic competence, social status, prowess, or age. Moreover, mutually cooperative relationships within peer-groups contribute to members' understandings of the social consensus on which situations are evaluated and the informal rules on which power relationships are developed and maintained.

The stability of the latency phase is distinguished by a generalization of the four role categories of a family to an extra-family context and the socializee's understanding the univeralistic and particularistic aspects of social roles. The four role categories are: (1) male, instrumental adult role; (2) male, instrumental childhood role; (3) female, expressive adult role; (4) female, expressive childhood role. In the latency phase each of these four is categorized from the perspective of universalistic standards and from the perspective of particularistic standards.

Maturity or genitality: Security within a family is challenged by expectations that an adolescent should be independent and autonomous. The equilibrium of the latency phase is disturbed and an adolsecent crisis ensues. Attitudes about parents change from those viewing parents as central to a child's private experiences to ones in which parents are thought of as adult members of the community. Persons who are not members of his family, such as educators, community leaders, peers, and representatives of occupations, are perceived as influential role models. Now, parents must share their socializing roles with others, and peers and persons of the opposite sex are especially significant in socializing an adolescent.

Resolution of the adolescent crisis occurs when a young person orients himself outside of his family of orientation, internalizes roles appropriate to his own family of procreation, and acquires an autonomous personal identity. That orientation requires the internalization of the qualitative and performance aspects of roles.

Prior to adolescence a young person has had a lot of contact with the qualitative aspects of roles. One of his earliest learning experiences dealt with qualities, the sex and age of persons in his family. Although many adolescent relationships are focused on qualitative characteristics of roles, such as relationships between the sexes, much adolescent behavior is also judged by performance or achievement standards. Indeed, some of the stress associated with the adolescent experience derives from a peer-group's emphasis on the performance aspect of adolescent roles. An adolescent is expected to know the culture of adolescence, acquire symbols which indicate that he associates with the "right crowd" and participates in status-enhancing activities. Whom one dates is evaluated as an indication of achievement or performance. These concerns foster an emphasis on vertical stratification. What is more, as indicators of performances, grades are important in order to get into college, and performances are judged relative to one's occupational aspirations. These expectations provoke differentiation and internalization of the performance (achievement) and quality (ascription) attributes of roles. Universalism-particularism has already been internalized in the latency phase and with the internalization of quality-performance, the phase of maturity (also called genital phase) is stabilized.

The last stage of socialization - maturity - culminates in a structured personal culture which regulates cathectic and cognitive orientations which are, to some degree, consistent with normative expectations of a society. An individual experiences his personal culture as a sense of integrity and identity. It legitimates to him his value-commitments. It articulates between personal and cultural values. It does not implement values; it is a base for coordinating them within a personality. Integrity is the ability to be cognitively consistent and integrated as an actor and as a social object. Identity is the core of meanings of a personality and because it is the base for an actor's internal dialogue, its reference is internal to personality. Identity's code is embedded in a pattern-maintenance subsystem and is the grounds for the integrative functions of a superego and conscience.

After the acquisition of the primary need-dispositions of nuturance, adequacy, conformity, and security, these need-dispositions become less specific in their focus. Although they do not form a permanent structure of a personality, they become the scaffolding on which other need-dispositions are acquired. Need-dispositions acquired after the maturity phase become more prominent in the structure of a personality than the elementary need-dispositions. Learning continues and adult learning involves ongoing changes in the structure of personality. The primary need-dispositions are transformed into performance and sanction norms similar to those presented in Chapter 3 (Figure 3-4). These sanction and performance norms are acquired in interactions with others in a variety of situations. Then they are organized into diverse patterns of motivations relevant to adult role performances. These topics are discussed in the following section.

Personality and Social Interaction

After a society's frames of reference have been internalized an individual and society interpenetrate. Norms are the nexus of the interpenetration and they are instrumental in further adult socialization. In discussing these issues Parsons postulated that as a result of social interaction the elementary need-dispositions of adequacy, nurturance, conformity, and security are transformed into the object and attitudinal norms similar to those set forth in Chapter 3. Adequacy becomes values of approval and achievement. Nurturance becomes values of response and appreciation. Conformity becomes values of esteem and accomplishment; security, acceptance and satisfaction.

Adult socialization involves learning new roles, adapting to new interaction situations, sanctioning others, and being sanctioned by them. In this context, new objects are internalized, and elementary need-dispositions are organized in new socially appropriate patterns.

Prior to maturity, the four need-dispositions are played out in families, peer groups, and schools. With maturity, an individual's frames of reference shift to include collectivities in his community, his society and its subsystems. He becomes less concerned with the elementary need-dispositions and more concerned with others' expectations about how he should behave. Moreover, he expresses his needs in a socially broader perspective.

In interactions with others an adult experiences needs as types of reactions or attitudes he expects to receive from others. The need-dispositions become sanction and performance values. A need for nurturance becomes a need for response from others or a need to be an object of gratification for others, as well as a tendency to respond to others. Security is experienced as a desire for acceptance by members of a group which symbolizes that one belongs. Adequacy is transformed into valuing approval from others and showing approval of others. If others approve of one's actions there is a feeling that one has performed a role in accordance with relevant standards. Finally, a personality desires a general positive evaluation from others. His need for social conformity is socially translated into a desire for others to regard him with esteem and an inclination to reciprocate.

There is a mutuality between actors; they desire similar attitudes, or sanctions, from each other. For instance, ego is expected to perform in order to warrant these types of reactions (sanctions) from others. Also, to some extent, he is expected to reciprocate; i.e., to show response to others and to give them esteem, for if he has these needs, so do they. He is expected to respond by giving gratification to others, providing others with response. He should accept and support group values and norms in order to receive acceptance. If he performs adequately he will receive approval, and if he exercises self-control and discipline by conforming to norms he may be viewed with esteem.

An actor's tendencies to comply with others' expectations and his proclivities to perform in order to receive satisfactory evaluations from others transform the need-dispositions into goals of a personality. These goals are: achievement, appreciation, accomplishment, and satisfaction. The sanction and performance values are similar to those given in Chapter 3 (Figure 3-4), although Parsons used different words to describe them. In social action systems, actors utilize attitudes of approval, response, esteem, and acceptance as positive sanctions. In order to receive these positive sanctions they strive in ways which will bring about achievement, appreciation, satisfaction, and accomplishment.

Since according to the postulates of Parsons' theory all systems must

solve the same four problems, the coincidence of a personality's acquir-
ing the same sanction and performance norms as those of a system of action (as set forth in Chapter 3) is derived from the postulates of the
theory of action systems. Parsons said that the coinciding of
personality's need-dispositions with the performance and sanction values of interaction systems was a demonstration of the interpenetration
of society and personality. The interpenetration was thought to be an
outcome of the mutuality of influences between actors' interacting in the
context of similar definitions of situations. Moreover, he set forth another demonstration of interpenetration between personality and interaction systems. The pattern variables describe the values underlying
the functional differentiations of personalities and these are the same
values underlying the functional differentiations of all social action systems. The interpentration of culture and society is indicated by the same
values, described by the pattern variables, which underly the four functional problems of all action systems. These demonstrations of interpen-
etrations between culture and society and society and personality are
schematically depicted in Figure 7-4.

In Figure 7-4 cultural values are described by combinations of the pattern variables which were used to describe the phase movements of a
system of action in Chapter 3 (Figure 3-3). The need-dispositions of a
personality are set forth and related to personality's four problems. The
performance and sanction values, as derived from elementary need-
dispositions, are set forth under the need-dispositions from which they
are derived. As can be read off of Figure 7-4, the pattern variables which
describe the four system problems of an action system also describe the
need-dispositions and sanction and performance values related to the
four system problems of personality. Pattern variables describe (1) cultural values, (2) personality's need-dispositions, (3) sanction norms, and
(4) performance norms as set forth in Figure 7-4 (see also Figure 3-4).

The general theory of action (Chapter 2) described Parsons' thoughts
about the four levels of meaning of action and his theoretical descriptions of relationships between culture, society, personality, and behavioral organism. The information in Figure 7-4 is a schematic representa-
tion of these four levels of meaning. The need-dispositions refer to personality's meanings. The theory of socialization described the instigating force for these need-dispositions as being organic energy. The cultural values described by the pattern variables indicate the cultural level
of meaning. Sanction and performance values are norms used by actors
in interaction situations. They represent a societal level of meaning.

Although in adulthood the elementary need-dispositions are transformed into normative expectations for sanctions and performances in

Figure 7-4

**Cultural Values of the Subsystems of a Social System;
Need-dispositions of a Personality;
Sanction and Performance Values of Social Interaction**

		Adaptation		*Goal-Attainment*
	Functions:	**instrumental**		**expressive**
		C universalism neutrality		C affectivity particularism
Environmental Focus:				
external				
C specificity performance		ND adequacy S approval P achievement		ND nurturance S response P appreciation (or gratification)
internal				
C quality diffuseness		ND conformity S esteem P accomplishment		ND security S acceptance P satisfaction
		Latency		*Integration*

Derived from *Family, Socialization and Interaction Process* (1955), Figure 2, pp. 172-173, and *Working Papers in the Theory of Action* (1953), Figure 2. p. 182; Figure 5, p. 203.

social interaction situations, the elementary need-dispositions do not disappear. They are links in an evolutionary chain. Internalizations of new objects and motivations have fibers and strands of the old, childhood objects and need-dispositions out of which they evolve.

After the four functional subsystems of a personality are differentiated, motivations become increasingly complex. They evolve into organized patterns associated with roles. An individual's roles become molds through which he experiences and expresses motivations, cognitions, cathexes, and evaluations. In any interaction situation, through role performances, a personality functions not as one motivation, but as a bundle of patterned motivational units. Within the bundle, the uniqueness of a role performance depends not only on the organization of the differentiated motivational units, but also, on the relative strengths of motivations within a pattern of organization. Motives underlying different roles are not necessarily different in kind, but different in their organizational patterns. However, whether or not a motivation is manifested in a role performance not only depends on its strength in the bundle, but also, it must be compatible with other motives within the bundle.

Diverse motivational components, bound together in role expectations, are the cross-beams of a personality structure. The same role performed by different persons may have the same or different motivations and their organizational patterns may differ. Also, several roles performed by the same person may tap the same motivations but the motives' distribution in each role may be different.

In performing any role an individual taps appropriate cognitions, expressive symbols, evaluations, and patterns of motivations. An integration of personality as a system permits multiple role performances and different orientations to many types of social objects. Appropriate role performances are conditioned on an integrated personality; they are also conditioned on an integrated system of interaction; that is, an integration of two persons who mutually influence each other. A system of interaction is integrated when actors have, at least, internalized: (1) the values of the collectivity within which their roles exist; (2) the values of the societal subsystem within which the collectivity is located; (3) one or more values in common with other roles in the collectivity; (4) values relevant to other roles in other subsystems and not commonly shared by the actors' role collectivity.

Expressive symbols signify two characteristics of each actor: firstly, as an actor seeking gratification in a relationship with alter, and secondly, as an object evaluated by alter or as an object to which alter is oriented. From these two perspectives actors view each other as roles or systems of action. There is a mutuality of influence in interaction between them facilitated by the fact that they have experienced similar socialization processes; they have internalized the same cultural values. Cultural values, learned in a family, are grounds for a sharing of role identities and meanings. Consequently, there is a commonality of values and need-dispositions which brings order to each personality and to interactions between them.

Nevertheless, despite their internalization of common values and their experiences of similar socialization processes, actors maintain their individuality. Individuality is possible and extant because the organization and weights of cognitive and cathective objects and motivations are variable as are the situations conditioning their internalization and functional articulation within different personality systems.

Although the contents and styles of role performances vary, as systems of action personalities function in accordance with the theoretical postulates set forth for all action systems. This is the topic of the next section.

Personality as a System

It will be remembered that in the latency phase of socialization four subsystems of a personality have been differentiated. As in all action systems, these subsystems are: adaptation, goal-attainment, latency or pattern-maintenance, and integration. Although the pattern-maintenance subsystem is differentiated in a latency phase of socialization, that subsystem is not fully developed. After an adolescent crisis, the genital or maturity phase of socialization stabilizes when there is further development of a personal culture resulting from an internalization of cultural values.

After the pattern-maintenance subsystem has been fully developed, new objects and motives are further differentiated and internalized. They are integrated with previously internalized objects and motives. Personality's structure is changed and reorganized. Each of its goals is of special interest to one of the subsystems. Adaptation is concerned with achievement; goal-attainment, appreciation; pattern-maintenance strives for accomplishment; and satisfaction is the province of integration.

Adaptation and goal-attainment functions are directed to environmental conditions external to a personality . Adaptation processes focus on the cognitive meanings of objects; goal-attainment, concerned with satisfying a personality's motives, concentrates on the cathectic meanings of objects.

Adaptive processes are more general than goal-attainment processes. The cognitive orientation of the former is concerned with a broader range of phenomena than the cathectic orientation of the latter. The cathectic orientation of a goal-attainment subsystem provokes specific interests in objects as well as motivations. It matches objects with motives, evaluating objects in the context of specific motivations.

Handling the problems of adaptation and goal-attainment requires the cognitive and cathectic differentiations of objects and motives. If goals are to be achieved then goal-attainment must be concerned with differentiation of motivations so that an individual knows what motives need to be satisfied and what objects can be used to satisfy specified motives. Consequently, the cathectic value of objects must be evaluated and compared. Adaptation means using objects in the environment for the benefit of personality. Therefore, objects must be cognitively evaluated in order to determine to what purposes and for what motives they can be used.

The adaptation subsystem receives information from the goal-attainment subsystem about personality's goals and motives and that type of information sensitizes it to be interested in objects which might satisfy goal-attainment. When it cognitively identifies objects which can be utilized for goals of a personality, achievement is experienced. Achievement is one of the goals of a personality system and one of the performance values in social interaction.

Goal-attainment involves a sorting-out process. Personality has many motives, some old, some new. It has previously internalized objects because of their cathectic values and old objects and old motives have been linked. Goal-attainment sorts out relationships between old and new objects and old and new motives, comparing cathectic values of objects relative to their gratificational potentiality. If new motives have been developed a reordering of motives may be required in that some motives may be given more importance than others. All needs cannot be satified at once and gratification is always selective; some needs are satisfied; others are not. The sorting-out process eventually results in some motives being rewarded and some being deprived of gratification. Appreciation follows from goal-attainment, from linking objects to motives.

Appreciation may initiate a chain of interactions among the subsystems of a personality system whereby old motives may be reinforced or inhibited or old objects may be subordinated to new ones. Changes in relationships between motivations and objects may ensue and these changes are the concerns of integration and pattern-maintenance.

Integrative and pattern-maintenance processes reorganize and consolidate new relationshhips between objects and motivations; hence, the two subsystems use integration processes. A pattern-maintenance subsystem is concerned with the cognitive meanings of objects. An integration subsystem is concerned with the cathectic, motivational meanings of objects.

The integration subsystem internalizes the cathexis of external objects, generalizes cathexis, and if conditions require it, reorders the relative importance of internalized objects and motivations. Reordering of internalized objects and motivations may require repressing categorizations of old objects and motivations, as well as changing linkages between them in order to minimize internal conflict and ambiguity.

One of the goals of personality and one of the performance values of social interaction, satisfaction, is experienced when cathexes are generalized, when new objects are internalized, and when internalized objects and motives are organized so that some are more dominant than others. The result is a change in the structure of the system and the internalization of a new structure. The type, amount or extent of change depends on situations. All of this is the problem of the integration subsystem of personality.

As a system, personality is in a state of disequilibrium if motivations are not ordered in such a way that some are more important than others. Of course, we should recall that the basis for organization of motives is roles, role expectations, personal identity, and an ego ideal. With motives organized into many bundles and each bundle signifying a role, within any motivational role structure some motives are more dominant than others. The integration subsystem of a personality creates, changes, and organizes such an organization of motivational bundles in accordance with a personality's role requirements.

When circumstances have required a change in the pattern of motivations and objects, a latency (pattern-maintenance) subsystem maintains the pattern of the organization. Maintenance of the organized internalized objects, values, and motivations is important for reinforcing motivational complexes so that they are consistent with multiple role performances; otherwise, internal conflict or confusion can result in disorganization or deviancy. The outcome of the latency subsystem's function, or its goal, is accomplishment. Accomplishment is one of personality's goals and one of the performance values of social interaction.

The pattern-maintenance subsystem is primarily concerned with objects internal to the system and with maintaining them in a stable organized pattern so as to lessen personality's tension or stress. The organized structures of objects and motives from the integration subsystem are inputs into the pattern-maintenance subsystem. The pattern-maintenance subsystem reinforces and maintains the organized structure. It uses values, beliefs, and knowledge to justify the pattern. A personal culture is thereby maintained, and since the pattern-maintenance subystem is relatively insulated as a system, as explained in Chapter 3, Figure 3-6, its organization is an anchor for a personal autonomy and identity which are not solely dependent on external support or external reinforcement.

A pattern-maintenance subsystem enforces its own style of morality. The pattern of morality which it consolidates and maintains provides a base from which a personality system can utilize self-imposed sanctions to maintain stability of the system's moral-normative-motivational structure. It manages tension created by a personality's multiple role performances. When this subsystem's mechanisms are functioning properly, an identity is maintained over time and space.

The functioning of personality's subsystems which were described above can be illustrated by using a rather mundane example drawn from ordinary experience. Activity can be initiated in any subsystem and the source of a stimulus necessitating a response can be internal or external to a personality. Let us assume a need to adapt to a new situation internal to a personality. For example, sometimes there are feelings of boredom and lethargy. Having few objects which are gratifying can be an occasion for boredom. We simply are not motivated and we seek out situations which we think may stimulate us to acquire some motivation. Using Parsons' theory, we can designate such an experience as deprivations of goal-attainment or lack of cathexis of objects. The deprivations can provoke an adaptation subsystem to become aware of new objects in the environment. New objects are investigated. For example, if an individual feels lethargic and lacks zest for normal everyday activity he may not experience gratification from objects which previously have been sources of gratification. This can provide sufficient frustration to stimulate his cognitively recognizing new objects in the environment, perhaps a new style of activity. Let us assume some physical activity, such as skiing is experienced. Perhaps we cathect a friend and go skiing with him. As a result of the experience, we are aware of a new object, the activity of skiing, and more information about skiing is obtained. The investigation of skiing is a function of the adaptation subsystem. If skiing becomes linked to a motive from the goal-attainment subsystem there is a sense of achievement.

The goal-attainment subsystem evaluates skiing for its gratificational potentiality as well as personality's motivations which have been previously acquired. Assuming that there is a motivation which physical activity can satisfy, the goal-attainment subsystem can evaluate the relative importance of this need, compare it to other needs, and compare skiing with other types of activity. If skiing is gratifying, the goal-attainment subsystem can match a motivation for physical activity with the object, skiing. If skiing is linked to a motivation for physical activity there is an experience of appreciation. However, in order to make the linkage, other motivations or objects may have to be inhibited.

The integration subsystem internalizes the association between a motivation for physical activity and the new object, skiing. The need and the object are incorporated into the object and motivational structure already present. This results in satisfaction. Since the system has other objects and needs, and since the zeal which frequently accompanies new experiences may provide a situation in which skiing is a dominant object because it satisfies a need, a previously dominant motivation may have to be subordinated to the need for physical activity. Motivations may be restructured. Such a restructuring process is the domain of the integration subsystem.

The pattern-maintenance subsystem maintains the new structure and relates it to an individual's sense of identity. This process may stimulate the individual to join a ski club or a physical-fitness club through which his personal belief about the benefits of physical exercise is shared with others. Thereby, his sense of identity is reinforced and a sense of accomplishment is experienced.

Deviancy and Personality

All of Parsons' theory, discussed in the foregoing sections, has assumed normative compatibilities between actors in social interaction. Once personality is developed as a system it is assumed that it has processes which maintain a patterned structure which is more or less consistent with the normative requirements of a particular culture of a society in which socialization has occurred. These ideas lead us to presume Parsons' theory was primarily concerned with normative behavior. On the contrary, the theory also accounted for deviancy. His most familiar statements explain deviancy as an interruption of the normative equilibrium of interaction between an ego and an alter. From that perspective, deviancy occurs because one of the actors does not comply with the other's expectations, which, presumably, are expectations that norms be compiled with; as a result, the noncompliant actor is deviant.

Parsons classified types of deviant behavior which could result from such a situation by considering whether or not a deviant controls the interaction situation. If he controls the situation, deviancy is active; if not, it is passive. Deviancy was also categorized as alienative or conformative and as directed to objects or norms. Explaining these types of deviant behaviors, arising in interactions, Parsons focused on relationships between two actors. The same types of deviancy were also attributed to imbalances and inadequacies in solutions to a personality's system problems. The latter perspective is the topic of this section.

Deviant tendencies may arise as a result of inadequate need-dispositions. As need-dispositions are differentiated there can be an emphasis on one and a deprivation of another. If there is such an imbalance, it has consequences for later development, and deviant tendencies may develop. It is assumed that imbalances in the differentiations of need-dispositions continue in adulthood. His theory of deviancy and personality development includes three assumptions, the implications of which are demonstrated in the following discussion of deviancy and personality adjustment:

1. A division of a need-disposition once made is irrevocable. A direction of specialization is established and it becomes irreversibly established.

2. Variations in motivations derive from the relative strengths of need-dispositions in each stage of socialization. Once established, the relative strength of a need-disposition is irrevocable.

3. Adult motivations may be traced to phases of differentiations of need-dispositions in childhood.

It was assumed that there are optimal balances in the interchanges between a personality's subsystems. Hence, deviancy may result from an inability of a personality to maintain internal stability of personality as a system. Also, inactivity or overactivity of subsystems can provoke deviancy.

Socialization processes establish the relative strengths of four need-dispositions. Parsons assumed that there had to be some optimal balance among the need-dispositions. If there are imbalances among them, if some are too weak or too strong tendencies to deviant behavior can occur. He discussed these imbalances and the resulting deviant tendencies: (1) as arising in the phase of childhood socialization and (2) as to their effects on the functioning of personality as a system.

If socialization produces a need-disposition which is underdeveloped, deviancy may stem from a lack of motivation for those objects or activities for which a child is expected to be motivated. For instance, if a child has an underdeveloped autonomy need-disposition he may be unable to initiate and participate in play activities appropriate to his age. If a need-disposition is overdeveloped, deviant behavior may stem from too much motivation for certain types of objects. For instance, if a child has an overdeveloped dependency need-disposition he may be too dependent on his mother.

Deviant tendencies may arise in three of the phases of socialization. A particular type of deviancy can arise in each of the phases. The phases and deviancies are: (1) the oral-dependency phase of socialization can produce either an alienative or a conforming type of deviancy; (2) the love-attachment phase can produce either an active or a passive type of deviancy: and (3) the latency phase can give rise to a type of deviancy which focuses either on objects or on norms.

In the oral-dependency phase of socialization an infant is very dependent on his mother for satisfying his needs. It will be remembered that Parsons emphasized that this is the first time a child is confronted with the requirement that he conform to some kind of social control; he is under the control of his mother. He can resist this control or he can conform to it. A tendency for a conforming or alienative type of deviancy is related to the degree to which a child submits to normative controls of his mother. If he is excessively compliant and conforming, the conforming type of deviancy can develop. If he excessively resists and opposes his mother's control the alienative type of deviancy can develop. The child with a conforming type of deviancy is excessively compliant with norms regulating interactions; the alienative type is excessive in his noncompliance. Perhaps the extremes of these types of deviancy occur when children over-conform to parental expectations and when children are habitually unwilling to comply with any parental expectations.

In the love-attachment phase of socialization a child must balance his needs for dependency and autonomy. Too much autonomy may provoke an active type of deviancy. Too much dependency may provoke a passive type of deviancy. In the case of the active type a child has too much initiative; in the case of the passive type there is too little initiative. The over-active child would be an example of the active type; the inactive child would be an example of the passive type. In interactions with other children the active type of deviant would be the child who takes total control of a play group and situation; the passive type of deviant would be the child who stands aside, watches, and who does not actively engage in the give-and-take of interactions with his peers. In altercations, the passive type gives in or withdraws. The active type seeks to have things go his way.

In the latency phase of socialization a child encounters new extra-family situations requiring that he match need-dispositions to new objects. There are two kinds of problems which can occur because his need-dispositions are inappropriately developed. Motivations can be too sophisticated for his developmental stage. Hence, he may behave in a precocious manner. He does things which a child of his age should not be doing. Violation of norms is a consequence of his precociousness. Driving a car without a driver's license is an example; a young child's crossing the street is an example. These are examples of norm-focused deviancy.

On the other hand, a child can have inadequately developed motivations. His undeveloped or underdeveloped motivations are inadequate and he does not respond to the objects to which he is expected to respond. Since in the latency phase a child is expected to begin to orient his actions to persons outside his family unit there may be an underdeveloped motivation for interactions with persons outside the family. His family may remain excessively dominant in its influence on him. A strong attachment to the family and an insensitivity to relationships with peers is an example of the object-focused deviancy. The young person is deviant because he directs too much motivational energy to the family as an object and too little motivational energy to a peer group as an object.

The functioning of the subsystems of personality may also provoke deviancy. The subsystem functions which provoke deviant tendencies are: adaptation, goal-attainment, and integration. As previously explained, each of these subsystems relates motives to objects. Deviant tendencies are provoked because of imbalances between motives and between motives and objects.

It will be recalled that cathecting objects reinforces motivations and may stimulate the acquisition of new motives. Hence, sensitivity to objects in the environment is very important for generating and maintaining motivation. Generation and maintenance of motivations are byproducts of goal-attainment and adaptation processes which relate objects to motivations. If motivations are inadequately differentiated or underdeveloped one can be insensitive to available or "appropriate" objects. The result is an imbalance between motives and objects and the imbalance can produce deviant tendencies.

Personality's integrative processes establish relationships between internalized objects, motivations, and values. Social interactions with others require that persons have internalized motives, objects, and values which are appropriate to situations in which interactions occur. If a person's behavior indicates that one has not internalized the appropriate motives, objects, or values the behavior may be categorized as deviant. Thus, the integration subsystem's internalized motives, objects, and values can result in deviant tendencies.

If personality's integration emphasizes some motives or values and neglects others, a conforming or alienative type of deviancy occurs. The result is an overcommitment or an undercommitment to internalized values. In the case of overcommitment the deviancy is of the conforming type; in the case of undercommitment the deviancy is of the alienative type. One who is overcommitted to his work so that he works sixteen hours a day, talks about nothing else and has no other interests may be the conforming type. On the other hand, there is also the noncommitted, the alienative type who is habitually mentally and physically disengaged from his occupational role.

Deviancy arising from personality's adaptation problem focuses on relationships between motives and objects. Object or norm-focused deviancy arises from the adaptation problem. It involves the question of whether or not there is a proper fit or match between motivations and objects. Are motivations appropriate for the objects in the environment, or conversely, are objects appropriate for the motivations available. At issue is the level of development of motivations; are they highly developed or underdeveloped. If motivations are too highly developed for the objects available behavior toward the objects can be too sophisticated. Sometimes we observe children who misbehave because they are bored; they are undisciplined in a classroom because the projects and assignments are too simplistic for their abilities. Instead of working a puzzle they may take it apart because that is more challenging than working it. Thus, their deviancy is object-focused. Alexander Pope wrote a verse about such a condition, describing a person as having motivations too refined to be satisfied by available objects.[1]

On the other hand, there can be objects in the environment for which motivations are not programmed. There are many such instances in everyday life experiences. Students do not have motivations for classroom activities. Persons are not motivated to participate in sports, social events, or political activities. Parsons assumed that there are normative expectations that persons should have motivation for certain objects. When they fail to respond to them their behavior is categorized as norm-focused deviancy.

Deviancy stemming from personality's goal-attainment problem also involves difficulties in matching motivations to objects. With regard to the goal-attainment, the problem is whether objects reinforce elementary motivations or stimulate new motives. There can be excesses in gratifications which reinforce elementary motivations to the extent that new motives are not acquired. For example, if children do not have other children to play with, they may not acquire social motives for peer-group relationships and they may remain dependent on their parents for nurturance. The result can be active types of deviancy, examples of which are children's temper tantrums which demand attention and care from their parents. A passive type of deviancy is exhibited when the children fail to fulfill social obligations or retreat from role responsibilities because they do not have motivations to participate in peer-group activities.

In summary, deviancy occurs as a result of inadequate solutions to personality's system problems. Imbalances among internalized motives, objects, and values involve the integration problem and can result in the

---

1. *Wise wretch! with pleasures too refin'd to please;*
   With too much spirit to be e'er at ease;
   With too much quickness ever to be taught;
   With too much thinking to have common thought;
   You purchase Pain with all that Joy can give,
   And die of nothing but a rage to live.

(**Moral Essays:** Epistle II, To A Lady)

conforming or alienative type of deviancy. Too simplistic or too highly developed motives affects personality's adaptation to objects in the environment and may result in norm or object-focused deviancy. Goal-attainment which entails gratifications from objects which reinforce elementary motivations to the extent that new motives are not developed may result in an active or passive type of deviancy.

References and Suggestions for Further Study

The writings of Parsons which have been primary sources for information in this chapter are:
"The Learning of Social Role-Expectations and the Mechanisms of Social Motivations," and "Deviant Behavior and the Mechanisms of Social Control," *The Social System* (1951), Chaps. VI and VII.
"Personality as a System of Action," *Toward a General Theory of Action* (1951), Chap. 2.
Family, Socialization and Interaction Process (1955), espec. Chaps. I-IV.
"An Approach to Psychological Theory in Terms of the Theory of Action" (1959).
"The Position of Identity in the General Theory of Action" (1968).
Technical Appendix to *The American University* (1973), espec. Figure A.6.

Social Structure and Personality (1964) contains a series of essays on the topic of socialization:
"The Superego and the Theory of Social Systems" (1952).
"The Incest Taboo in Relation to Social Structure and the Socialization of the Child" (1954).
The Father Symbol: An Appraisal in Light of Psychoanalytic and Sociological Theory" (1954).
"Social Structure and the Development of Personality: Freud's Contribution to the Integration of Psychology and Sociology" (1958).
"The School Class as a Social System: Some of its Functions in American Society" (1959).
(with Winston White) "The Link Between Character and Society" (1961).
"Youth in the Context of American Society" (1962).
See also: "Psychoanalysis and Social Science with Special Reference to the Oedipus Problem" (1953):
"Higher Education, Changing Socialization, and Contemporary Student Dissent" (1972).
"General Education and Studentry Socialization: The Undergraduate College," *The American University* (1973), Chap. 4.

A recent extension of Parsons' personality theory has been stated by Muench, *Sociological Inquiry* 51 (1981): 311-54.

Gordon (1968) has presented operational definitions of an individual's sense of self as it relates to the four system problems of personality.

Chapter 8

Epilogue: Problems and Prospects

The persistence of Parsons' pursuit of a general theory in the social sciences has been awesome. He has been highly praised for his scholarship, the wide-ranging scope of phenomena with which his theory dealt, and for bringing coherency and order to disparate concepts. As stated in the Preface, the major purpose of this work was to provide a nonevaluative statement of Parsons' general theory. It was thought that students would better understand the theory if explanations of it were not confounded by others' evaluative comments. There was an attempt not to commingle evaluations of the theory with statements about what the theory says. Since the goal has been to provide the reader with an understanding of Parsons' theory a detailed critique of it has been outside the scope and plan of the book. The purpose of this final chapter is to summarize a few of the general evaluations of the Parsonian perspective. Considering the amount written about the theory it is probably impossible to offer any evaluations which have not already been stated. The cments here refer to the general theoretical perspective and are addressed primarily to undergraduate students. Those who are interested in detailed evaluations of the specifics of the theory should use the list of references which contains evaluations more thorough than those presented here, documentation of others' evaluations, and Parsons' responses to his critics. Since there has been a paucity of research evidence from which to judge the empirical status of the theory the appraisal of it here is limited to philosophical and logical issues. Although my evaluations are primarily addressed to the theory's assumptions and logical consistency, for illustrative purposes most comments refer to Parsons' theory of society.

The classification of Parsons' theory as structural-functional theory early in his career initiated arguments about the usefulness and relevancy of the theory compared to the Marxian conflict perspective. Although after working with the system problems Parsons said he did not think the classification appropriate, the structural-functional designation remained. He said he thought "functional analysis" was the appropriate classification.

The assumption that subsystems of a society are functionally differentiated is the reference point for the structural-functional classification. The subsystems and their relationships define the structure of a society. This structure does something — functions — for society. The structure functions for society, and the theory is accordingly classified as structural-functional theory.

The most frequently discussed criticisms of structural-functional theory have addressed three general issues: (1) the conceptual validity of a theory about a society; (2) the cultural primacy thesis; and (3) the teleological explanation implied by the organic analogy.

A description of the structure of society was derived from an assumption that all action systems have four needs. When society was analyzed Parsons was primarily interested in defining the subsystems which contributed to satisfaction of these needs. Consequently, his discussion of the contributions of the subsystems to the needs of a society was interpreted as an indication that he was more concerned with the welfare of society than with the welfare of individuals. Some critics have preferred the Marxian stance which analyzes society from the vantage point of individuals who have opposing economic interests. They question the conceptual validity of a description of society which does not account for collective or individual interests. Parsons' critics think he should have explained how a society meets the needs of individuals. Such expectation is unreasonable to us; it places a burden on Parsons' theory to answer a Marxian-conflict-type question. And in so doing, it poses questions for Parsons' theory the answers to which would violate the theory's assumptions.

Parsons was insistent that a society is analytically different from an individual. When he studied society he did so from the perspective of a society as a system, not from the perspective of an individual as a member of a society. The absurd consequence of an outright rejection of studying a society from that viewpoint is a rejection of the feasibility of the study of a society as an object of scientific inquiry. There is considerable utility to Parsons' approach. His analytically distinguishing society has contributed to our understanding of the multifaceted relationships between individuals and their society. Such a perspective does not depreciate the social or political efficacy of individuals. Rather, it informs about the complexity of the organizational contexts through which individuals are related to a society.

According to Parsons, any individual's goals are not directly provided for by a society, nor are his effects on society direct. They are channeled through groups, collectivities, organizations, and institutions. So for individuals, the impact of their actions on society takes place in the context of some interaction in or affiliation with groups or organizations.

There is never a one-to-one relationship between an individual's goals or desires and those of a group or an organization with which he is associated. When persons join a group or an organization to attain their goals the ends of the group or the organization and the ends of the persons are not the same. In the first place, there are other members of a group who also have goals, and in a collective effort to realize several individuals' goals, it is reasonable that, from a group's view, individual goals come to be redefined. The redefinition comes about merely as a result of social interaction between members of a group who have similar goals. Moreover, in any group there must be some leadership, someone who is concerned with maintaining the group and who speaks on behalf of the group as a whole so that it remains a viable vehicle for its members. These leaders are concerned with issues and goals of the group as a whole; these are not precisely the same as members' goals.

The importance of recognizing differences in the perspectives of action from the vantage points of individuals and of groups or collectivities was repeatedly emphasized by Parsons. It is equally important to recognize the differences in the vantage points of a society and individuals. Although he wrote a theory about a society he was keenly aware of the selectivity in his description of it. Furthermore, he thought that it was impossible for any theory to describe accurately a society in its totality. His analysis was not conceived as such a description, nor was it viewed as the only conceptually valid one.

Parsons' failure to address issues important to individuals arose from his interest in describing and explaining societies as an object of study. The explanation was from the perspective of a theory of social action systems. If we disagree with the assumptions of that theoretical perspective that disagreement is not a sound foundation for attributing an anti-individual bias to him. Certainly, there is no basis for assuming he was insensitive to individuals' interests. More than most was his recognition of the multitude of those interests. He also acknowledged the futility of viewing society as a summation of individuals who have conflicting interests. As a result, his theory avoided the biases of theories which presume to account for relationships between individuals' interests and societal processes. Invariably, a theory which attempts such an explanation produces ideological biases because it can only address some interests of some individuals to the exclusion of other interests and individuals.

Marxian conflict theorists also have been critical of Parsons' cultural primacy thesis, stating a preference for explanations which emphasize the importance of economic factors. For the Marxian conflict theorists, distributions of economic resources are thought to have dominant influence over societal processes; however, Parsons recognized not only the importance of economic factors but also the importance of power, values, and normative control. For a time this issue was debated with regard to why some occupations in society receive higher rewards than others. Parsons' theory permitted the explanation of higher rewards to occupations arising from the fact that some positions are more important to society than are other positions. For instance, in a particular society, if health issues are highly valued and since physicians are dealing with health issues their rewards are high. The critics argue that, on the contrary, since physicians receive high income, their positions are valued for economic reasons, because they are offered high economic rewards.

Another issue attending the structural-functional/conflict debate calls attention to the purposive, teleological slant of the organic analogy. Teleological explanation exists when a future event, state of affairs, design, or purpose is used to explain present or past events. Structural-functional theory is especially threatened with the teleological accusation because when it is said that subsystems solve problems it appears that future problems cause present structures. For example, since the subsystems of a society comprise a society's structure and solve the four system problems, it appears that the problems cause the structure.

The accusation that Parsons' theory is teleological has focused on the organic system postulate and lost sight of the fact that all of Parsons' tory was based on a theory of action. It will be remembered that in action theory actors are assumed to be future oriented in that they use present means to attain future ends. In all social action systems including society, social structures, such as the subsystems of a society, are created and organized for the purpose of solving future problems. Although in describing the structural units of society (the subsystems), Parsons did not specify the role of individuals as actors, they are presumed to be members of organizations the functions of which comprise the subsystems. Hence, all subsystems are made up of organizations' activities. Role performances in the organizations anticipate future states of affairs, future problems, and future goals. For instance, in many, many political organizations the perceptions of leaders about future problems of a society eventually define a society's goals. They also create structures which they think will attain the goals. The problems or goals do not cause the structures, but persons' perceptions of problems stimulate them to devise ways to solve problems. In doing so, they create social structures in anticipation of future problems. This pragmatic understanding of the composition of the subsystems of society is a foundation for a conclusion that the teleological issue is based on an erroneous interpretation of the theory of social action systems.

Discussions of the teleological aspects of the theory of social action systems have fomented some misconceptions about Parsons' methodology. One, discussed above, originated from an emphasis on the organic analogy and a disregard of action theory. Another misconception has arisen out of different judgments about the time interval between means and ends and structures and goals. Evaluators who have found teleological explanation have presumed that the system problems are in the future and that the system structures exist in the present or the past. With such a time interval between structures and problems, the theory is presumed to be nonscientific because it uses something which has not yet occurred, the future problems, to explain the present or past structures. That point of view is often based on a presumption that scientific explanation should involve prediction so that present events are used to predict future events.

Parsons used a historical analysis which involved retrospective prediction. He wrote his theory from the perspective of an observer who knew what had happened, knew that the problems existed and knew that they had been solved. Then, working backward in time, he, the observer, asked, how were the problems solved, what structures of a system contributed to their solutions? Some of us think that this type of explanation has advantages over prediction. At least, an observer knows what has happened. And knowing the event which is explained actually did occur directs an inquiry to find the factors which influenced it. With knowledge of the event to be explained, there is a much better chance that factors which influenced it may be found; whereas, from a predictive stance, the event which is to be explained has not occurred. It is predicted that it will occur in the future. Not only is it difficult to predict something which will occur at some future time, it is also difficult to speculate about the things which are expected to influence events that are expected to occur at some future time. Thus, a predictive study is most appropriate to laboratory experiments in which influencing factors and outcomes can be controlled. It is impossible to put a society or a noncontrived social action system into a laboratory.

Parsons admitted no empirical problems resulting from a commitment to retrospective prediction and a commitment to analytical abstraction. However, there is one. It exists because it is the conceptual categories of the theory which are retroactively predicted. As previous chapters herein have demonstrated, Parsons did not find it disconcerting to use his theory, to define and interpret reality. Some social scientists do find it disconcerting. The constraints imposed by interpreting reality in accordance with analytical concepts are unacceptable to scientists interested in the empirical status of a theory. If there is a great deal of knowledge about the subject being analyzed the concepts can be based on knowledge, if not, the empirical validity of the interpretation is suspect. Understanding society by theoretically analyzing it can be only as accurate as the knowledge from which theory was derived. Problems with Parsons' interpretation of society arise from the fact that analytical categories were derived from a generous use of analogies, not from empirical evidence.

Most of Parsons' ideas were arrived at by using analogies from biology and economics. If the analogies are inappropriate, they depreciate his theory. Parsons had far too much confidence that his analogies were appropriate. He used them as though they provided evidence of the abstractions he wanted to explain and thereby seemed to avoid explaining the empirical phenomena to which his theory was addressed. He also borrowed liberally from pre-existing theory, using his own words to denote concepts in others' theories. To those of us who subscribe to the view that sociology should have a technically specialized language and that knowledge should be cumulative, Parsons' use of new words for old ideas neither advanced knowledge nor sociology as a specialized discipline.

In reading Parsons one has the impression that theoretical concepts are intended as universally applicable. The universality derives from the assumptions of the theory, not from the characteristics of phenomena. As Parsons was critical of the misplaced concreteness in others' theories, we can criticize his universal application of the theory of social action systems as misplaced concreteness. Also, the theory's generality can be mistakenly judged to contribute to its validity. Since it is used to analyze many empirical situations it can be concluded that it must be empirically valid. The widespread application of it does not validate it. To presume that because a theory can be used to interpret many empirical situations it has empirical validity is similar to Whitehead's fallacy of "misplaced concreteness." The only appropriate external criteria for judging the empirical status of a theory is an assessment of the weight of empirical evidence supporting its propositions.

Those who prefer the inductive method for arriving at theoretical concepts think that greater validity can be obtained by empirically testing propositions, and then, if warranted by the evidence, the propositions are revised so that they are consistent with the empirical evidence. But in order to test propositions they must be stated in a manner that one can gather evidence about them. Parsons' theory does not present propositions in that form. Ideally, a proposition should specify relationships between concepts. It should also state conditions under which the relationships are expected to exist. To state them as propositions would require that it be possible to observe their absence, i.e., when does legitimation or mobilization of resources not occur, or what are the conditions under which there is more or less integration, mobilization or legitimation? The theory does not specify the conditions. Nevertheless, an abundance of ideas has provided a fertile area for others to arrive at hypotheses deduced from the theory.

Although the theory does not contain formally stated propositions, Parsons' legacy could be the plethora of hypotheses suggested by the theory. For instance, his view of the structure of motivations in roles could be investigated. One question could be: For effective interactions what are the most advantageous similarities or dissimilarities of motivational structures of role partners? Deviancy could be investigated from the outlook of personality as a system. The theory has been criticized because it cannot account for social change. On the contrary, evolutionary theory provides many statements about conditions internal to a society under which change and conflict are most likely to occur. These statements could be used to investigate change and conflict in institutions, organizations or bureaucracies. In modern societies, with the increasing importance of the mass media as channels for symbolic communication, investigations of the symbolic aspects of money, power, influence, and value-commitments are timely. If problems with the theory are viewed as a challenge to resolve the difficult questions which Parsons attempted to answer, however unsatisfactorily to some, then his works could invigorate knowledge in the social sciences. The scope and abstractness of his theory present social scientists with the methodological challenge of constructing operational definitions and instruments of observation which bring precision to the theory.

There is a tendency for writers who devote a lifetime to developing a theory, such as Marx, Freud, and Parsons, to become engulfed by their conceptual schemes. At some point in the process of developing their ideas they become fixatedly focused on their analytical categories and lose sight of the problem or issue which had been the instigator of their pursuit. The instigating issue for Parsons was the problem of how to explain social order brought about by the normative regulation of behavior. It began as an attempt to identify processes which maintain coordinative relationships between values, institutions, norms, and roles. After postulating the four problems for all social action systems his attention was deflected from the instigating problem and the institutional and group level of analysis was subsumed under the rubric of the sub-systems of systems. Thereafter, he seemed engulfed by the four system problems, concentrating on preserving their logical status in the theory.

In using analytical categories to describe empirical systems, Parsons insisted that different words should be used to signify theoretical concepts when they described different empirical systems. In the context of the theory, definitions of the concepts are the same, the words used to denote them change. One gets the impression that when a word is found to plug into the scaffold of a theory about empirical systems, the validity of the original theory is enhanced. We dispute — it is not. The four system problems are analytically the same problems whether they are applied to a university, a society, an economy, or a personality. For example, merely by finding some activities in a university, in a family, in an economy, in a personality, and also in a society, all of which can be categorized as concerned with problems of adaptation, does not increase the empirical validity of adaptation or of the theory from which the concept was derived.

A theory should be logically consistent and there are many points of logical consistencies in the theory, but, inconsistencies stem from the assumptions that systems are open and that they are sensitive to exter-nal environments. It will be recalled that two of the system problems are defined as concerned with a system's external environment. However, there is a failure to specify the external environmental conditions. In dcriptions of the subsystems and their relationships to each other, the internal environment is emphasized. Accounting for the maintenance of a system by merely postulating that it adapts to its external environment while, at the same time, not specifying conditions in the external envi-ronment to which it is supposedly adapting is a vacuous statement.

A basic postulate of the theory, derived from the biological analogy, is that social action systems are open and that they have interchanges with the external environment. Systems theory was viewed as useful because of its ability to account for systems' sensitivities to environmental conditions and their ability to be self-maintaining. Failure to define alternative environmental conditions to which a system, and especially a society, is supposedly adapting is an avoidance of a question for which the theory is most capable of answering.

The avoidance of the crucial question about external conditions also ex-ists in Parsons' evolutionary theory. As has been previously explained, evolutionary theory accounts for changes in system structures not as a consequence of a system's adaptation to changing environmental condi-tions. On the contrary, there is a focus on internal dimensions of systems and structural change results from differentiations internal to a system.

There was failure to direct attention to the external conditions to which systems were presumably adapting and coincidentally undergoing structural change. External environmental conditions are not even recognized as important factors in instigating change.

The assumption that living systems are sensitive to environmental conditions is essential to the biological analogy and the evolutionary perspective. By slighting external conditions and concentrating on a system's internal organization and integration, Parsons treated societies as if they were closed, whereas the theory was proposed as one especially capable of explaining systems' adaptation to external environments. The logical consistency of the theory is diminished by his treating systems as closed and still assuming that they are open.

The inconsistency is especially problematical with respect to socialization theory. In the theory of personality development all motivations stem from the first one, oral-dependency. It seems inconsistent with the concept of an open system that a personality would be so restricted in its adaptability. The theory leaves an individual out in the cold, so to speak, with only four basic motivations, initially rooted in one, from which to construct enough motives to take on the many roles throughout a human life-span. Using cell division as an analogy to account for differentiation of units restricts the degrees of freedom available to an open system. It will be recalled that the analogy accounts for initiation of growth by one need-disposition dividing into two and each of those two dividing to produce four. In biology there is the presumption that there are genes in a cell adequate for an organism's growth. Despite Parsons' grasp of the analogy, there is no evidence that personalities, or for that matter, social action systems generally, have such an adequate supply of "genetic" materials. Hence, the cell-division analogy seems inappropriate to account for socialization processes. It provides a view of personality as being closed, with limited potentialities for arriving at novel solutions to problems.

With respect to the theory of social change, Parsons' choice of historical events to demonstrate the theory diminished its empirical relevancy. Providing an example of the evolution of modernity, Parsons conceived the continent of Europe and England as comprising one system out of which evolved a system of modern societies. A superficial analysis of European history selected events to demonstrate the differentiation of subsystems illustrative of modernity. Historical events in Austria, Spain, Switzerland, Prussia, Italy, Holland, the Holy Roman Empire, Bohemia, Russia, France, Germany, Roman Catholicism, and Protestantism were selected. It is hard to glean from the analysis an understanding of the precise units comprising the "system of modern societies." Apparently, such a system is an analytical system made up of various aspects of historical events in Europe and England, but it cannot be identified as any one empirical society. He called it a "system of modern societies." The analytical system of modern societies was then analyzed using another analytical system, the theory of the evolution of social action systems. The resulting concatenation of analytical abstraction produced a transcendental interpretation of social change.

Since World War II social change has been contracted. Some of the most significant questions for the social sciences have arisen out of the historical circumstances of synthetic communities' needs to build institutions out of the vacuums resulting from decolonization. There have been numerous instances of nations attempting to organize themselves into social systems, trying to do in thirty years what once took nations a century to do. The ex-colonies, such as Laos, Viet Nam, India and the nations on the continent of Africa, provided empirical instances to which such a theory could have been applied with more concrete empirical evidence available. Furthermore, an empirical system of modern societies could have been identified by recognizing the political, economic, and military interdependencies of post-World War II societies. However, Parsons' choices of 17th and 18th centuries and an analytical "system of modern societies" demonstrated a reluctance to address the significant empirical problem of relationships between specific societies which in fact comprise an empirical system of modern societies.

Integration is the dominant independent variable in Parsons' theory. Every system has its own version of it. Admittedly, with respect to American society, the postulate flies in the face of commonsense. If American society is integrated, we wonder what all the protests are about. To those persons who are aware of the debates, protests, strikes, class action lawsuits, political action committees, and political campaigns the value-normative integration of the total society is incomprehensible. Parsons has been criticized for writing his theory to fit the culture of American urban, middle-class society. On the contrary, unable to find congruence between integration of American society and its institutionalized individualism, as proposed by Parsons, I can surmise that the theory is most appropriately applied to a society with a long history of totalitarianism in which brainwashing and thought -control are the dominant goals. Alternatively, perhaps the integration postulate is comprehended from such a distant long-range historical view of social processes that the details of current events are not relevant, as facial features are irrelevant in a bas-relief sculpture.

For purposes of discussion, let us assume, in the context of the theory, that American society is integrated. Turning our attention to integration as explained in the theory, the relationships between the elements in the hierarchy of control are postulated; they are not explained by the theory. Using the example of relationships between values, norms, and role performances, each of these concepts has different degrees of generality and abstractness. Values are most abstract and vague, norms are general guidelines for behavior, and role performances are specific behaviors. While Parsons admitted the differences in the levels of abstraction, in using the concepts in his theory, conflicts arising out of the differences in the levels of abstraction are ignored. Apparently he did not think it necessary or important to explain how to translate abstract values into role performances or how to legitimate norms so as to be consistent with the abstractness of values. An example to the point has been the American dilemma of integrating norms and behavior with the value of equality of opportunity so far as blacks are concerned.

Action theory could be used to investigate social processes through which values are transformed into norms. Empirical investigations of legitimating processes in different institutions in the same society or of the same institutions in different societies could provide some knowledge and understanding of the processes which establish relationships between values and norms, and concomitantly, legitimation and integration. However, the important question was avoided by Parsons' putting a direct relationship between values, norms, and roles, and in application, viewing the differences in their abstractness and generality as nonproblematical. In the analysis of society, by assuming that integration stems from both values and norms the theory deflects attention away from the problematic relationships between values, norms and roles. In the United States there have been war, riots, protests, assassinations and killings of protesters, civil and criminal cases directed to bridging the gap between the abstract values of civil rights and equal opportunities and behavior which complies with those values. Parsons addressed the black issue, but the empirical evidence of non-integration between values, norms, and behavior did not disturb the integration postulate. Taking the high road of his analytical theory, he viewed the issue as one of ongoing evolutionary processes of the society's trying to include blacks into the societal community.

Parsons had a proclivity for observing balance, equilibrium, and integration in processes which others might interpret as imbalance, disequilibrium, and nonintegration. An example can be demonstrated from his theory of the balancing of equality and inequality in the United States. One could as easily draw the conclusion that the coexistence of equalities and inequalities with respect to power, achievements, and authority bring about imbalances, contradictions, and non-integration in American society.

When integration fails, the Parsonian long-time perspective introduces the idea of fluctuations between states of equilibrium and disequilibrium. Eventually, a state of equilibrium is reached at which point a society can be said to have become integrated. By focusing on relationships between a society's subsystems instead of processes underlying those relationships, tough questions are avoided. Disagreements, actions which violate norms and values, conflicting interests, divergent political ideologies, illegitimate uses of power are inconsequential to Parsons' theory because its generality and abstractness are so great that it does not cast a net fine enough to apprehend historically specific events.

Parsons' explaining the value-integration of social action systems put him in the company of the many scholars who have also grappled with the problem. Some of the inadequacies of his explanation can be attributed to the difficulty of the problem and to the monumental task of studying a complex society. Many of the theory's critics have tried to avoid the problem. Those of a behavioristic persuasion eschew it by casting it out of the realm of the scientific enterprise. They think that cultural elements are mental states, nonmaterial and metaphysical, inaccessible to scientific investigation. Defining behavior as material and as involving some bodily movements they think observations of behavior and the external environmental factors which affect it are the only feasible subjects for scientific study. These beliefs are grounds for rejecting cultural elements as not appropriate for scientific study.

Another rejection of the importance of cultural elements stems from Marxian philosophy which also distinguishes between material and nonmaterial factors. Material elements, and especially economic factors, are believed to be dominantly important in explaining social relationships. Economic processes are then used to account for all institutions, processes, and structures of a society. There is a rejection of the idea of value-integration because of a preference for the study of the disequilibrium and conflict which arise from the inequitable distribution of economic resources. Parsons' ideas that both society and personality have similar cultural elements is also rejected. Cultural elements are viewed as arising out of different economic interests, the consequence of which is socialization according to economic class interests. It is then concluded that a society is not value-integrated, that values are as stratified and differentiated as are economic interests. A second conclusion is that integration stems not from socialization, but from the societal-wide power of those who control the major social institutions because of their superior economic positions.

Rejection of the value-integration proposition does not obviate the study of values and the cultural elements. They are significant and important aspects of human experience. One of Parsons' many contributions has been the conceptualization of culture as an autonomous subject for study. Except for the study of opinions and attitudes as they relate to behaviors and styles of life, in the recent past social scientists in the United States have not been much interested in nor have they investigated the structure of values and beliefs as distinct entities. In analytically distinguishing culture from the other subsystems of action Parsons indicated that culture, as such, is a legitimate object of study. A by -product of that was his ingenuity in arriving at the idea of value -commitments as one type of symbolic media. He thereby demonstrated that there is another form of domination besides influence, power, and money. Perhaps there are others, the discovery of which, to paraphrase Parsons, would expand our understanding of the many ways in which subordinate and superordinate relationships are created, perpetuated, and institutionalized.

The concept of value-commitments is not the only example of Parsons' ingenuity. There are many more. If, by chance, negative evaluations of the Parsonian perspective result in anyone's ignoring Parsons' many contributions to our understanding of social phenomena a warning is needed that such should not be the case. Even though the theory has its dubious aspects they are not intractable, nor are there any less dubious theories in the social sciences. This work has covered only the basic structure of Parsons' general theory. In its limited objective, many of the details of Parsons' analyses of institutions and social processes were ignored. Ignoring his ideas or categorically rejecting them because of disagreement with his overall perspective, in my opinion, is an exercise of obstinate closed-mindedness.

References and Suggestions for Further Study

Some compilations of others' evaluations of the theory are:
  Adriaansens (1980); Barber and Inkeles (1971); Bershady (1973); Black (1961); Bourricaud (1977, 1981); Demerath and Peterson (1967); Isajiw (1968); Martindale (1965); Mulkay (1971); Savage (1981); Smith (1973); Turk and Simpson (1971).

Alexander (1983) surveys the development of Parsons' theory, works related to Parsons', Parsons' critics, and analyses by others who have used Parsons' perspective.

The debate about the structural-functional theory of stratification can be found in:
  Davis and Moore (1945); Davis (1942, 1953, 1959); Tumin (1953); Simpson (1956); Wrong (1945, 1961); Schwartz (1955); Buckley (1958, 1959); Huaco (1963); Moore (1963); Stinchcombe (1963); Bershady (1970); Cullen (1979).

Jonathan H. Turner (1978) discusses the teleological nature of structural-functional theory in a broader perspective than presented here.

Buckley (1967) provides a thought-provoking discussion of analyses subsumed under systems theory.

Merton (1957) proposed methodological refinements for structural-functional theory and discussed inadequacies of grand theories.

Parsons discussed: the issue of race in "Full Citizenship for the Negro American?" (1965); retrospective prediction in "Cause and Effect in Sociology" (1965); structural-functional analysis in "The Present Status of 'Structural-Functional' Theory in Sociology" (1975); and "Some Problems of General Theory in Sociology" (1970).

The following discuss social change:
  Barber and Inkeles (1971); Berk (1972); Bock (1963); Boskoff (1964); Cancian (1960); Eisenstadt (1964); Granovetter (1979); Henry (1955); Smelser (1959); Smith (1973).

Bibliography

I. General References

Bales, Robert F., *Interaction Process Analysis.* Cambridge, MA.: Addison-Wesley, 1950.

Hoffer, Eric, *The True Believer.* N.Y.: New American Library, 1958.

Nisbet, Robert A., *Twilight of Authority.* N.Y: Oxford University Press, (1975).

Pope, Alexander, *Moral Essays: Epistle II, To A Lady,* ed., Henry W. Boynton. Boston: Houghton Mifflin, 1903.

Tocqueville, Alex De, *Democracy in America.* N.Y: Knopf, 1944.

II. Publications by Talcott Parsons

1928 Capitalism in Recent German Literature: Sombart and Weber. I.*J. of Political Economy* 37 (6): 641-61.

1929 Capitalism in Recent German Literature: Sombart and Weber. II. *J. of Political Economy* 37 (1): 31-51.

1930 tr. Max Weber, *The Protestant Ethic and the Spirit of Capitalism.* London: Allen & Unwin; N.Y.: Scribner's.

1931 Wants and Activities in Marshall. *Qrtly. J. of Econ.* 46 (1(: 101-40.

1932 Economics and Sociology: Marshall in Relation to the Thought of His Time. *Qrtly. J. of Econ.* 46 (2(: 316-47.

1933 Malthus. *Encyclopedia of the Social Sciences.* 10: 68-69. N.Y.: Macmillan.
   Pareto. *Ibid.,* 11: 576-78.

1934   Some Reflections on 'The Nature and Significance of Economics.' *Qrtly. J. of Econ.* 48: 511-45.

Service. *Encyclopedia of the Social Sciences.* 13: 672-74. N.Y.: Macmillan. Society. *Ibid.* 14:225-31.

Sociological Elements in Economic Thought. I. *Qrtly. J. of Econ.* 49:414-53.

1935   Sociological Elements in Economic Thought. II. *Qrtly. J. of Econ.* 49: 645-67.

The Place of Ultimate Values in Sociological Theory. *Intrntl. J. of Ethics* 45: 282-316.

H.M. Robertson on Maxweber and His School. *J. of Political Economy* 43: 688-96.

1936   Pareto's Central Analytical Scheme. *J. of Social Philosophy* 1 (3): 244-62.

On Certain Sociological Elements in Professor Taussig's Thought. In Jacobs Viner, ed., *Explorations in Economics: Notes and Essays Contributed in Honor of F.W. Taussig,* pp. 352-79. N.Y.: McGraw-Hill.

1937   *The Structure of Social Action.* N.Y.: McGraw-Hill; reprinted Free Press, N.Y.: 1949.

Education and the Professions. *Intrntl. J. of Ethics* 47: 365-69.

1938   The Role of Theory in Social Research. *Amer. Soc. Rev.* 3: 13-20.

The Role of Ideas in Social Action. *Amer. Soc. Rev.* 3: 653-64.

1939   The Professions and Social Structure. *Social Forces* 17 (4): 457-67.

Comte. *J. of Unified Science* 9:77-83.

1940   An Analytical Approach to the Theory of Social Stratification. *Amer. J. of Soc.* 45: 841-62.

The Motivation of Economic Activities. *Canadian J. of Economics and Political Science* 6: 187-203.

1942   Max Weber and the Contemporary Political Crisis. *Rev. of Politics* 4: 61-76, 155-72.

The Sociology of Modern Anti-Semitism. In J. Graeber and Stuart Henderson Britt, eds., *Jews in a Gentile World,* pp. 101-122. N.Y.: Macmillan.

Age and Sex in the Social Structure of the United States. *Amer. Soc. Rev.,* 7: 604-16.

Propaganda and Social Control. *Psychiatry* 5 (4): 551-72.

Democracy and Social Structure in Pre-Nazi Germany. *J. of Legal and Political Sociology* 1: 96-114.

Some Sociological Aspects of the Fascist Movement. *Soc. For.* 21: 138-47.

1943 The Kinship System of the Contemporary United States. *American Anthropologist* 45: 22-38.

1944 The Theoretical Development of the Sociology of Religion. *J. of the History of Ideas* 51: 176-90.

1945 The Present Position and Prospects of Systematic Theory in Sociology. In Georg Gurvitch and Wilbert E. Moore, eds., *Twentieth Century Sociology,* pp. 42-69. N.Y.: Philosophical Library.

The Problem of Controlled Institutional Change: An Essay on Applied Social Science. *Psychiatry* 8: 79-101.

Racial and Religious Differences as Factors in Group Tensions. In Louis Finkelstein, *et al.,* eds., *Unity and Difference in the Modern World.* N.Y.: Conference on Science, Philosophy and Religion in Their Relation to the Democratic Way of Life.

1946 The Science Legislation and the Role of the Social Sciences. *Amer. Soc. Rev.* 11: 653-66.

Population and Social Structure of Japan. In Douglas E. Haring, ed., *Japan's Prospect,* pp. 87-114. Cambridge, MA: Harvard Univ. Press.

Certain Primary Sources and Patterns of Aggression in the Social Structure of the Western World. *Psychiatry* 10: 167-81.

Some Aspects of the Relations between Social Science and Ethics. *Social Science* 22: 213-17.

1947 Science Legislation and the Social Sciences. *Polit. Sci. Qrtly.* 62 (2): 241-49.

Max Weber: The Theory of Social and Economic Organization. ed. and tr. with A.M. Henderson. N.Y.: Oxford Univ. Press (reprinted by Free Press, N.Y.: 1957).

Note on the Science Foundation Bill in the 80th Congress. *Amer. Soc. Rev.* 12: 601-03.

1948 Sociology 1941-1946. with Bernard Barber. *Amer. J. of Soc.* 53: 245-57.

The Position of Sociological Theory. *Amer. Soc. Rev.* 13: 156-71.

1949 *Essays in Sociological Theory: Pure and Applied.* (A collection of previously published essays.) N.Y.: Free Press.

The Rise and Decline of Economic Man. *J. of Gen. Educ.* 4: 47-53.

Social Classes and Class Conflict in the Light of Recent Sociological Theory. *Amer. Econ. Rev.* 39: 16-26.

1950 The Prospects of Sociological Theory. *Amer. Soc. Rev.* 15: 3-16.

The Social Environment of the Educational Process. *Centennial,* pp. 36-40. Washington, DC: Amer. Assn. for the Advancement of Science.

Psychoanalysis and the Social Structure. *Psychoanalytic Qrtly.* 19: 371-84.

1951 *The Social System.* N.Y.: Free Press.

Toward a General Theory of Action. ed. with Edward A. Shils. (contributors: Edward Tolman, Gordon W. Allport, Clyde Kluckhohn, Henry A. Murray, Robert R. Sears, Richard C. Sheldon, Samuel A. Stouffer). Cambridge, MA: Harvard Univ. Press (reprinted Harper Torchbooks, N.Y., 1962).

Graduate Training in Social Relations at Harvard. *J. of Gen. Educ.* 5: 149-57.

Illness and the Role of Physician: A Sociological Perspective. *Amer. J. of Orthopsychiatry* 21: 452-60.

1952 The Superego and the Theory of Social Systems. *Psychiatry* 15: 15-25.
    Religious Perspectives in College Teaching: Sociology and Social Psychofy. In Hoxie N. Fairchild, ed., *Religious Perspectives in College Teaching,* pp. 286-337. N.Y.: Ronald Press.
    A Sociologist Looks at the Legal Profession. *Conference on the Profession of Law and Legal Education,* conference series, no. II, pp. 49-63. Chicago: The Law School, University of Chicago.

1953. *Working Papers in the Theory of Action.* with Robert F. Bales and Edward A. Shils. N.Y.: Free Press (reissued, 1967).
    Psychoanalysis and Social Science with Special Reference to the Oedipus Problem. In Franz Alexander and Helen Ross, eds., *Twenty Years of Psychoanalysis,* pp. 186-215. N.Y.: W.W. Norton.
    A Revised Analytical Approach to the Theory of Social Stratification. In Reinhard Bendix and Seymour Lipset, eds., *Class, Status, and Power: A Reader in Social Stratification,* pp. 92-129. N.Y.: Free Press.
    Therapy and the Modern Urban American Family. with Renee C. Fox. *J. of Social Issues* 8: 31-44.
    Some Comments on the State of the General Theory of Action. *Amer. Soc. Rev.* 18 (6): 618-31.

1954 The Father Symbol: An Appraisal in the Light of Psychoanalytic and Sociological Theory. In Lyman Bryson, Louis Finkelstein, R.M. MacIver, and Richard McKeon, eds., *Symbols and Values: An Initial Study,* pp. 523-44. N.Y.: Harper and Row.
    Essays in Sociological Theory [*revised*]. (A reprint of all except three of the 1949 collection of *Essays,* and additional essays published prior to 1954.) N.Y.: Free Press.
    Psychology and Sociology. In John P. Gillin, ed., *For A Science of Social Man.* N.Y.: Macmillan.
    The Incest Taboo in Relation to Social Structure and the Socialization of the Child. *British J. of Soc.* 5 (2): 101-17.
    McCarthyism and American Social Tension: A Sociologist's View. *Yale Rev.* 44: 226-45.

1955 *Family, Socialization and Interaction Process.* with Robert F. Bales, James Olds, Morris Zelditch, and Philip E. Slater. N.Y.: Free Press.

1956 *Economy and Society.* with Neil J. Smelser. N.Y.: Free Press; London: Routledge & Kegan Paul.
    Suggestions for a Sociological Approach to the Theory of Organizations. *Admin. Sci. Qrtly.* Part I, 1: 63-85; Part II, 1: 225-39.

1957 The Distribution of Power in American Society. *World Politics* 10: 123-43.
    Malinowski and the Theory of Social Systems. In Raymond Firth, ed., *Man and Culture.* London: Routledge & Kegan Paul.

Man in His Social Environment - As Viewed by Modern Social Science. *Centennial Review of Arts & Sciences.* 1 (1): 50-69. E. Lansing, MI: Mich. State Univ.

The Mental Hospital as a Type of Organization. In Milton Greenblatt, Daniel J. Levinson and Richard H. Williams, eds., *The Patient and the Mental Hospital.* N.Y.: Free Press.

1958 Authority, Legitimation, and Political Action. In C.J. Friedrich, ed., *Authority.* Cambridge, MA: Harvard Univ. Press.

Definitions of Health and Illness in the Light of American Values and Social Structure. In E. Gartly Jaco, ed., *Patients, Physicians and Illness: Sourcebook in Behavioral Science and Medicine.* N.Y.: Free Press.

Social Structure and the Development of Personality. *Psychiatry* 21: 321-40.

Some Ingredients of a General Theory of Formal Organization. In Andrew W. Halpin, ed., *Administrative Theory in Education.* Chicago: Midwest Admin. Center, Univ. of Chicago.

Some Reflections on the Institutional Framework of Economic Development. In *The Challenge of Development: A Symposium.* Jerusalem: The Hebrew Univ.

Some Trends of Change in American Society: Their Bearing on Medical Education. *J. of Amer. Med. Assn.* 167 (1): 31-36.

The Pattern of Religious Organization in the United States. *Daedalus* 87: 65-85.

The Concepts of Culture and of Social System. with A.L. Kroeber. *Amer. Soc. Rev.* 23 (5): 582-83.

1959 An Approach to Psychological Theory in Terms of the Theory of Action. In Sigmund Koch, ed., *Psychology: A Study of a Science.* vol. 3: 612-711. N.Y.: McGraw-Hill.

The Role of General Theory in Sociological Analysis: Some Case Materials. *Sociological Inquiry* 29: 12-38.

General Theory in Sociology. In Robert K. Merton, Leonard Broom and Leonard S. Cottrell, eds., *Sociology Today,* pp. 3-38. N.Y.: Basic Books.

Rejoinder to Levy's "Some Questions About 'The Concepts of Culture and of Social System'." *Amer. Soc. Rev.* 24: 248-49.

The Principal Structures of Community: A Sociological View. In C.J. Friedrich, ed., *Community.* N.Y.: Liberal Arts Press.

Voting and the Equilibrium of the American Political System. In Eugene Burdick and Arthur Brodbeck, eds., *American Voting Behavior.* N.Y.: Free Press.

Durkheim's Contribution to the Theory of Integration of Social Systems. In Kurt H. Wolff, ed., *Emile Durkheim, 1858-1971: A Collection of Essays with Translations and a Bibliography.* Columbus, OH: Ohio State Univ. Press.

Some Problems Confronting Sociology as a Profession. *Amer. Soc. Rev.* 24: 547-58.

The School Class as a Social System. *Harvard Educ. Rev.* 29: 297-318.

Comment on 'American Intellectuals: Their Politics and Status.' *Daedalus* 88: 493-95.

An Approach to the Sociology of Knowledge. *Proceedings of the Fourth World Congress of Sociology.* (Milan, Italy) 4: 25-49.

A Short Account of My Intellectual Development. *Alpha Kappa Delta* 29: 3-12.

1960 Mental Illness and 'Spiritual Malaise:' The Roles of the Psychiatrist and of the Minister of Religion. In Hans Hofmann, ed., *The Ministry and Mental Health*. N.Y.: Association Press.

Structure and Process in Modern Societies. (Essays on formal organization, authority, industrial societies, power, social strains, education, religion, and community.) N.Y.: Free Press.

Pattern Variables Revisited: A Response to Robert Dubin. *Amer. Soc. Rev.* 25: 467-83.

Toward a Healthy Maturity. *J. of Health and Human Behavior* 1: 163-73.

In memoriam: 'Clyde Kluckhohn, 1905-1960.' *Amer. Soc. Rev.* 25: 960-62.

Commentary on *The Mass Media and the Structure of the American Society*. with Winston White. *J. of Soc. Issues* 16: 67-77.

The Physician in a Changing Society. *What's New* 220: 11-12.

Social Structure and Political Orientation: A review of *Political Man* by Seymour Lipset and *The Politics of Mass Society* by William Kornhauser. *World Politics* 13: 112-28.

Review of *Max Weber: An Intellectual Portrait* by Reinhard Bendix. *Amer. Soc. Rev.* 25: 750-52.

1961 *Theories of Society*. coed. with Edward A. Shils, Kaspar D. Naegele, and Jesse R. Pitts. Vols I and II. N.Y.: Free Press.

The Contributions of Psychoanalysis to the Social Sciences. *Science and Psychoanalysis* 4: 28-38.

Comment on 'Preface to a Metatheoretical Framework for Sociology' by Llewellyn Gross. *Amer. J. of Soc.* 67: 136-40.

In memoriam: 'Alfred L. Kroeber, 1876-1960.' *Amer. J. of Soc.* 67: 616-17.

Clyde Kluckhohn, Anthropologist. *Science* 144: 1584.

Some Principal Characteristics of Industrial Societies. In C.E. Black, ed., *The Transformation of Russian Society since 1861*. Cambridge, MA: Harvard Univ. Press.

The Link Between Character and Society. with Winston White. In Seymour M. Lipset and Leo Lowenthal, eds., *Culture and Social Character*. N.Y.: Free Press.

Polarization of the World and International Order. In O. Wright, W.M. Evan and M. Deutsch, eds., *Preventing World War III*. N.Y.: Simon & Schuster.

The Point of View of the Author. In Max Black, ed., *The Social Theories of Talcott Parsons*, pp. 311-63. Englewood Cliffs, NJ: Prentice-Hall.

The Problem of International Community. In James N. Rosenau, ed., *International Politics and Foreign Policy*. N.Y.: Free Press.

Some Considerations on the Theory of Social Change. *Rural Sociology* 26: 219-39.

A Sociologist's View. In Eli Ginzberg, ed., *Values and Ideals of American Youth*. N.Y.: Columbia Univ. Press.

1962 Clyde Kay Maben Kluckhohn, 1905-1960. with Evon Z. Vogt. *Amer. Anthropologist* 64: 140-48.

Individual Autonomy and Social Pressure: An Answer to Dennis H. Wrong. *Psychoanalysis and Psychoanalytic Review* 49: 70-79.

Youth in the Context of American Society. *Daedalus* 91: 97-123.

The Aging in American Society. *Law and Contemporary Problems* 27 (1): 22-35.

Review of *Law and Social Process* by Hurst. *J. of the History of Ideas* 23: 558-65.

The Law and Social Control. In William M. Evan, ed., *Law and Society*, pp. 56-72. N.Y.: Free Press.

In memoriam: Richard Henry Tawney, 1880-1962. *Amer. Soc. Rev.* 27: 888-90.

Review of *Reason in Society: Five Types of Decisions and Their Social Conditions* by Paul Diesing. *Industrial and Labor Relations Rev.* 16: 630-31.

The Cultural Background of American Religious Organization. In Harlan Cleveland and Harold D. Lasswell, eds., *Ethics and Bigness: Scientific, Academic, Religious, Political, and Military*, pp. 141-67. N.Y.: Conference on Science, Philosophy, and Religion in Their Relation to the Democratic Way of Life.

1963 Social Strains in America: A Postscript - 1962. In Parsons, *Politics and Social Structure*, pp. 179-84. 1969 N.Y.: Free Press.

Introduction to Max Weber's *The Sociology of Religion*, (tr. by Ephraim Fischoff from *Wirtschaft und Gesellschaft*]. In Parsons, *Sociological Theory and Modern Society*, pp. 35-78. N.Y.: Free Press, 1967.

Christianity and Modern Industrial Society. In Edward A. Tiryakian, ed., *Sociological Theory, Values and Sociocultural Change: Essays in Honor of Pitirim A. Sorokin*, pp. 33-70. N.Y.: Free Press.

On the Concept of Influence. *Public Opinion Qrtly.* 27 (1): 37-62.

Rejoinder to Bauer and Coleman ("On the Concept of Influence"). *Public Opinion Qrtly.* 27: 87-92.

On the Concept of Political Power. *Proceedings of the Amer. Phil. Soc.* 107 (3): 232-62.

Social Change and Medical Organization in the United States: A Sociological Perspective. *Annals of Amer. Acad. of Pol. and Soc. Sci.* 346: 22-33.

Old Age as Consummatory Phase. *Gerontologist* 3 (2): 53-54.

1964 Evolutionary Universals in Society. *Amer. Soc. Rev.* 29 (3): 339-57.

Social Structure and Personality. Essays published between 1952 and 1962; contains previously unpublished essays:

Some Reflections on the Problems of Psychosomatic Relationships in Health and Illness;

Some Theoretical Considerations Bearing on the Field of Medical Sociology.

N.Y.: Free Press.

Sociological Theory. *Encyclopedia Britannica*. Chicago: Encyclopedia Britannica, Inc.

La Theorie de la Societe. *Les Etudes philosophiques, perspectives sur la philosophie nord-americaine.* 3: 537-47.

Some Reflections on the Place of Force in Social Process. In Harry Eckstein, ed., *Internal War: Basic Problems and Approaches*. N.Y.: Free Press.

Levels of Organization and the Mediation of Social Interaction. *Sociological Inquiry* 34 (2): 207-20.

Youth in the Context of American Society. In Henry Borow, ed., *Man in a World at Work*. Boston: Houghton Mifflin.

The Sibley Report on Training in Sociology. *Amer. Soc. Rev.* 29: 747-48.

"Comment" (on Kolb's "Images of Man and the Sociology of Religion"). *J. for the Sci. Study of Relig.* 1: 22-29.

Recent Trends in Structural-Functional Theory. In E.W. Count and G.T. Bowles, eds., *Fact and Theory in Social Science*, pp. 140-58. Syracuse, NY: Syracuse Univ. Press.

1965 Cause and Effect in Sociology. In Daniel Lerner, ed., *Cause and Effect*, pp. 51-73. N.Y.: Free Press.

Unity and Diversity in the Modern Intellectual Disciplines: The Role of the Social Sciences. *Daedalus* 94 (1): 39-65.

Changing Family Patterns in American Society. *The American Family in Crisis* 3: 4-10. Forest Hospital, Des Plaines, IL: Forest Hospital Publictions.

Max Weber, 1864-1964. *Amer. Soc. Rev.* 30: 171-75.

Evaluation and Objectivity in the Social Sciences: An Interpretation of Max Weber's Contributions. In Parsons, *Sociological Theory and Modern Society*, pp. 79-101. 1967 New York: Free Press.

An American Impression of Sociology in the Soviet Union. *Amer. Soc. Rev.* 30: 121-25.

Full Citizenship for the Negro American. *Daedalus* 94: 1009-54.

1966 Societies: Evolutionary and Comparative Perspectives. Englewood Cliffs, NJ: Prentice-Hall.

The Negro American. coed. with Kenneth Clark. Boston: Houghton Mifflin.

The Concept of 'Social System' as a Theoretical Device. with Charles Ackerman. In Gordon J. DiRenzo, ed., *Concepts, Theory, and Explanation in the Behavioral Sciences*, pp. 24-40. N.Y.: Random House.

Religion in a Modern Pluralistic Society. *Rev. of Relig. Res.* 7: 125-46.

The Political Aspect of Social Structure and Process. In David Easton, ed., *Varieties of Political Theory*, pp. 71-116. Englewood Cliffs, NJ: Prentice-Hall.

1967 Death in American Society. with Victor M. Lidz. In Edwin Schneidman, ed., *Essays in Self-Destruction*. N.Y.: Science House.

The Nature of American Pluralism. In Theodore Sizer, ed., *Religion and Public Education*. Boston: Houghton Mifflin.

Social Science and Theology. In William A. Beardslee, ed., *America and the Future of Theology*. Philadelphia: Westminster Press.

Sociological Theory and Modern Society. Essays published between 1959 and 1965 and a previously unpublished essay:
Some Comments on the Sociology of Karl Marx.
N.Y.: Free Press.

1968 Components and Types of Formal Organization. In Preston L. LeBreton, ed., *Comparative Administrative Theory.* Seattle, WA: Univ. of Washington Press.
   Christianity.
   Emile Durkheim
   Interaction: Social Interaction.
   Vilfredo Pareto: Contributions to Economics
   Professions
   Systems Analysis: Social Systems
   Utilitarians: Social Thought
      International Encyclopedia of the Social Sciences. N.Y.: Macmillan.
   The Position of Identity in the General Theory of Action. In Chad Gordon and Kenneth J. Gergen, eds., *The Self in Social Interaction,* pp. 11-23. N.Y.: John Wiley.
   On the Concept of Value-Commitments. *Sociological Inquiry* 38 (2): 135-59.
   Commentary on "Religion as a Cultural System" by Clifford Geertz. In Donald R. Cutler, ed., *The Religious Situation: 1968.* Boston: Beacon.
   Order as a Sociological Problem. In Paul G. Kuntz, ed., *The Concept of Order.* Seattle, WA: Univ. of Washington Press.
   Cooley and the Problem of Internalization. In Albert J. Reiss, Jr., ed., *Cooley and Sociological Analysis.* Ann Arbor, MI: Univ. of Michigan Press.
   The Problem of Polarization on the Axis of Color. In John Hope Franklin, ed., *Color and Race.* Boston: Houghton Mifflin.
   Considerations on the American Academic System. with Gerald M. Platt. *Minerva* 6 (4): 497-523.
   Law and Sociology: A Promising Courtship. In Arther E. Sutherland, ed., *The Path of the Law from 1967. Harvard Law School Sesquicentennial Papers.* Cambridge, MA: Harvard Univ. Press.
   The Disciplines as a Differentiating Force. with Norman Storer. In Edward B. Montgomery, ed., *The Foundations of Access to Knowledge.* Syracuse, NY: Syracuse Univ. Div. of Summer Sessions.

1969 Research with Human Subjects and the "Professional Complex." *Daedalus* 98 (2): 325-360.
      Politics and Social Structure. A selection of essays previously published between 1942 and 1969 on politics; contains essays not previously published:
   Polity and Society: Some General Considerations.
   Postscript to Chapter 15 (On the Concept of Influence).
   N.Y.: Free Press.
   On Stinchcombe's Conceptualization of Power Phenomena: A Review of *Constructing Social Theories* by Arthur L. Stinchcombe. *Sociological Inquiry* 39: 226-31.

1970 Theory in the Humanities and Sociology. *Daedalus* 99 (2): 495-523.
   Some Problems of General Theory in Sociology. In John McKinney and Edward A. Tiryakian, eds., *Theoretical Sociology: Perspectives and Development,* pp. 27-68. N.Y.: Appleton-Century-Crofts.
   Age, Social Structure and Socialization in Higher Education. with Gerald M. Platt. *Soc. of Educ.* 43 (1): 1-37.

Decision-making in the Academic System: Influence and Power Exchange. In Carlos E. Kruytbosch and Sheldon L. Messinger, eds., *The State of the University: Authority and Change*. Beverly Hills, CA: Sage Publications.

The Impact of Technology on Culture and Emerging New Modes of Behavior. *Intrntl. Soc. Sci. J.* 22 (4): 607-27.

Equality and Inequality in Modern Society, or Social Stratification Revisited. *Sociological Inquiry* 40: 13-72.

On Building Social System Theory: A Personal History. *Daedalus* 99 (4): 826-81.

Some Considerations on the Comparative Sociology of Education. In Joseph Fischer, ed., *The Social Sciences and the Comparative Study of Educational Systems*. Scranton, PA: International Textbook Co.

1971   *The System of Modern Societies*. Englewood Cliffs, NJ: Prentice-Hall.

Kinship and the Associational Aspects of Social Structure. In Francis L.K. Hsu, ed., *Kinship and Culture*. Chicago: Aldine.

The Strange Case of Academic Organization. *J. of Higher Educ.* 42 (6): 486-95.

Comparative Studies and Evolutionary Change. In Ivan Vallier, ed., *Comparative Methods in Sociology*, pp. 97-139. Berkeley, CA: Univ. of California Press.

The Normal American Family. In Bert N. Adams and Thomas Weirath, eds., *Readings on the Sociology of the Family*, pp. 53-66. Chicago: Markham.

Commentary. In Herman Turk and Richard L. Simpson, eds., *Institutions & Social Exchange: The Sociologies of Talcott Parsons & George C. Homans*, pp. 380-99. Indianapolis, IN: Bobbs-Merrill.

Belief, Unbelief and Disbelief. In Rocco Caporale and Antonio Grumelli, eds., *The Culture of Unbelief: Studies and Proceedings from the First International Symposium on Belief* (Rome, 1969), pp. 207-45. Berkeley, CA: Univ. of California Press.

Value-freedom and Objectivity. In Otto Stammer and Kathleen Morris, eds., *Max Weber and Sociology Today*, pp. 2750. N.Y.: Harper & Row.

1972   Higher Education as a Theoretical Focus. In Turk and Simpson, *Ibid.*, pp. 233-52.

Commentary on 'Structural-Functionalism, Exchange Theory, and the New Political Economy: Institutionalization as a Theoretical Linkage' by Terry Clark. *Sociological Inquiry* 42: 299-308.

Higher Education, Changing Socialization, and Contemporary Student Dissent. with Gerald M. Platt. In Matilda W. Riley, Marilyn E. Johnson and Anne Foner, eds., *Aging and Society, Vol. 3: A Sociology of Age Stratification*. N.Y.: Russell Sage Foundation.

Readings on Premodern Societies. ed. with Victor Lidz. Englewood Cliffs, NJ: Prentice-Hall.

Field Theory and Systems Theory: With Special Reference to the Relations Between Psychological and Social Systems. In Daniel Offer and Daniel X. Freedman, eds., *Modern Psychiatry and Clinical Research: Essays in Honor of Roy R. Grinker, Sr.* N.Y.: Basic Books.

Review of *Scholarship and Partisanship* by Reinhard Bendix and Guenther Roth. *Contemporary Soc.* 1: 200-03.

The "Gift of Life" and Its Reciprocation. with Renee C. Fox and Victor Lidz. *Social Research* 39 (3): 367-415.

Culture and Social System Revisited. *Soc. Sci. Qrtly.* 53 (2): 253-66.

1973 Durkheim on Religion Revisited: Another Look at the Elementary Forms of the Religious Life. In Charles Y. Glock and Phillip E. Hammond, eds., *Beyond the Classics? Essays in the Scientific Study of Religion*, pp. 156-80. N.Y.: Harper & Row.

The American University. with Gerald M. Platt and Neil J. Smelser. Cambridge, MA: Harvard Univ. Press.

Clyde Kluckhohn and the Integration of Social Science. In Walter W. Taylor, John L. Fischer and Evon Z. Vogt, eds., *Culture and Life: Essays in Memory of Clyde Kluckhohn*, pp. 30-57. Carbondale, IL: Southern Illinois Univ. Press.

The Social Concept of the Present Civilization. *Tribuna Medica* 25: 19-20.

The Bellah Case: Man and God in Princeton, New Jersey. *Commonweal* 98 (11): 256-59.

Religious Symbolization and Death. In Allan Eister, ed., *Changing Perspectives in Scientific Study of Religion.* N.Y.: Wiley-Interscience.

Some Reflections on Post-Industrial Society. *Japanese Soc. Rev.* 24 (2): 109-13.

Review of *A Critique of Max Weber's Philosophy of Social Science* by W.G. Runciman. *Pol. Sci. Qrtly.* 88: 345-48.

Review of *Sociology and Philosophy* by L.T. Hobhouse. *Sociological Inquiry* 43: 85-87.

Review of *Capitalism and Modern Social Theory: An Analysis of the Writings of Marx, Durkheim, and Max Weber* by Anthony Giddens. *Amer. Pol. Sci. Rev.* 67: 1358-60.

1974 The University 'Bundle': A Study of the Balance Between Differentiation and Integration. In Neil J. Smelser and Gabriel Almond, eds., *Public Higher Education in California: Growth, Structural Change, and Conflict.* Berkeley, CA: Univ. of California Press.

The Institutional Function in Organizational Theory. *Organization and Administrative Sciences* 5 (1): 3-16.

Sigmund Freud: The Interpretation of Dreams. *Daedalus.* 103: 91-96.

Stability and Change in the American University. *Daedalus.* 103: 269-77.

Review of *A God Within* by Rene Dubos. *Commonweal* 100: 42-44.

Review of *Ideology and Social Knowledge* by Harold J. Bershady. *Sociological Inquiry* 44: 215-21.

Review of *Social Organization: A General Systems and Role Theory Perspective* by Alvin L. Bertrand. *Social Forces* 53: 126-27.

Comment on 'Current Folklore in the Criticisms of Parsonian Action Theory' by Turner and Beeghley. *Sociological Inquiry* 44: 55-58.

Religion in Postindustrial America: The Problem of Secularization. *Social Research* 41: 193-225.

1975 The Present Status of 'Structural-Functional' Theory. In Lewis A. Coser, ed., *The Idea of Social Structure.* N.Y.: Harcourt Brace Jovanovich.

The Sick Role and the Role of the Physician Reconsidered. *Milbank Memorial Fund Quarterly* 53 (3): 257-78.

Social Structure and the Symbolic Media of Interchange. In Peter M. Blau, ed., *Approaches to the Study of Social Structure,* pp. 94-120. N.Y.: Free Press.

Some Theoretical Considerations on the Nature and Trends of Ethnicity. In Nathan Glazer and Daniel F. Moynihan, eds., *Ethnicity: Theory and Experience.* Cambridge, MA: Harvard Univ. Press.

Commentary on 'Classic on Classic: Parsons' Interpretation of Durkheim' by Whitney Pope, and 'Moral Freedom through Understanding in Durkheim' by Jere Cohen. *Amer. Soc. Rev.* 40: 106-11.

Commentary on 'De-Parsonizing Weber: A Critique of Parsons' Interpretation of Weber's Sociology' by Cohen, Hazelrigg, and Pope. *Amer. Soc. Rev.* 40: 666-69.

Commentary on 'A Radical Analysis of Welfare Economics and Individual Development' by Herbert Gintis. *Qrtly. J. of Econ.* 89: 280-90.

Comment on 'Parsons as a Symbolic Interactionist' by Jonathan Turner. *Sociological Inquiry* 45: 62-65.

1976 Faculty Teaching Goals, 1968-1973. with Gerald M. Platt and Rita Kirshstein. *Social Problems* 24 (2): 298-307.

Vico and History. *Social Research* 43 (4): 881-85.

Social Science: The Public Disenchantment. *The American Scholar* 45 (4): 580-81.

Reply to Cohen, Hazelrigg and Pope, with Special Reference to Their Statement 'On the Divergence of Weber and Durkheim: A Critique of Parsons' Convergence Thesis.' *Amer. Soc. Rev.* 41: 361-64.

The Relations Between Biological and Socio-Cultural Theory. *Bulletin of the Amer. Academy of Arts and Sciences* 29 (8): 14-18.

Some Considerations on the Growth of the American System of Higher Education and Research. In T.N. Clark and J. Ben-David, eds., *Culture and Its Creators: Essays in Honor of Edward Shils.* Chicago: Univ. of Chicago Press.

The Sociology and Economics of Clarence E. Ayers. In William Patton Culbertson and William Breit, eds., *Science and Ceremony: The Institutional Economics of Clarence E. Ayers.* Austin, TX: Univ. of Texas Press.

1977 Law as an Intellectual Stepchild. *Sociological Inquiry* 47: 11-58.

The Evolution of Societies. (ed., Jackson Toby). Englewood Cliffs, NJ: Prentice-Hall.

Two Cases of Social Deviance: Addiction to Heroin, Addiction to Power. with Dean R. Gerstein. In Edwin Sagarin, ed., *Deviance and Social Change.* Beverly Hills, CA: Sage.

Social Systems and the Evolution of Action Theory. (Essays previously published after 1957.) N.Y.: Free Press.

Comment on Burger's Critique: A Reply to Thomas Burger, 'Talcott Parsons, The Problem of Order in Society, and the Program of an Analytical Sociology.' *Amer. J. of Soc.* 83: 335-39.

1978 Undergraduate Teaching Environments: Normative Orientations to Teaching Among Faculty in the Higher Educational System. with Gerald M. Platt and Rita Kirshstein. *Sociological Inquiry* 48 (1): 3-21.

Action Theory and the Human Condition. Essays previously published after 1968 on health, disease, death, religion, and education; contains:

A Paradigm of the Human Condition.

N.Y.: Free Press.

Death in the Western World. *Encyclopedia of Bioethics* 1: 255-61.

Health and Disease: A Sociological and Action Perspective. *Encyclopedia of Bioethics* 2: 590-99.

Letter to Editor (re: introduction to Weber's *The Protestant Ethic and the Spirit of Capitalism,* 1976 publication by Allen and Unwin). *Contemporary Sociology* 7: 117.

Epilogue in Eugene B. Gallagher, ed., *The Doctor-Patient Relationship in the Changing Health Scene,* pp. 445-55. Washington, DC: U.S. Govt. Printing Office, DHEW.

1979 The Symbolic Environment of Modern Economies. *Social Research* 46 (3): 436-53.

Religious and Economic Symbolism in the Western World. *Sociological Inquiry* 49: 1-48.

1980 The Circumstances of My Encounter with Max Weber. In Robert K. Merton and Matilda W. Riley, eds., *Sociological Traditions from Generation to Generation,* pp. 37-43. Norwood, NJ: Ablex.

1981 Revisiting the Classics Throughout a Long Career. In Rhea Buford, ed., *The Future of the Sociological Classics,* pp. 183-94. Boston: Allen & Unwin.

Letter to Edward Tiryakian (re Weber's 'Iron Cage'). *Sociological Inquiry* 51: 35-36.

1986 *The Integration of Economic and Sociological Theory* [*The Marshall Lectures, Cambridge, 1953*]. Richard Swedberg, ed. Uppsala: Sociologiska institutionen.

III. References: Investigations, Evaluations, and Extensions of Parsons' Theory

Abel, T. and J.P. Spiegel, "Two Comments on the Review of *The Social System.*" *Amer. Soc. Rev.* 18 (1953): 322-23.

Aberle, D.F., A.K. Cohen, A.K. Davis, M.J. Levy, and F.X. Sutton, "The Functional Prerequisites of a Society." *Ethics* 60 (1950): 100-11.

Abrahamson, M., Review of *Action Theory and the Human Condition. Soc. Sci. Qrtly.* 60 (1979): 530.

Adriaansens, Hans P., *Talcott Parsons and the Conceptual Dilemma.* Boston: Routledge & Kegan Paul, 1980.

Alexander, Jeffrey C., "Formal and Substantive Voluntarism in the Work of Talcott Parsons: A Theoretical and Ideological Reinterpretation." *Amer. Soc. Rev.* 43 (1978): 177-98.

"The French Connection: Revisionism and Followership in Interpretation of Parsons." *Contemporary Sociology* 10 (1981): 500-05.

"Revolution, Reaction, and Reform: The Change Theory of Parsons' Middle Period." *Sociological Inquiry* 51 (1981): 267-80.

The Modern Reconstruction of Classical Thought: Talcott Parsons. Berkeley, CA: Univ. of California Press, 1983.

"The Parsons Revival in Germany." In Randall Collins, ed., *Sociological Theory 1984,* pp. 394-412. San Francisco, CA: Jossey-Bass, 1984.

NeoFunctionalism. Beverly Hills, CA: Sage, 1985.

Alker, H.A. and N. Kogan, "Effects of Norm-oriented Group Discussion on Individual Risk Taking and Conservatism." *Human Relations* 21 (1968): 393-403.

Almond, Gabriel A., "Comparative Political Systems." *J. of Politics* 18 (1956): 391-409.

"Introduction: A Functional Approach to Comparative Politics." In Gabriel A. Almond and James S. Coleman, eds., *The Politics of the Developing Areas,* pp. 3-64. Princeton, NJ: Princeton Univ. Press, 1960.

Almond, Gabriel A. and Sidney Verba, *The Civic Culture.* Boston: Little, Brown, 1965.

Back, Kurt W., "Biological Models of Social Change." *Amer. Soc. Rev.* 36 (1971): 660-67.

Reply to Berk. *Amer. Soc. Rev.,* 37 (1972): 238.

Review of *Action Theory and the Human Condition. Annals of Amer. Acad. of Pol. and Soc. Sci.* 450 (1980): 295-96.

Barber, Bernard and Alex Inkeles, eds., *Stability and Social Change.* Boston: Little, Brown, 1971.

Bauer, Raymond A., "Communication As A Transaction: A Comment 'On the Concept of Influence'." *Public Opinion Qrtly* 27 (1963): 83-7.

Baum, Rainer C., "Values and Democracy in Imperial Germany." *Sociological Inquiry* 38 (1968): 179-96.

"The System of Solidarities." *Indian J. of Social Research* 16 (1975): 306-53.

"A Revised, Interpretive Approach to the Religious Significance of Death in Western Societies." *Sociological Analysis* 43 (1982): 327-49.

Baum, Rainer C. and F.J. Lechner, "National Socialism: Towards an Action-Theoretical Interpretation." *Sociological Inquiry* 51 (1981): 281-308.

Bealer, Robert C., "Ontology in American Sociology: Whence and Whither" In William E. Snizek, Ellsworth R. Fuhrman and Michael K. Miller, *Contemporary Issues in Theory and Research: A metasociological perspective,* pp. 85-105. Westport, CT: Greenwood Press, 1979.

Becker, Howard, Review of *The Social System. Social Forces* 30 (1952): 463.

Review of *Toward a General Theory of Action. Loc. cit.*

Bellah, Robert, "Religious Evolution." *Amer. Soc. Rev.* 29 (1964): 358-74.

"The World is the World through Its Theorists — In Memory of Talcott Parsons." *Amer. Sociologist* 15 (1980): 60-2.

Berger, Bennett, "On Talcott Parsons." *Commentary* 34 (1962): 507-13.

Berger, J., M. Zelditch, A.J. Gregor and J.F. Scott, Review of *Sociological Theory and Modern Society. Amer. Soc. Rev.* 33 (1968): 446-50.

Berk, Richard A., "Some Comments on Biological Models of Social Change." *Amer. Soc. Rev.* 37 (1972): 237-8.

Berkhofer, Jr., Robert F., "Models and Systems and the Problem of Wholes" (Chap. 8) and "Systems Analysis and the Organization of the Observer's Viewpoint" (Chap. 9). In Robert F. Berkhofer, Jr., *A Behavioral Approach to Historical Analysis,* pp. 169-210. N.Y.: Free Press, 1969.

Bernard, Jessie, Review of *Family, Socialization and Interaction Process. Social Forces* 34 (1955): 181.

Bershady, Harold J., "On Davis and Moore Again, or: Dissensus and the Stability of Social Systems." *British J. of Soc.* 21 (1970): 446-54.

Ideology and Social Knowledge. N.Y.: Wiley, 1973.

Bierstedt, Robert, "The Means-Ends Schema in Sociological Theory." *Amer. Soc. Rev.* 3 (1938): 665-71.

Review of *Essays in Sociological Theory. Amer. Soc. Rev.* 14 (1949): 700.

Review of *Essays in Sociological Theory,* rev. ed. *Amer. Soc. Rev.* 20 (1955): 124-5.

Review of *Economy and Society. Amer. Soc. Rev.* 22 (1957): 345.

Black, Max., ed. *The Social Theories of Talcott Parsons.* Englewood Cliffs, NJ: Prentice-Hall, 1961.

Blain, Robert R., "A Critique of Parsons' Four-Function Paradigm." *Sociological Qrtly.* 11 (1970): 157-68.

"An Alternative to Parsons' Four-Function Paradigm as a Basis for Developing General Sociological Theory." *Amer. Soc. Rev.* 36 (1971): 678-92.

Blau, Peter M., Review of *Family, Socialization and Interaction Process. Amer. Soc. Rev.* 61 (1956): 488.

"Operationalizing A Conceptual Scheme: The Universalism-Particularism Pattern Variable." *Amer. Soc. Rev.* 27 (1962): 159-69.

Bluth, B.J., *Parsons' General Theory of Action: A Summary of The Basic Theory.* Granada Hills, CA: NBS, 1982.

Bock, Kenneth E., "Evolution, Function, and Change." *Amer. Soc. Rev.* 28 (1963): 229-37.

Borgatta, Edgar F., "Functionalism and Sociology." *Amer. Soc. Rev.* 25 (1960): 267.

"Reply" (to Ogles). *Ibid.,* 25 (1960): 559-61.

Boskoff, Alvin, "The Systematic Sociology of Talcott Parsons." *Social Forces* 28 (1950): 393-400.

Review of *Structure and Process in Modern Societies. Ibid.,* 39 (1960): 84.

Review of *Theories of Society. Ibid.,* 41 (1962): 83.

"Functional Analysis as a Source of a Theoretical Repertory and Research Tasks in the Study of Social Change." In George K. Zollschan and Walter Hirsch, eds., *Explorations in Social Change,* pp. 213-43. Boston: Houghton Mifflin, 1964.

"Stratification, Power, and Social Change." In Herman Turk and Richard L. Simpson, *Institutions & Social Change: The Sociologies of Talcott Parsons & George C. Homans,* pp. 289-308. Indianapolis, IN: Bobbs-Merrill, 1971.

Bottomore, T.B., "Out of This World: The Sociological Theories of Talcott Parsons." In T.B. Bottomore, *Sociology as Social Criticism,* pp. 29-43. N.Y.: Random House, 1975.

Boulding, Kenneth E., Review of *Economy and Society. Amer. J. Soc.* 63 (1958): 427-28.

Bourricaud, Francois, *The Sociology of Talcott Parsons.* Paris: Presses Univ. de France. tr. Arthur Goldhammer. Chicago: Univ. of Chicago Press, 1981.

Bredemeier, Harry C., "The Methodology of Functionalism." *Amer. Soc. Rev.* 20 (1955): 173-180.

"Law as an Integrative Mechanism." In William M. Evan, ed., *Law and Sociology,* pp. 73-90. N.Y.: Free Press, 1962.

Bredemeier, Harry C. and Richard M. Stephenson. *The Analysis of Social Systems.* N.Y.: Holt, Rinehart & Winston, 1962.

Brownstein, Larry, *Talcott Parsons' General Action Scheme.* Cambridge, MA: Schenkman, 1981.

Bryant, C. "Who Now Reads Parsons." *Sociological Rev.* 31 (1983): 337-49.

Buck, Gary L. and Alvin L. Jacobson, "Social Evolution and Structural-Functional Analysis: an empirical test." *Amer. Soc. Rev.* 33 (1968): 343-55.

Buckley, Walter, "Structural-Functional Analysis in Modern Sociology." In Howard Becker and Alvin Boskoff, *Modern Sociological Theory,* pp. 236-59. N.Y.: Holt, Rinehart & Winston, 1957.

"Social Stratification and the Functional Theory of Social Differentiation." *Amer. Soc. Rev.* 23 (1958): 369-75.

"A Rejoinder to Functionalists Dr. Davis and Dr. Levy." *Amer. Soc. Rev.* 24 (1959): 84-5.

"Social System Models." In Walter Buckley, *Sociology and Modern Systems Theory,* pp. 7-40. Englewood Cliffs, NJ: Prentice-Hall, 1967.

Burger, Thomas, "Talcott Parsons, the Problem of Order in Society, and the Program of an Analytical Sociology." *Amer. J. Soc.* 83 (1977): 320-34.

Butts, Stewart, "Parsons, Weber and the Subjective Point of View." *Sociological Analysis and Theory* 5 (1975): 185-217.

"Talcott Parsons' Ideas on the Relation Between Theory and Analysis." *Sociological Analysis* 1 (1970): 41-50.

Buxton, William, *Talcott Parsons and the Capitalist Nation-State.* Toronto: Univ. of Toronto Press, 1985.

Cancian, F., "Functional Analysis of Change." *Amer. Soc. Rev.* 25 (1960): 818-27.

"Functional Analysis: varieties of functional analysis." *International Encyclopedia of the Social Sciences.* 6: 21-43. N.Y.: Crowell, Collier & Macmillan, 1968.

Catton, William, Jr., "Flaws in the Structure and Functioning of Functional Analysis." *Pacific Soc. Rev.* 10 (1961): 3-12.

Christenson, Harold T., Review of *Family, Socialization and Interaction Process. Amer. Soc. Rev.* 21 (1956): 96-7.

Clark, S.D., Review of *The Social System. Amer. J. of Soc.* 58 (1953): 103.

Review of *Structure and Process in Modern Societies. Amer. Soc. Rev.* 25 (1960): 971-72.

Clark, Terry N., "Structural-Functionalism, Exchange Theory, and the New Political Economy: Institutionalization as a Theoretical Linkage." *Sociological Inquiry* 42 (1972): 275-98.

"Institutions and an Exchange with Professor Parsons." *Ibid.,* 42 (1972): 309-11.

Cohen, Jere, "Moral Freedom Through Understanding Durkheim." *Amer. Soc. Rev.* 40 (1975): 104-06.

Cohen, Jere, Lawrence E. Hazelrigg and Whitney Pope, "De-Parsonizing Weber: A Critique of Parsons' Interpretation of Weber's Sociology." *Amer. Soc. Rev.* 40 (1975): 229-41.

"Reply to Parsons." *Amer. Soc. Rev.* 40 (1975): 670-74.

Coleman, James, "Comment on 'On the Concept of Influence'." *Pub. Opin. Qrtly.* 27 (1963): 63-82.

"Social Structure and a Theory of Action." In Peter M. Blau, ed., *Approaches to the Study of Social Structure*, pp. 76-93. N.Y.: Free Press, 1975.

Coser, Lewis A. Review of *Essays in Sociological Theory: Pure and Applied. Amer. J. of Soc.* 55 (1950): 502.

Crano, W.D. and J. Aronoff, "A Cross-cultural Study of Expressive and Instrumental Role Complementarity in the Family." *Amer. Soc. Rev.* 43 (1978): 463-71.

Crespi, J. "Comments on Parsons' 'The Prospects of Sociological Theory'." *Amer. Soc. Rev.* 15 (1950): 432.

Cullen, John B. and Shelley M. Novick, "The Davis-Moore Theory of Stratification: A Further Examination and Extension." *Amer. J. of Soc.* 84 (1979): 1424-37.

Dahrendorf, Ralf, "Out of Utopia: Toward a Reorientation of Sociological Analysis." *Amer. J. of Soc.* 64 (1958): 115-27.

Davis, Arthur K., Review of *Essays in Sociological Theory: Pure and Applied. Soc. For.* 28 (1949): 90.

Davis, Kingsley, "A Conceptual Analysis of Stratification." *Amer. Soc. Rev.* 7 (1942): 309-21.

"Reply to Tumin." *Amer. Soc. Rev.* 18 (1953): 394-97.

"The Myth of Functional Analysis as a Special Method in Sociology and Anthropology." *Amer. Soc. Rev.* 24 (1959): 757-71.

"The Abominable Heresy: A Reply to Dr. Buckley." *Amer. Soc. Rev.* 24 (1959): 82-83.

Davis, Kingsley and Wilbert E. Moore, "Some Principles of Stratification." *Amer. Soc. Rev.* 10 (1945): 242-49.

Dawe, Alan, "Theories of Social Action." In Tom Bottomore and Robert A. Nisbet, *A History of Sociological Analysis*, pp. 362-417. N.Y.: Basic Books, 1978.

Dean, Lois, "The Pattern Variables: Some Empirical Operations." *Amer. Soc. Rev.* 26 (1961): 80-90.

Five Towns: A Comparative Community Study. N.Y.: Random House, 1967.

Demerath, N.J., Review of *Essays in Sociological Theory. Soc. For.,* 33 (1954): 193.

Demerath, N.J. and Richard A. Peterson, *System, Change, and Conflict: A Reader on Contemporary Sociological Theory and the Debate Over Functionalism.* N.Y.: Free Press, 1967.

Deutsch, K.W., "Mechanism, Organism, and Society: Some Models in Natural and Social Science." *Philosophy of Science* 18 (1951): 230-52.

"Integration and the Social System: Implications of Functional Analysis." In Philip E. Jacob and James V. Toscana, eds., *The Integration of Political Communities*, pp. 179-208. Philadelphia: Lippincott, 1964.

DiTomasco, Nancy, "Sociological Reductionism from Parsons to Althusser." *Amer. Soc. Rev.* 47 (1982): 14-28.

Dixon, Keith, *Sociological Theory: Pretense and Possibility.* London: Routledge & Kegan Paul, 1973.

Review of *Social Systems and the Evolution of Action Theory* and *Action Theory and the Human Condition. Ethics* 90 (1980): 608-11.

Dore, Ronald P., "Function and Cause." *Amer. Soc. Rev.* 26 (1961): 843-53.

Drake, Joseph T., Review of *The Negro American. Soc. For.* 45 (1966): 303.

Dubin, Robert, "Parsons' Actor: Continuities in Social Theory." *Amer. Soc. Rev.* 25 (1960): 457-66.

"Causality and Social System Analysis." *Int. J. General Systems* 2 (1975): 107-13.

Easton, David, "Limits of the Equilibrium Model in Social Research." *Behavioral Sci.* 1 (1956): 96-104.

A Systems Analysis of Political Life. N.Y.: Wiley, 1965.

Eckstein, Harry, "A Perspective of Comparative Politics, Past and Present." In Harry Eckstein and David E. Apter, eds., *Comparative Politics,* pp. 26-29. N.Y.: Free Press, 1963.

Edel, Abraham, "The Concept of Levels in Social Theory." In Llewellyn Gross, ed., *Symposium on Sociological Theory,* pp. 167-95. N.Y.: Harper & Row, 1959.

Effrat, Andrew, "Editor's Introduction" (to *Sociological Inquiry* 38 (2) 1968 on Applications of Parsonian Theory). *Sociological Inquiry* 38 (1968): 97-103.

Eisenstadt, S.N., *The Political Systems of Empires. The Rise and Fall of the Historical Bureaucratic Societies.* N.Y.: Free Press, 1963.

"Social Change, Differentiation, and Evolution." *Amer. Soc. Rev.* 29 (1964): 375-86.

Ellis, Desmond P., Review of *Sociological Theory and Modern Society. Soc. For.* 47 (1968): 90.

Embree, Lester, "Methodology is Where Humanists, Scientists, and Philosophers Can Meet: Reflections of the Schutz-Parsons Exchange." *Human Studies* 3 (1980): 367-74.

Emmet, Dorothy, *Function, Purpose, and Powers.* N.Y.: Macmillan, 1958, 1972.

Erasmas, Charles J., "Obviating the Functions of Functionalism." *Soc. For.* 45 (1967): 319-28.

Etzioni, Amitai, "The Functional Differentiation of Elites in the Kibbutz." *Amer. J. of Soc.* 64 (1959): 476-87.

Falding, H., "Toward a Reconciliation of Mills with Parsons." *Amer. Soc. Rev.* 26 (1961): 778-80.

Faris, Ellsworth, Review of Parsons' *The Social System. Amer. Soc. Rev.* 18 (1953): 103-6.

Rejoinder to Abel and Spiegal. *Amer. Soc. Rev.* 18 (1953): 323.

Feibleman, James, and Julius Weis Friend, "The Structure and Function of Organization." *Phil. Rev.* 54 (1945): 19-44.

"Theory of Integrative Levels." *Brit. J. for Phil. of Sci.* 5 (1954): 59-66.

Feuer, Lewis, "The Social Theories of Talcott Parsons: A Critical Examination." *J. of Phil.* 59 (1962): 182-93.

Ford, Joseph Brandon, "Parsons versus Comte: On Positivism." *Indian J. of Social Research* 15 (1974): 77-100.

Foss, Daniel, "The World View of Talcott Parsons." In Maurice Stein and Arthur Vidich, eds., *Sociology on Trial*, pp. 96-126. Englewood Cliffs, NJ: Prentice:Hall, 1963.

Freeman, Linton C. and Robert F. Winch, "Societal Complexity: An Empirical Test of a Typology of Societies." *Amer. J. of Soc.* 62 (1957): 461-66.

Gallagher, Eugene B., "Lines of Reconstruction and Extension in the Parsonian Sociology of Illness." *Soc. Sci. & Med.* 10 (1976): 207-18.

Gerstein, D.R., "A Note on the Continuity of Parsonian Action Theory." *Sociological Inquiry* 45 (1975): 11-15.

"Cultural Action and Heroin Addiction." *Ibid.,* 51 (1981): 355-70.

"A Reminiscence of Talcott Parsons, September 1970 to April 1979." *Ibid.,* 51 (1981): 166-70.

Gettys, Warner R. Review of *The Structure of Social Action. Soc. For.* 17 (1939): 425.

Getzels, J.W., and E.G. Guba, "Role, Role Conflict, and Effectiveness." *Amer. Soc. Rev.* 19 (1954): 164-75.

Giddens, Anthony H., "'Power' in the Recent Writings of Talcott Parsons." *Sociology* 2 (1968): 257-72.

Goode, William J., "Functionalism: The Empty Castle." In William J. Goode, *Explorations in Social Theory*, pp. 64-94. N.Y.: Oxford Univ. Press, 1973.

Gordon, Chad, "Systemic Senses of Self." *Sociological Inquiry* 38 (1968): 161-77.

Gould, Mark, "Parsons versus Marx: 'An earnest warning...'." *Sociological Inquiry* 51 (1981): 197-218.

Gouldner, Alvin W., "Some Observations on 'Systematic Theory' 1945-1955." In Hans Zetterberg, ed., *Sociology in the United States of America*, pp. 34-42. Paris: UNESCO, 1956.

"Reciprocity and Autonomy in Functional Theory." In L. Gross, ed., *Symposium on Sociological Theory*, pp. 241-70. N.Y.: Harper & Row, 1959.

"The Norm of Reciprocity." *Amer. Soc. Rev.* 25 (1960): 161-78.

"The World of Talcott Parsons." In Alvin W. Gouldner, *The Coming Crisis of Western Sociology*, pp. 167-338. N.Y.: Basic Books, 1970.

"Talcott Parsons." *Theory and Society 8 [1979]: 299-301.*

Granovetter, Mark, "The Idea of 'Advancement' in Theories of Social Evolution and Development." *Amer. J. of Soc.* 85 (1979): 489-515.

Grathoff, Richard, ed., *The Theory of Social Action: The Correspondence of Alfred Schutz and Talcott Parsons*. Bloomington, IN: Indiana Univ. Press, 1978.

Gregor, A.J. Review of *Sociological Theory and Modern Society. Amer. Soc. Rev.* 33 (1958): 450-53.

Gross, Llewellyn, "Preface to a Metatheoretical Framework in Sociology." *Amer. J. of Soc.* 67 (1961): 125-40.

"Rejoinder" (to Parsons). *Ibid.,* pp. 140-44.

Review of *Theories of Society: Foundations of Modern Sociological Theory,* Vol. I. *Amer. Soc. Rev.* 27 (1962): 259-60.

Gusfield, Joseph, "Review Symposium, *The American University*." *Contemporary Sociology* 3 (1974): 291-95.

Habermas, Jurgen, "Talcott Parsons: Problems of Theory Construction." *Sociological Inquiry* 51 (1981): 173-96.

Hagen, Everett E., "Analytical Models in the Study of Social Systems." *Amer. J. of Soc.* 67 (1961): 144-51.

Hall, John R., "The Problem of Epistemology in the Social Action Perspective." In Randall Collins, ed., *Sociological Theory 1984*, pp. 253-89. San Francisco: Jossey-Bass, 1984.

Halpern, Ben, Review of *Societies: Evolutionary and Comparative Perspectives. Amer. Soc. Rev.* 32 (1967): 678-79.

Hamilton, Peter, *Talcott Parsons.* N.Y. Methuen, 1983.

Hayes, Adrian C., "A Comparative Study of the Theoretical Orientations of Parsons and Levi-Strauss." *Indian J. of Soc. Res.* 15 (1974): 101-11.

"A Semi-formal Explication of Talcott Parsons' Theory of Action." *Sociological Inquiry* 50 (1980): 39-56.

"Structure and Creativity: The Use of Transformational-Generative Models in Action Theory." *Ibid.,* 51 (1981): 219-39.

Hempel, Carl G., "The Logic of Functional Analysis." In Llewellyn Gross, ed., *Symposium on Sociological Theory,* pp. 271-307. N.Y.: Harper & Row, 1959.

Henry, Jules, "Homeostatis, Society, and Evolution: A Critique." *Scientific Monthly* 81 (1955): 300-09.

Heydebrand, Wolf, Review of *The System of Modern Societies. Contemporary Soc.* 1 (1972): 387-95.

Hinkle, R.C., "Antecedents of the Action Orientation in American Sociology Before 1935." *Amer. Soc. Rev.* 28 (1963): 705-15.

Holmwood, J.M., "Action, System and Norm in the Action Frame of Reference: Talcott Parsons and His Critics." *Sociological Rev.* 31 (1983): 310-36.

Holton, Robert J. and Bryan S. Turner, *Talcott Parsons on Economy and Society.* N.Y.: Routledge & Kegan Paul, 1986.

Homans, George C., "Bringing Men Back In." *Amer. Soc. Rev.* 29 (1964): 809-18.

Horne, William C., and Gary Long, "Effects of Group Discussion on Universalistic-Particularistic Orientations." *J. Exper. Soc. Psych.* 8 (1972): 236-46.

Hoult, Thomas Ford, "Functionalism: A Brief Clarification." *Sociological Inquiry* 33 (1963): 31-33.

House, Floyd N., Review of *The Structure of Social Action: A Study in Social Theory with Specific Reference to a Group of Recent European Writers. Amer. J. of Soc.* 55 (1950): 504.

Huaco, George A., "A Logical Analysis of the Davis-Moore Theory of Stratification." *Amer. Soc. Rev.* 28 (1963): 801-3.

Isajiw, Wsevolod W., *Causation and Functionalism in Sociology.* London: Routledge & Kegan Paul, 1968.

Jackson, Toby, "Social Evolution and Criminality: A Parsonian View." *Soc. For.* 26 (1979): 386-91.

Jacobs, Harold, "Aspects of the Political Sociology of Talcott Parsons." *Berkeley J. of Soc.* 14 (1969): 58-72.

Jacobson, A.L. , "A Theoretical and Empirical Analysis of Social Change and Conflict Based on Talcott Parsons' Ideas." In Herman Turk and Richard L. Simpson, *Institutions & Social Exchange: The Sociologies of Talcott Parsons & George C. Homans,* pp. 344-60. Indianapolis, IN: Bobbs-Merrill, 1971.

Johnson, Benton, *Functionalism in Modern Sociology: Understanding Talcott Parsons.* Morristown, NJ: General Learning Press, 1975.

Johnson, Chalmers, *Revolutionary Change,* 2nd ed. Stanford, CA: Stanford Univ. Press, 1982.

Johnson, Harry M., *Sociology: A Systematic Introduction.* N.Y.: Harcourt, Brace & World, 1960.

"Talcott Parsons and the Theory of Action: The Generalized Symbolic Media in Parsons' Theory." *Soc. and Soc. Res.* 57 (1973): 208-21.

"Editorial Introduction" (to special issue of *Sociological Inquiry*]. *Sociological Inquiry* 51 (1981): iii-xvii.

Jules-Rosette, Benetta, "Talcott Parsons and the Phenomenological Tradition in Sociology: An Unresolved Debate." *Human Studies* 3 (1980): 311-30.

Kallen, H., "Functionalism." *Ency. Soc. Sci.* 6 (1934): 523-35.

Kaminsky, Elijah Ben-Zion, "Talcott Parsons and The Study of Comparative Politics." *Indian J. of Soc. Res.* 15 (1974): 137-47.

Kaplan, Harold, "The Parsonian Image of Social Structure and Its Relevance for Political Science." *J. of Politics* 30 (1968): 885-909.

Klausner, Michael and Mary Ann Groves, "Empirical Application of Parsonian Theory." *Sociological Inquiry* 51 (1981): 243-65.

Kolb, William L., "Images of Man and the Sociology of Religion." *J. for the Scientific Study of Religion* 1 (1964): 5-22.

Landau, Martin, "On the Use of Functional Analysis in American Political Science." *Social Research* 35 (1968): 48-75.

Lawlicht, J., "Role Conflict, the Pattern Variable Theory, and Scalogram Analysis." *Soc. For.* 33 (1955): 250-54.

Lazarsfeld, Paul F., "Historical Notes on the Empirical Study of Action: An Intellectual Odyssey." In Paul F. Lazersfeld, *Qualitative Analysis: Historical and Critical Essays,* pp. 53-105. Boston: Allyn & Bacon, 1972.

Lessnoff, M.H., "Parsons' System Problems." *Soc. Rev.* 16 (1968): 185-215.

Review of *Action and the Human Condition* and *Social Systems and the Evolution of Action Theory. Brit. J. of Soc.* 31 (1980): 300-02.

Levine, Donald N., *Simmel and Parsons.* N.Y.: Arno Press, 1980.

Levy, Marion J., *The Family Revolution in Modern China.* Cambridge, MA: Harvard Univ. Press, 1949.

"Some Questions about 'The Concepts of Culture and of Social System'." *Amer. Soc. Rev.* 24 (1959): 247-48.

The Structure of Society. Princeton, NJ: Princeton Univ. Press, 1966.

Lidz, Victor, "Conceptions of Value-Relevance and the Theory of Action." *Sociological Inquiry* 51 (1981): 371-408.

"Religion and Cybernetic Concepts in the Theory of Action." *Sociological Analysis* 43 (1982): 287-305.

Lilienfeld, Robert, "Systems Theory as an Ideology." *Sociological Research* 42 (1975): 637-60.

Lipset, Seymour Martin, *The First New Nation.* N.Y.: Basic Books, 1963.

"Social Structure and Social Change." In Peter Blau, ed., *Approaches to the Study of Social Structure,* pp. 172-209. N.Y.: Free Press, 1975.

Lipset, Seymour Martin and Everett Carll Ladd, "The Politics of American Sociologists." In Robert K. Merton, *et al.,* eds., *Varieties of Political Expression in Sociology,* pp. 67-104. Chicago: Univ. of Chicago Press, 1972.

Little, D., Review of *Action Theory and the Human Condition. Sociological Analysis* 42 (1981): 77-78.

Lockwood, David, "Some Remarks on the Social System." *Brit. J. of Soc.* 7 (1956): 134-46.

"Social Integration and System Integration." In G.K. Zollschan and W. Hirsch, eds., *Explorations in Social Change,* pp. 244-57. Boston: Houghton Mifflin, 1964.

Loomis, Charles P. and John C McKinney, "System Differences Between Latin-American Communities of Family Farms and Large Estates." *Amer. J. of Soc.* 61 (1956): 404-12.

Lopreato, Joseph, "The Concept of Equilibrium: Sociological Tantalizer." In Herman Turk and Richard L. Simpson, eds., *Institutions & Social Exchange: The Sociologies of Talcott Parsons & George C. Homans,* pp. 309-43. Indianapolis, IN: Bobbs-Merrill, 1971.

Loubser, Jan J., Rainer C. Baum, Andrew Effrat and Victor Meyer Lidz, *Explorations in General Theory in Social Science: Essays in Honor of Talcott Parsons.* Vols. I and II. N.Y.: Free Press, 1976.

Luhmann, Niklas, "Talcott Parsons: The Future of a Theory." In Niklas Luhman, *The Differentiation of Society,* pp. 47-65. N.Y.: Columbia Univ. Press, 1982.

Lundberg, George, "Some Convergences in Sociological Theory." *Amer. J. of Soc.* 62 (1957): 21-27.

Maniha, John K., "Universalism and Particularism in Bureaucratizing Organizations." *Admin. Sci. Qtrly.* 20 (1975): 177-90.

Marsh, Robert M., Review of *Societies. Soc. For.* 45 (1967): 589.

Martel, Martin U., "Some Controversial Assumptions in Parsons' Approach to Social Systems Theory." *Alpha Kappa Deltan* 29 (1959): 53-63.

"Talcott Parsons." *International Encyclopedia of the Social Sciences, Biographical Supplement* 18: 609-30. N.Y.: Crowell, Collier & Macmillan, 1979.

Martel, Martin U. and Adrian C. Hayes, "Some New Directions for Action Theory." *Sociological Inquiry* 49 (1979): 77-82.

Martindale, Don, "Talcott Parsons' Theoretical Metamorphosis from Social Behaviorism to Macrofunctionalism." *Alpha Kappa Deltan* 29 (1959): 38-46.

Functionalism in the Social Sciences. Philadelphia: Amer. Acad. of Pol. and Soc. Sci., 1965.

"Titans of American Sociology: Talcott Parsons and C. Wright Mills." In Don Martindale, *Personality and Milieu: The Shaping of Social Science Culture,* pp. 60-103. Houston: Cap and Gown Press, 1982.

Mayhew, Leon, "Ascription in Modern Societies." *Sociological Inquiry* 38 (1968): 105-20.

"Action Theory and Action Research." *Soc. Problems* 15 (1968): 420-31.

"Stability and Change in Legal Systems." In Bernard Barber and Alex Inkeles, *Stability and Social Change,* pp. 197-210. Boston: Little, Brown, 1971.

Talcott Parsons on Institutions and Social Evolution. Chicago: Univ. of Chicago Press, 1982.

"In Defense of Modernity: Parsons and the Utilitarian Tradition." *Amer. J. of Soc.* 89 (1984): 1273-05.

McKinney, John C., "Methodological Convergence of Mead, Lundberg, and Parsons." *Amer. J. of Soc.* 59 (1954): 565-74.

Merton, Robert K., "Discussion of Parsons' 'Position of Sociological Theory'." *Amer. Soc. Rev.* 13 (1949): 1648.

"A Paradigm for Functional Analysis." in Robert K. Merton, *Social Theory and Social Structure.* N.Y.: Free Press, 1957, and 3rd ed., 1968.

Michelson, William, "A Parsonian Scheme for the Study of Man and Environment, or What Human Ecology Left Behind in the Dust." *Sociological Inquiry* 38 (1968): 197-208.

Mitchell, William C., "The Polity and Society: A Structural-Functional Analysis." *Midwest J. of Pol. Sci.* 2 (1958): 403-20.

Sociological Analysis and Politics: The Theories of Talcott Parsons. Englewood Cliffs, NJ: Prentice-Hall, 1967.

Modelski, George, "Agraria and Industria: Two Models of the International System." *World Politics* 14 (1961): 119-43.

Moore, Jr., Barrington, "The New Scholasticism and the Study of Politics." *World Politics* 8 (1955): 1-19.

Moore, Wilbert E., "But Some are More Equal than Others." *Amer. Soc. Rev.,* 28 (1963): 13-18.

"Functionalism." In Tom Bottomore and Robert Nisbet, *A History of Sociological Analysis,* pp. 321-61. N.Y.: Basic Books, 1978.

Morrione, T.J., "Symbolic Interactionalism and Social Action Theory." *Soc. and Soc. Res.* 59 (1975): 201-18.

Moulyn, Adrian C., *Structure, Function, and Purpose.* N.Y.: Liberal Arts Press, 1957.

Muench, Richard, "Talcott Parsons and the Theory of Action. I. The Structure of the Kantian Core." *Amer. J. of Soc.* 86 (1981): 709-39.

"Socialization and Personality Development from the Point of View of Action Theory: The Legacy of Emile Durkheim." *Sociological Inquiry* 51 (1981): 311-54.

"Talcott Parsons and The Theory of Action. II. The Continuity of Development." *Amer. J. of Soc.* 87 (1982): 771-826.

"From Pure Methodological Individualism to Poor Sociological Utilitarianism." *Canadian J. of Soc.* 8 (1983): 45-76.

Mulkay, M.J., "Structural-functionalism as a Theoretical Alternative: Parsons; An Assessment of Parsons' Scheme." In M.J. Mulkay, *Functionalism, Exchange, and Theoretical Strategy,* pp. 36-93 (chaps. 3, 4). N.Y.: Schocken Books, 1971.

Mullins, Nicholas C. and Carolyn J. Mullins, "Standard American Sociology." In N.C. Mullins and C.J. Mullins, *Theories and Theory Groups in Contemporary American Sociology,* pp. 40-74 (chap. 3), N.Y.: Harper & Row, 1973.

Murphy, J.W., "Talcott Parsons and Niklas Luhmann: Two Versions of The Social System." *Intrntl. Rev. of Mod. Soc.* 12 (1982): 291-301.

Nagel, Ernest, "Teleological Explanation and Teleological Systems." In H. Feigl and M. Brodbeck, *Readings in the Philosophy of Science,* pp. 537-58. N.Y.: Appleton-Century-Crofts, 1953.

"A Formalization of Functionalism." In Ernest Nagel, *Logic without Metaphysics,* pp. 247-83. N.Y.: Free Press, 1956.

Neal, Marie Augusta, *Values and Interests in Social Change.* Englewood Cliffs, NJ: Prentice-Hall, 1965.

Newcomb, Theodore M., "Discussion." *Amer. Soc. Rev.* 13 (1948): 168-71.

Nock, Steven, and Peter H. Rossi, "Ascription versus Achievement in the Attribution of Family Social Status." *Amer. J. of Soc.* 84 (1978): 565-90.

Ogles, R.H., "Programmatic Theory and the Critics of Talcott Parsons." *Pac. Soc. Rev.* 4 (1961): 53-56.

"Comments on 'The Concepts of Culture and of Social System'." *Amer. Soc. Rev.* 24 (1959): 246-47.

"A Complete Bibliography of Talcott Parsons and Selected Reviews and Critiques of his Work." *Alpha Kappa Deltan* 29 (1959): 73-80.

"On Borgatta's Use of 'Functionalist'." Amer. Soc. Rev. 25 (1960): 559-61.

Olds, James, *The Growth and Structure of Motives.* N.Y.: Free Press, 1956.

O'Neill, John, "The Hobbesian Problem in Marx and Parsons." In John O'Neill, ed., *Sociology as a Skin Trade: Essays Towards a Reflexive Sociology,* pp. 177-208. N.Y.: Harper & Row, 1972.

Pedraza-Bailey, S., "Talcott Parsons and Structural Marxism: Functionalist Theories of Society." *Current Perspectives in Social Theory* 3 (1982): 207-24.

Pinney, Howard, "The Structure of Social Action." *Ethics* 50 (1940): 164-92.

Platt, Gerald M., *"The American University:* Collaboration with Talcott Parsons." *Sociological Inquiry* 51 (1981): 155-65.

Pope, W., "Classic on Classic: Parsons' Interpretation of Durkheim." *Amer. Soc. Rev.* 38 (1973): 399-415.

"Parsons on Durkheim Revisited: Reply to Cohen and Parsons." *Amer. Soc. Rev.* 40 (1975): 111-15.

"Reply to Parsons." *Amer. Soc. Rev.* 42 (1977): 809-11.

Pope, W., J. Cohen and L. Hazelrigg, "On the Divergence of Weber and Durkheim: A Critique of Parsons' Convergence Thesis." *Amer. Soc. Rev.* 40 (1975): 417-27.

Pope, W. and J. Cohen, "On R. Stephen Warner's 'Toward a Redefinition of Action Theory: Paying the Cognitive Element Its Due." *Amer. J. of Soc.* 83 (1978): 1359-67.

Proctor, Ian, "Parsons' Early Voluntarism." *Sociological Inquiry* 48 (1978): 37-48.

"Voluntarism and Structural-Functionalism in Parsons' Early Work." *Human Studies* 3 (1980): 331-46.

Rehorick, David Allen, "Schutz and Parsons, Debate or Dialogue?" *Human Studies* 3 (1980): 347-56.

Reynaud, Jean-Daniel and Pierre Bourdieu, "Is a Sociology of Action Possible?" In Anthony Giddens, ed. *Positivism and Sociology,* pp. 101-13. London: Heinemann, 1974.

Ritzer, G., Review of *The Evolution of Societies. Soc. and Soc. Res.* 64 (1980): 447-48.

Robertson, Roland, "Talcott Parsons on Religion: A Preface." *Sociological Analysis* 43 (1982): 283-85.

"Parsons on the Evolutionary Significance of American Religion." *Ibid.,* pp. 307-25.

Robertson, Roland and M. Cavanaugh, "Bibliography of Talcott Parsons' Writings on Religion." *Ibid.,* pp. 369-73.

Rocher, Guy, *Talcott Parsons and American Sociology.* N.Y.: Barnes and Noble, 1975.

Rossi, Ino, Review of Toby's edited version of Parsons' *The Evolution of Societies. Cont. Soc.* 8 (1979): 644-45.

Rubenstein, D., "The Concept of Action in the Social Sciences." *J. for Theory of Soc. Behav.* 7 (1977): 209-36.

Russett, Cynthia Eagle, *The Concept of Equilibrium in American Social Thought.* New Haven, CT: Yale Univ. Press, 1966.

Savage, Stephen P., *The Theories of Talcott Parsons: The Social Relations of Action.* N.Y.: St. Martin's Press, 1981.

Review of *Action Theory and the Human Condition* and *Social Systems and the Evolution of Action Theory. Soc. Rev.* 28 (1980): 204-07.

Scarr, Harry A., "Measures of Particularism." *Sociometry* 27 (1964): 413-32.

Schrag, Clarence, Review of *Toward a General Theory of Action. Amer. Soc. Rev.* 17 (1952): 247-49.

"Comments on the General Theory of Action." *Alpha Kappa Deltan* 29 (1959): 46-52.

Schutz, Alfred, "The Social World and the Theory of Social Action." *Soc. Res.* 27 (1960): 203-21.

"Subjective and Objective Meaning." In Anthony Giddens, ed., *Positivism and Sociology,* pp. 33-52. London: Heinemann, 1974.

Schwanenberg, Enno, "The Two Problems of Order in Parsons' Theory: An Analysis from Within." *Soc. For.* 49 (1971): 569-81.

Schwartz, R., "Functional Alternatives to Inequality." *Amer. Soc. Rev.* 20 (1955): 424-30.

Sciulli, David, "Talcott Parsons's Analytical Critique of Marxism's Concept of Alienation." *Amer. J. of Soc.* 90 (1984): 514-40.

"The Practical Groundwork for Critical Theory: Bringing Parsons to Habermas (and vice versa)." In Jeffrey C. Alexander, ed., *Neofunctionalism,* pp. 21-50. Beverly Hills, CA: Sage, 1985.

"Voluntaristic Action as a Distinct Concept: Theoretical Foundations of Societal Constitutionalism." *Amer. Soc. Rev.* 51 (1986): 743-66.

Sciulli, David and Dean Gerstein, "Social Theory and Talcott Parsons in the 1980s." *Annual Rev. of Soc.* 11 (1985): 369-87.

Scott, F.G., "Action Theory and Research in Social Organization." *Amer. J. of Soc.* 64 (1959): 386-95.

Scott, John Finley, "The Impossible Theory of Action: Some Questions on Parsons' Prewar Classifications of Action Theories." *Berkeley J. Soc.* 7 (1962): 51-62.

"The Changing Foundations of the Parsonian Action Schema." *Amer. Soc. Rev.* 28 (1963): 716-35.

Review Symposium of T. Parsons' *Sociological Theory and Modern Society. Amer. Soc. Rev.* 33 (1968): 453-56.

"Interpreting Parsons' Works: A Problem in Method." *Sociological Inquiry* 44 (1974): 58-60.

Selznick, Philip,, Review of *Social Theories of T. Parsons,* M. Black, ed. *Amer. Soc. Rev.* 26 (1961): 932-35.

Sexton, Patricia Cayo, Review of *The American University. Cont. Soc.* 3 (1974): 296-300.

Sibley, Elbridge, "Parsons on the Sibley Report." *Amer. Soc. Rev.* 30 (1965): 110.

Simich, J.L. and R. Tilman, "On the Use and Abuse of Thorstein Veblen in Modern American Sociology: David Riesman's Reductionist Interpretation and Talcott Parsons' Pluralist Critique." *Amer. J. of Economics and Sociology* 42 (1983): 417-29.

Simpson, Richard L., "A Modification of the Functional Theory of Social Stratification." *Soc. For.* 35 (1956): 132-37.

Sinclair, Peter, Review of *Economy and Society. Soc. For.* 36 (1957): 177.

Sklair, Leslie, "The Fate of the 'Functional Requisites' in Parsonian Sociology." *Brit. J. of Soc.* 21 (1970): 30-42.

Smelser, Neil J. *Social Change in the Industrial Revolution: An Application of Theory to the British Cotton Industry 1770-1840.* Chicago: Univ. of Chicago Press, 1959.

  Theory of Collective Behavior. N.Y.: Free Press, 1963.

  "Some Personal Thoughts on the Pursuit of Sociological Problems." *Sociological Inquiry* 39 (1969): 155-67.

  "Epilogue: Social Structural Dimensions of Higher Education." In Talcott Parsons and Gerald N. Platt, with Neil J. Smelser, *The American University,* pp. 389-422. Cambridge, MA: Harvard Univ. Press, 1973.

  "On Collaborating with Talcott Parsons: Some Intellectual and Personal Notes." *Sociological Inquiry* 51 (1981): 143-54.

Smith, Anthony D., *The Concept of Social Change: A Critique of the Functionalist Theory of Social Change.* Boston: Routledge & Kegan Paul, 1973.

Smith, M.B., Review of *Toward a General Theory of Action. J. Abn. & Soc. Psych.* 48 (1953): 215-18.

Sprott, W.J.H., "Principia Sociologica." *Brit. J. of Soc.* 3 (1952): 203-21.

  "Principia Sociologica, II." *Brit. J. of Soc.* 14 (1963): 307-20.

Stinchcombe, Arthur L., "Specious Generality and Functional Theory." *Amer. Soc. Rev.* 26 (1961): 929-30.

  "Some Empirical Consequences of the Davis-Moore Theory of Stratification." *Amer. Soc. Rev.* 28 (1963): 805-08.

  "A Parsonian Theory of Traffic Accidents." *Sociological Inquiry* 45 (1975): 27-30.

Stouffer, Samuel A. and Jackson Toby, "Role Conflict and Personality." *Amer. J. of Soc.* 56 (1951): 395-405.

Sutton, F.X., "Social Theory and Comparative Politics." In Harry Eckstein and David E. Apter, eds., *Comparative Politics,* pp. 67-81. N.Y.: Free Press, 1963.

Swanson, Guy E., "The Approach to a General Theory of Action by Parsons and Shils." *Amer. Soc. Rev.* 18 (1953): 125-34.

  Review of *Working Papers in the Theory of Action. Amer. Soc. Rev.* 19 (1954): 95-7.

  Review of *Social Structure and Personality. Amer. J. of Soc.* 70 (1965): 275.

Tartar, Donald E., "Toward Prediction of Attitude-Action Discrepancy." *Soc. For.* 47 (1969): 398-405.

Tausky, C., "Parsons on Stratification: An Analysis and Critique." *Soc. Qrtly.* 6 (1965): 128-38.

Tibbetts, Paul, "The Issue of Human Subjectivity in Sociological Explanation: the Schutz-Parsons Controversy." *Human Studies* 3 (1980): 357-66.

Tiryakian, Edward A., Review of *Politics and Society. Soc. For.* 49 (1970): 327.

"Post-Parsonian Sociology." *Humboldt J. of Social Relations* 7 (1979): 17-32.

"The Significance of Schools in the Development of Sociology." In William E. Snizek, Ellsworth R. Fuhrman and Michael K. Miller, *Contemporary Issues in Theory and Research: a metasociological perspective,* pp. 211-33. Westport, CT: Greenwood Press, 1979.

"Puritan America in the Modern World: Mission Impossible?" *Sociological Analysis* 43 (1982): 351-67.

Toby, Jackson, "Universalistic Factors in Role Assignment." *Amer. Soc. Rev.* 18 (1953): 134-41.

"Parsons' Theory of Social Evolution." *Cont. Soc.* 1 (1972): 395-401.

"Gouldner's Misleading Reading of the Theories of Talcott Parsons." *Ibid.,* pp. 109-10.

"Societal Evolution and Criminality: A Parsonian View." *Soc. Problems* 26 (1979): 286-91.

Touraine, Alain, "Towards a Sociology of Action." In Anthony Giddens, ed., *Positivism and Sociology,* pp. 75-100. London: Heinemann, 1974.

Tumin, Melvin J., "Some Principles of Stratification: A Critical Analysis." *Amer. Soc. Rev.* 18 (1953): 387-93.

"Reply to Kingsley Davis." *Ibid.,* pp. 672.

Turk, Austin T., "An Examination of the Kroeber-Parsons Distinction between 'Culture' and 'Society'." *Soc. Qrtly.* 3 (1962): 135-40.

"On the Parsonian Approach to Theory Construction." *Soc. Qrtly.* 8 (1967): 37-50.

Turk, Herman and Richard L. Simpson, eds., *Institutions & Social Exchange: The Sociologies of Talcott Parsons & George C. Homans.* Indianapolis, IN: Bobbs-Merrill, 1971.

Turner, Jonathan H., "Parsons as a Symbolic Interactionist - Comparison of Action and Interaction Theory." *Soc. Qrtly.* 44 (1974): 283-94.

"A Strategy for Reformulating the Dialectical and Functional Theories of Conflict." *Soc. For.* 53 (1975): 433-44.

The Structure of Sociological Theory, rev. ed. Homewood, IL: Dorsey Press, 1978.

"Parsons on the Human Condition." *Cont. Soc.* 9 (1980): 380-82.

Turner, Jonathan H. and Leonard Beeghley, "Current Folklore in the Criticisms of Parsonian Action Theory." *Sociological Inquiry* 44 (1974): 47-55.

Turner, Jonathan H. and Alexandra Maryanski, *Functionalism.* Menlo Park, CA: Benjamin/Cummings Publ. Co., 1979.

Turner, Ralph H., Review of *Social Structure and Personality. Amer. Soc. Rev.* 30 (1965): 788-89.

Turner, Terence S., "Parsons' Concept of Generalized Media of Social Action and Its Relevance for Social Anthropology." *Sociological Inquiry* 38 (1968): 121-34.

Udy, Jr., Stanley H., Review of *Structure and Process in Modern Societies. Amer. J. of Soc.* 66 (1961): 96.

Vallier, I., "Empirical Comparisons of Social Structure: Leads and Lags." In I. Vallier, ed., *Comparative Methods in Sociology.* Berkeley, CA: Univ. of California Press, 1971.

Valone, James J., "Parsons' Contributions to Social Theory: Reflections on the Schutz-Parsons Correspondence." *Human Studies* 3 (1980): 375-86.

van den Berghe, Pierre L., "Dialectic and Functionalism: Toward a Theoretical Synthesis." *Amer. Soc. Rev.* 28 (1963): 695-705.

Vogt, Evon A., "On the Concepts of Structure and Process in Cultural Anthropology." *Amer. Anthrop.* 62 (1960): 18-33.

Vucinich, Alexander, "Marx and Parsons in Soviet Sociology." *Russian Review* 33 (1974): 1-19.

Wagner, Halmut R., "Reflections on Parsons' 1974 Retrospective Perspective on Alfred Schutz." *Human Studies* 3 (1980): 387-403.

Wallace, Walter L., "Structure and Action in the Theories of Coleman and Parsons." In Peter M. Blau, ed., *Approaches to the Study of Social Structure,* pp. 121-34. N.Y.: Free Press, 1975.

"Hierarchic Structures in Social Phenomena." In Peter M. Blau and Robert K. Merton, eds., *Continuities in Structural Inquiry,* pp. 191-234. Beverly Hills, CA: Sage, 1981.

Warner, R. Stephen, "Toward a Redefinition of Action Theory: Paying the Cognitive Element Its Due." *Amer. J. of Soc.* 83 (1978): 1317-49.

Review Essay: "Parsons' Last Testament" (review of *Action Theory and the Human Condition*). *Amer. J. of Soc.* 87 (1981): 715-21.

Wearne, B.C., "Talcott Parsons' Appraisal and Critique of Alfred Marshall." *Soc. Res.* 48 (1981): 816-51.

Weinstein, Fred and Gerald M. Platt, *The Wish to be Free.* Berkeley, CA: Univ. of California Press, 1969.

Psychoanalytic Sociology. Baltimore: Johns Hopkins Univ. Press, 1973.

Wiley, Norbert, "The Rise and Fall of Dominating Theories in American Sociology." In William E. Snizek, Ellsworth R. Fuhrman and Michael K. Miller, *Contemporary Issues in Theory and Research: a metasociological perspective,* pp. 47-77. Westport, CT: Greenwood Press, 1979.

Williams, Jr., Robin M., "Friendship and Social Values in a Suburban Community: an exploratory study." *Pac. Soc. Rev.* 2 (1959): 3-10.

Review of *Social Structure and Personality. Soc. For.* 43 (1964): 108.

Wirth, Louis, Review of *The Structure of Social Action. Amer. Soc. Rev.* 4 (1939): 399-404.

Wolff, Kurt H., Review of *American Sociology. Soc. For.* 47 (1968): 224.

"Introduction" (to Special Issue in Memory of Talcott Parsons). *Human Studies* 3 (1980): 309-10.

Wood, James L., "The Role of Systematic Theory in Parsons' General Theory of Action: The Case of the Pattern Variables." *Berkeley J. of Soc.* 13 (1968): 28-41.

Wrong, Dennis H., "The Functional Theory of Stratification: Some Neglected Considerations." *Amer. Soc. Rev.* 10 (1945): 242-49.

"The Oversocialized Conception of Man in Modern Sociology." *Amer. Soc. Rev.* 26 (1961): 183-93.

"The Uses of Power." In Dennis H. Wrong, *Power: Its Forms, Bases, and Uses,* pp. 218-57. N.Y.: Harper & Row, 1980.

Review of *Action Theory and the Human Condition. Soc. For.* 58 (1980): 1339-41.

Zetterberg, Hans, Review of *Theories of Society: Foundations of Modern Sociological Theory. Amer. J. of Soc.* 67 (1962): 707.

Zurcher, Jr., Louis A., Arnold Meadow and Susan Lee Zurcher, "Value Orientation, Role Conflict, and Alienation from Work: a cross:cultural study." *Amer. Soc. Rev.* 30 (1965): 539-48.

Special Publications

"Tributes to Talcott Parsons: 1902-1979," by Renee C. Fox, Neil J. Smelser and Matilda White Riley. *ASA Footnotes,* August, 1979.

"Talcott Parsons, 1902-1979, The Man and His Work." Memorial Session of the American Sociological Association, August 18, 1979, by Robert N. Bellah, Jesse R. Pitts, Robin M. Williams, Jr., John W. Riley, Jr., and Robert K. Merton. *American Sociologist* 15 (1980): 2.

INDEX

201